Toward a Science of Man: Essays in the History of Anthropology

World Anthropology

General Editor

SOL TAX

Patrons

CLAUDE LÉVI-STRAUSS
MARGARET MEAD
LAILA SHUKRY EL HAMAMSY
M. N. SRINIVAS

MOUTON PUBLISHERS · THE HAGUE . PARIS
DISTRIBUTED IN THE USA AND CANADA BY ALDINE, CHICAGO

Toward a Science of Man

Essays in the History of Anthropology

Editor

TIMOTHY H. H. THORESEN

MOUTON PUBLISHERS · THE HAGUE · PARIS
DISTRIBUTED IN THE USA AND CANADA BY ALDINE, CHICAGO

General Editor's Preface

The "natural history" of history begins with people who live and do, unconscious that their everyday activities might some day appear significant. So they are careless of records and of summations. Then a succeeding generation searches for their identity and reconstructs a suitable past which might assure them of a posterity. However mythological the reconstruction, succeeding generations now see that they have a valued past to explore, and that they must preserve for posterity the records of the present. Now also somebody of the new generation attacks as false some central part of what has been accepted as the conventional story; and the need is recognized for trained and disinterested observors. These—the first historians—proceed to research specific pieces of genuine information, from which to make a history that will eventually replace the storied past. This is the stage at which anthropology finds itself, and the present book is a sample of the kinds of pieces which will make our history. The collection is international both because anthropology has been from its beginning unusually international and because the book responds to an invitation to an unusual international Congress.

Like most contemporary sciences, anthropology is a product of the European tradition. Some argue that it is a product of colonialism, with one small and self-interested part of the species dominating the study of the whole. If we are to understand the species, our science needs substantial input of scholars from the variety of cultures on all continents. It was a deliberate purpose of the IXth International Congress of Anthropological and Ethnological Sciences to provide impetus in this direction. The books of *World Anthropology* therefore provide a first glimpse of a future all-human human science. Each is designed to be a

self-contained book with its own updated part of the world's scientific
knowledge, written by specialists from every part of the world. They
must be read and reviewed individually as books on their particular
subjects. The set together may tell us what changes are in store for anthropology as scholars of the developing countries join in studying the
species of which we are all part.

The IXth Congress was planned not only to include as many as possible of the scholars of every part of the world, but with a view to producing
good books. Previous Congresses invited scholars to bring papers to be
read out loud. They were necessarily limited in length; many were only
summarized. Even so, it took so much time to read or speak them that
there was little time for discussion. Moreover, this sparse discussion was
not systematically translated into the various languages of the Congress.
For the IXth Congress, all of this was changed. Papers were written to be
interchanged before the Congress, and not read aloud; the time of the
Congress could be devoted to discussion; professional simultaneous
translation in five languages was provided. Papers were from the beginning designed for publication in this set of books. Although some papers
now published were not delivered in time to be interchanged in advance,
and others which were discussed are not being published, the set of
books comprising *World Anthropology* contains over two thousand papers
which were prepared for the Congress and which now are presented as a
substantial sample of world anthropology.

The method of eliciting the papers was designed to make it as representative a sample as allowable when scholarly creativity—hence self-selec-
tion—is critically important. Scholars of the world were asked to propose
both papers of their own and also topics for sessions of the Congress
which they might edit into books. All were then informed of all the suggestions, and encouraged to re-think their own papers. From study of
all of the other papers, colleagues discovered new topics for sessions and
books which reflect the changing reality which the original proposals
brought to light.

As might have been foreseen, in the first post-colonial generation the
large majority of the Congress papers (82%) are the work of scholars
identified with the industrialized world which fathered our traditional
discipline and the institution of the Congress itself: Eastern Europe (15%);
Western Europe (16%); North America (47%); Japan, South Africa,
Australia and New Zealand (4%). Only 18% are from developing areas:
Africa (4%); Asia-Oceania (9%); Latin America (5%). Aside from the
large representation from the U.S.S.R. and the other nations of Eastern
Europe, a significant difference between this corpus of written material

and all others is the addition of the substantial proportion of contributions from Africa, Asia and Latin America. "Only 18%" is two, three or four times that of previous Congresses; moreover, 18% of 2,000 papers is 360 papers, 10 times the number of "Third World" papers presented at previous Congresses. In fact, these 360 papers are more than the total of *all* papers published after the last International Congress of Anthropological and Ethnological Sciences which was held in the U.S.A. (Philadelphia, 1956). Even the beautifully organized Tokyo Congress in 1968 counted less than a third as many members from developing nations, including those of Asia.

The significance of the increase is not simply quantitative. The input from areas which have been a principal subject matter represents both feedback and also long-awaited theoretical contributions from the perspective of very different cultural, social, historical traditions. Many who attended the Congress were convinced that anthropology would not be the same again. The fact that the next Congress (in India in 1978) will be our first in the Third World may be symbolic of the change. Meanwhile, sober consideration of the present set of books, almost all of which contain papers by the whole variety of scholars, will show how much, and just where and how, our disciplines are being revolutionized.

This particular book was generated by the quarter of the Congress devoted to professional problems, and will be read in relation to others which deal with what anthropology is, what anthropologists do, and how our knowledge may be useful to others. These other books deal with particular subjects—geographic areas or special topics—on which they frequently provide background history. But it is the present volume, reflecting the growing self-awareness of our disciplines which provides guideposts for the coming history of world anthropology.

Chicago, Illinois   SOL TAX
May 6, 1975

Table of Contents

For Alice, of course

Preface

The papers included in this volume were contributed to a IXth ICAES session entitled "Current Prolems of the Profession in Historical Perspective." That session was briefer than most of the participants felt was wise. At the time I agreed and yet today I am not so sure. In the discussion we exposed several issues that could not have been satisfactorily resolved without pre-empting the whole of the Congress itself – national traditions of anthropological research; political implications of different kinds of historiography; the important and yet individually incomplete consequences of working through biography, or philosophy, or institutions, or bibliography, or subdisciplinary issues; the place of a historical perspective in contemporary theory construction; and, cross-cutting all of this, the possibility of "doing" anthroplogy through study of the history of anthropology itself. Appropriately, Jacob Gruber has developed his response to the various papers and to the session as a whole by raising more questions than he answers. Personally I am convinced that what I will call a historical perspective is and must be an essential component of the anthropological attitude. But such a perspective begins by asking the right questions. I will be satisfied if this volume will provoke at least some of those questions.

For their part in arranging the Congress and in seeing through the publication of this volume, I wish to thank Sol Tax and the members of his staff, especially Gay Neuberger and Roberta MacGowan; for their roles as the formal discussants during the session itself, I thank Jacob Gruber and Ray Fogelson; and for their cooperation and patience as I have learned something about editing, I thank the persons who contributed the papers to this volume.

Austin, Texas and Berkeley, California   TIMOTHY H. H. THORESEN

Introduction

JACOB W. GRUBER

In its emergence and development as an investigative discipline in its own right, with its own goals and logic, the history of anthropology has followed a path already marked out by a more general history of science; and that, by a still more inclusive intellectual history. This is not surprising since a history of anthropology is but one part of that attempt to understand the pattern of changes in ideas about the world which always structure those systems of thought which precede action. The fact of anthropology, the existence of the discipline, is itself an instance of the rise of a human self-consciousness which has sought to know the processes by which man became human and, thereby, to understand the hallmarks of his humanity. That particular form of the intellectual search, a particular way of looking at the world and man within it – science – is itself an important feature of the more recent cultural history of "Western" man.

It is an indication, I think, of the cultural lag within our own intellectual traditions that it has only been in this century that the serious study of the role science has played in history has come to warrant the respectable attention accorded other aspects of history whose problems and methods have a much longer genealogy in classical studies. The once common charge of the brutalizing or dehumanizing effects of science and mechanics affected not only the status of its practitioners but also the respectability accorded the study of its history. In any case, earlier attempts at a history of science were generally of an antiquarian sort. They were chronicles of events within, at best, the flimsiest of conceptual

I should like to express my appreciation for Dr. Timothy Thoresen's invitation to participate as discussant in this conference, and my thanks to Dr. Raymond Fogelson and Dr. Elmer Miller for reading and commenting upon the draft.

or theoretical schemes. Where it was not the exaltation of personal heroes or the creation of genius – as in the cases of Galileo, Newton, or Darwin – it was the search for the historical routes of development for the great truths which science had created; but always these were the truths which fit the present. It was a craft of collectors with little interest in process, with scant awareness of the intricate relationships which bound the institution within the culture as a whole. A precision and bibliographical thoroughness was demanded by George Sarton whose very intensity of commitment has accorded him the mythic role of the founder of the history of science. But he, too, was encumbered by an apparatus which stressed the accumulation of data and a search for its sources, which, thus, obscured process and blurred institutional structure.[1]

The practice of a history of anthropology has gone through a similar growth, albeit a half century later. Its very recency as a self-conscious discipline (with its own specialists, journals, and meetings) has seemed to evade the historical question – an interesting reflection of the ahistorical attitude among anthropologists, who were immersed in the sociological processes of a present devoid of an easily controlled or readily available past. It is just barely possible that the emergence of a sense of history OF the field is related to the recent development of a sense of history WITHIN the field.

It is not unlikely, however, that the very recency of its own establishment as a self-conscious discipline, its own particular process of professionalization, impeded the development of an historical awareness of its growth. It is difficult to transform real persons into historical personages and to translate real experiences into historical events. There is perhaps a sound logic which dictates that only the dead may be memorialized in the names of ships or the portraits of stamps. Chronological distance and experiential detachment provide the necessary requirements for both a historical dispassion and the sense of diachronic process. While today's events are tomorrow's history, their very extension distorts the order in whose creation they played their part. It is only in this generation that the distance between anthropology's "founders" and its present practitioners is sufficient to provide the opportunity, if not the anonymity, for the processual ordering of anthropology's experiences. And attempting to see process and order extracted from the particular and the aggregate, we speak of history rather than of chronicle or of record.

[1] The much more recent development of a sociology of science, in which Merton has been a significant leader, serves to emphasize the relative simplicity of the traditional historical approach. (See e.g. Merton 1973; Thackray and Merton 1972.)

There have been histories of anthropology for over a century. From Bendyshe's "The history of anthropology" in 1863 (1865) to Harris's *The rise of anthropological theory* (1968) a century later, there has been an occasional reflection of the desire to look back along the travelled track to see whence we have come, however scant the interest in where we are going. The Bendyshe and Harris works do in fact illustrate two kinds of traditional "history": the first a chronicle of events, the sign-posts along the road of discovery, each marked for its anticipation of some present truth; the second, polemical in tone and in argument, pointing out for the traveller the false starts and blind alleys, the sub-versions of a past which has given up the clarity of the present only with the greatest of difficulty. Both chronicle and polemic are similar in their lack of historicism, in their presentist view not of the historical process itself so much as of the hardly realized way in which one ideology sup-plants another[2]. History, however, if it is in fact an important tool for an understanding of the human condition through an awareness of the hu-man process, is neither chronicle nor polemic; it is neither the product of the antiquarian nor the revelation of the ideologue. History is not the demonstration of present truth through the documentation of past error. It is not a record of the red-letter days on the calendar of becoming. The history of our anthropology as institutional history, as intellectual history, is, in fact, one phase in a cultural anthropology of the West, one means to probe both the structure and the meaning of that culture in which we as anthropologists participate. It is such a possibility that provides contemporary interest, excitement, and value in the history of anthro-pology.[3]

Although the fragments of a history of anthropology were occasionally produced throughout the field's development – often as a by-product of more particular research, sometimes as a summing-up for ritual occasions – it was only in the History of Anthropology Conference, sponsored by the Social Science Research Council in 1962, that the prob-lems of such an interdisciplinary field were faced by both anthropolo-gists, sociologists of science, and historians. The papers written for the conference, as well as the extended discussions they stimulated, indicated

---

[2] For the idea of "presentism" and its distorting effect on the history of anthropology, see Stocking (1965).
[3] As historians and anthropologists begin to pursue particular traditions or local histories of either a formalized anthropology or anthropological concerns — note, for instance, studies of folklore in Central and Southern Europe from at least the nine-teenth century to the present — such "histories of anthropology" may well contribute to the separate cultural histories an understanding of the separate cultures themselves.

the wide range of possible approaches and the pitfalls.[4] The conclusion that a history of anthropology could not be optimally exploited by either anthropologist or historian alone did little to solve the problem of approach, nor was there any solution in the arguments over the role of history in anthropology – archival, ethnohistorical,interpretive, or what – which played a part in the demise of the short-lived AAA committee on the history of anthropology. The fact is, that, given existing discipline lines and particular career patterns and opportunities in each field, it is difficult for either anthropologists or historians to do good or continuous history of anthropology. Within anthropology there is still a bias against the treatment of the Western cultural tradition and, consequently, against the effective training in the methods of historical research; and in history, there is an essential lack of understanding or awareness of anthropological problems and traditions – an effect in general which led Sarton to demand of the historian of science some essential commitment to or training in one of the sciences. The discovery of Western culture as a respectable subject for anthropological inquiry and the revolutionary inroads which sociological concepts have made in professional history provide a promising opportunity for the emergence of a more sophisticated history of anthropology. Nevertheless, the peripheral position of the history of science within history, and of the history of anthropology within anthropology still do not provide sufficient professional stimuli to the commitment necessary to insure an effective body of scholarly activity.[5]

What can a history of anthropology be in order to insure the relevance of its problems and interpretations? If the history of anthropology is not chronicle, what is it? If its function is not to memorialize the accomplishments (and errors) of the past, what role has it? If it is not just another form of ancestor worship, how does it link past to present? Is there some worth in its pursuit other than an antiquarian search which often provides a useful justification for an evasion of the present and an avoidance of the future?

---

[4] It is perhaps some indication of the difficulties still inherent in the definition of a professionalized "field" of the history of anthropology that the papers of the conference were never published as a single entity, in contrast to the proliferation of volumes of proceedings in more traditionally defined areas of investigative concern.

[5] Although there has been a recent increase in the offering of courses in the history of anthropology, most of these are still surveys of a chronicle sort; and I believe that there is still only one major academic appointment of an avowed historian of anthropology charged with the development and pursuit of the field. In no department of anthropology is the history of anthropology considered a "major field" — in contrast to a service area — and rarely have doctoral dissertations been approved or written, within an anthropology department, in the history of the field.

I believe that to pursue a history of anthropology is to contribute with some significance not only to an understanding of the nature of Western culture but also to an understanding of the intellectual organization of the more particular behavior or "culture" of anthropologists, of the more particular institution of anthropology. As Hallowell has suggested earlier (1965), a history of anthropology can be a significant part of an anthropology of anthropology, in that it deals with the development in Western culture of a characteristic and abiding intellectual focus on and preoccupation with the nature of man.

Within such an overall historical interest there are several emphases, each of which etches in greater relief the nature of the field – both in its internal discipline and in its relationships to the larger social system of which it is a part.

Anthropology, as a discipline with established means for the pursuit of its objectives, exists as one of several complementary institutions each with its characteristic "charter, personnel, and proscribed activities." Merton on several occasions has attempted to describe the structure of the institution of science as a whole and the means by which it maintains it norms and imposes them upon its practitioners (Merton 1973).

The recency of anthropology's establishment makes possible detailed studies of the nature of the institution and the conditions of its growth. What are those unifying features in method, goal, and substance which have constituted its "charter?" Is it "charter" or "charters"? If in fact anthropology constitutes a common enterprise – and this is, I think, an important investigative question – what are the relationships of its "schools"? What is the history of its organization? What have been the lines of cleavage? Who have constituted its personnel? What have been the lines of communication and the processes of socialization through which the institution has maintained itself? Questions such as these are essentially anthropological questions which need to be asked about any social system. In asking them and in searching for their answers, we move toward an understanding of the process of a disciplined and structured intellectual activity which has arisen in response to a series of problems framed by an interest of man in his own nature. We can know something of ourselves, both as anthropologists and as men, through an increasingly sophisticated understanding of the institution which disciplines our own formal intellectual participation.

But we can go further. In that the practice of anthropology is institutionalized, to the extent that its activities are functionally distinct from comparable and analogous institutionalized areas and activities which seek to comprehend other particularized facets of the universe, anthropology is a constituent part of a more extended socio-cultural system which provides its validation and legitimacy. As a particular instance, as a recent instance whose origins and development are available for documented investigation, anthropology's history is a tool through which to examine its enclosing culture.

As an institution with the elucidation of a part of nature – the most "unnatural part" – as a goal, anthropology is a part of a wider structure. Its assumptions and its methods are a part of an interactional set in which influences are hardly clear cut and not always empirically demonstrable; rather they are diffused and situational, the effects of diverse historical and social events and realities. They are multi-factorial. To understand them requires the patient unravelling of the many strands which form, at one particular point, the knot of recognition and effect. The growth of anthropology viewed as a selection of problems which are a product of existing concepts and methods, and of the availability of the data can be examined in the context of a changing intellectual milieu without which neither field nor focus exists. It is something more than the general understanding (to which we all subscribe) that anthropology is itself a social product, a kind of artifact of our own culture. Like all artifacts, anthropology can be seen as the focal point or node of a system of relationships, the product of a continuing process, a reification of an historical moment. Examined in this light, the product not only leads to its own clarification but provides also the means to elaborate and thereby to understand the system which gave it rise. Comparing it with analogous intellectual concerns in other traditions, we may be better able to understand the nature of our own culture and theirs. For the notion of man, even as artifact, is central to the organization of human behavior.

Overworked as it has come to be, an ecological view is rewarding in that it demands that we test the development of anthropology against and within the more extended "community" – that paradigm of paradigms which orders thought and action in any human society which is the momentary expression of an ongoing tradition. How does the in-institution with the changing definition of its problems reflect the changing nature of the culture itself? Has, for instance, the interest in the exotic and the culturally marginal provided a respectable and institutionalized haven for those who themselves were marginal to their culture? Do shifts in anthropological problem reflect some deeper, less accessible shifts in the value orientations of the society itself? Do different "national" experiences throw up different anthropologies? What has been the role of anthropology in the establishment of social attitudes or in the validation of an existing normative system? Its subject matter, the reason for its being, makes of anthropology a sensitive barometer for the description of changes of pressure in the social atmosphere. Social concerns are basically human concerns; and the nature of anthropology is such that its history is a continuing reflection of their history.

Apart from the substantive objectives of a history of anthropology, there are also questions of methods, questions which are both of anthropological and historical concern. Any system is a continuing product of the informing tradition and of the individual's particular reaction to and enaction of it. It is, in fact, this ability to observe the individual within his tradition (so apparent in small-scale societies) which has provided cultural or social anthropology with so much of its particular value and interest in the understanding of human system and of human nature. Conversely, it is the lack of similar opportunities which makes it necessary to depersonalize so much of history. The recency of an institutionalized anthropology, however, provides a body of historical materials which give the opportunity for historical observations analogous to those of the ethnographic observer. Elsewhere, I have discussed the utility of life histories of anthropologists for an understanding of the history of the field (Gruber 1966). It is only necessary here to suggest that, in contrast to much of the history of science, there is an accumulated mass of individual materials – most of which are uncollected and uncollated – which can provide important insights into the interactional processes which alter the tradition. Cannon has suggested, after working with these kinds of informal materials, that "the study of private papers is one of the most suggestive ways of becoming aware of the problems in the field... But ... the private papers do little to solve the intellectualist problems... [which] can be solved only... by going to the published materials" (1964: 30–31). He is too cautious, I think, in making the distinction between the intellectualist problems and those which we might regard as interactional. His own work has gone far to indicate the utility of an examination of the more personal aspects of the lives of scientists and of the ephemeral documents which describe them for an understanding of the patterns of scientific activity.

As Kuhn has noted in his own seminal revamping of the history of science (1962), once the historian dispenses with an accumulation (for which read chronicle) model for the making of science, he begins to ask not for the relationship of past error to present truth but rather for the relationship of the views of the scientist to those of his group, to that particular version of the socio-intellectual milieu of which he is a part and from which he may strain to part. Such an "historiographic revolution in the study of science," as Kuhn calls it, is as apt for the history of anthropology as it is for the physical sciences which are his concern and source. Perhaps it is even more apt, for the subject matter of anthropology ties it more firmly to that range of values and passions, opinions and traditions whose very strengths translate so easily the novel into the ideological. No matter. To understand the development of the field, to understand a system in which "truth" can supplant "truth" in the absence of demonstrable error, to understand the meaning of discipline where parallel and sometimes contradictory systems of method and theory make their claims to allegiance, it is necessary to see the emergence of ideas and concepts as the products of men in constant interaction with their contemporaries and all within the relatively coherent thought system which nourished them. Novelty is a form of abnormality, innovation is a challenge to the normative system; and in order to understand the nature and the extent of the abnormal and the innovative, it is necessary to know the normal. If one is to appreciate the significance of a shift in paradigms, it is necessary to construe the paradigms themselves and in themselves.

In discussing the relationships which exist between history and anthropology – one of the continuing themes, incidentally, in the history of the field itself – Lévi-Strauss writes that "anthropology cannot remain indifferent to historical processes and to the most highly conscious expressions of social phenomena. But if the anthropologist brings to them the same scrupulous attention as the historian, it is in order to eliminate, by a kind of backward course, all that they owe to the historical process and to conscious thought. His goal is to grasp, beyond the conscious and always shifting images which men hold, the complete range of unconscious possibilities ... [while anthropologists are interested in literate peoples] he is above all interested in unwritten data, not so much because the peoples he studies are incapable of writing, but because that with which he is principally concerned differs from everything men ordinarily think of recording on stone or on paper (1967:23–26).

Upon such a distinction we can build another and, I think, a more significant concept of the role of the history of anthropology. As the present is not only the literal product of the historical consciousness whose description is the legitimate goal of formal history, so the present of anthropology is not the literal product of a succession of describable events which make up the conscious level of a succession of pasts. There is a latent structure which provides some order to the diachronic sequence of events which constitute history. Call it tradition or a "feel of the field" or a set of unstated assumptions acquired through practice and the association with adult models, it is the product of a continuing process of anthropologizing – the work and ideas which constitute the corpus, the body, of the field. It is the emergent frame which is constantly being reified for each moment by specific acts of behavior. It is the sense of the discipline which provides the locus for identification of the practitioner. The search for this underlying institutional structure which provides a system of reference for those engaged in the anthropological enterprise is an anthropological task. Its data are the ephemeral elements which constitute the constant products of a continuing interaction within the bounds of an already existing system. The nature of that system at any moment in time and the pattern and mode of its changes are related goals in a history of anthropology.

As anthropology itself, the history of anthropology seems to hang on the horns of a methodological dilemma: Is it to be institutional analysis and history or is its focus that of the enclosing culture itself? Does it describe a static succession of presents, each the subject of its own description and analysis, or does it seek to understand process, the sometimes hidden path which has led from past to present and stretches to the future? The various papers which make up this volume illustrate both the problem and the promise of the history of anthropology as a discipline with its own logic and its own goals. Read as contributions to the METHOD as well as to the substance of a history of anthropology, they are instructive documents for the furtherance of understanding.

Biography is one of the more usual defective modes of writing history. Often the life of a man, too often only his name, is invoked as some pseudo-focus to locate a more traditional chronicle or explication of ideas. This should not be surprising. Despite the insights that a life history can provide, even one devoted to the arbitrarily limited area of profession, the easy availability of the published works, in all the formalism and logic of their studied selectivity, provides them with a permanence and reality which the scattered documents of life do not possess. Of the seven papers which at least pretend to some personal focus, only Modell's interesting attempt to see Ruth Benedict's anthropology as a function of her self uses biographical method as a means of gaining significant insights into the forces which forged a discipline. As Modell indicates, Benedict's ideas and her life are so inflexibly linked that the anthropology she helped to create can only be fully understood and appreciated – at least historically and, I think, intellectually as well – by a continuing reference to that life. Modell makes the necessary assumption that it is important to regard any field, any system of ideas, as a part of the lives of those who made it – or the converse, that it is in the life of the practitioner that that system receives some coherent reality. Unless we can accept such a view, biography has little to contribute except titillating gossip. The articles by Stocking and Thoresen, on the other hand, represent an antithetical notion; they are intellectualist in their intent and in their result. Like the natural philosophers of an earlier century who ordered nature so that they could understand the order of God's intellect, so here the products of mind are analyzed to reveal the order, the creating intellect, of their creators. It is a useful method. It is interesting to see through Thoresen's analysis that the epistemologically useful distinction between theorist and empiricist, between conceptualist and experimentalist, which is so clear in the physical sciences, finds an expression in Kroeber's own continuing attempts to work out the ways of anthropology. As Thoresen's treatment concerns problems of anthropology within the context of the scientific mode, Stocking's analysis of the ideas of Lord Kames ties some historically central anthropological theory to a much more extensive intellectual system. His paper raises interesting questions regarding the nature of the change of which human history was only a part, a change which was more sweeping than that suggested by the surface arguments over progress or degeneration, monogenesis or polygenesis; rather as the works of Lord Kames indicate, the essential question was that of a shift from a concern with man as mind (a rational and moral creature) to man as animal – a shift from a definition of the nature of man to that of man in nature. It is from such sources that the more specific problems of a later anthropology emerged; and the loss of the source makes it difficult to understand if it does not in fact distort the particular problems themselves and the excitement their pursuit inspired.

The articles by Bieder and Tax provide useful and interesting historical resumés based upon the work of Gallatin and Squier. They seem to me too cautious in their use of the biographical tool and thus Gallatin and Squier seem hardly more than pegs upon which to hang some intellectual history. Gallatin's position within the Establishment provides a valuable opportunity to explore further the emergence of the structure of an institutionalized anthropology; and his European and essentially conservative theoretical orientation offer an interesting case study in the ideological conflicts between an older European tradition and one which was emerging in America at a time of intellectual isolationism. The Holtzman and Belaj articles are little more than descriptive statements although the latter suggests something of the role of the individual savant and the process of the "independent development" of anthropological theory. It serves as an interesting datum for a consideration of the hardly explored area of the role of national traditions and nationalism in the history of anthropology.

Of a different sort are the papers by de Brigard, Fowler, Vidyarthi, Nemeskéri, and Sozan. These are essentially institutional histories, contributions to our understanding of the development of a method and approach which can form a coherent frame which may be the defining element of the field.

The brief sketch by Nemeskéri points up some of the deficiencies as well as the possibilities of historical study when approached from a traditional chronological point of view. As it stands, it is a chronicle of individual achievements by a few historical figures. Apparent nevertheless is the interesting problem of the diffusion of an Anglo-French definition of the anthropological method and problem. It would be interesting to pursue the manner in which such a tradition came to be specialized or normalized within the Hungarian social milieu. To what extent was it in fact related to a continuing nationalist strain which had its political expressions from at least the middle of the nineteenth century? What was the reason for its decline at the turn of the century? What concept of anthropology or of science led to the reorganization of the field after the second World War? Such problems can be generalized, of course, beyond the Hungarian experience; for a developing anthropology in the nineteenth century was fostered by the emergent nationalisms of central and eastern Europe, whose most popular expressions today are the various folk museums and the particular kind of ethnography which they have fostered. The deficiencies of a chronicle such as that of Nemeskéri's are emphasized by Sozan's valuable paper in which he does indeed document the historical circumstances of the establishment of Hungarian anthropology. The effect of conflicting ideologies upon so sensitive a field as ethnography emerge quite clearly from his summary of the trials of the Hungarian Ethnographic Society. Sozan's historically sound description and analysis serves as a very useful case study of the "social ecology" of the field's development.

Vidyarthi's compact, informed, and informing description of the history of Indian anthropology summarizes some of those problems of a history of anthropology which historical vignettes only illustrate. As in anthropology generally, the use of one system aids in the clarification of another. Seeing anthropology as an institution with an historical life, Vidyarthi attempts to manage its history – to create it, in fact – through the construction of a series of growth periods which are defined essentially by their respectively different methodological approaches to the collection and analysis of data. It is an historical approach, but one, I would argue, that is essentially sterile. Periodization is itself a method – a way of organizing phenomena preliminary to their explication, as is typology in archeological analysis. It may work as a kind of history, but not as anthropology. Vidyarthi is aware of the anthropological problems – the effect of first British and then American anthropology upon the development of Indian practice; or the related notion of the logic of an INDIAN anthropology as opposed to an anthropology of India. As in America or in Britain, the institution in India is sufficiently vast to provide the opportunity for an understanding of its dynamics, its relationship to the sociocultural system of which it is a part and which it serves. If in fact anthropology in India is a foreign excrescence, that is a significant datum for an understanding both of anthropology and of Indian culture.

The articles by de Brigard and Fowler are excellent contributions to the historiography of anthropology. Fowler's is a detailed bibliographical essay on the use of the standardized schedule for the collection of comparable cultural data. Along with Urry's recently published account (1973), it goes a long way toward the establishment of a model for the manner in which the analysis of methodological developments affect and reflect the continually changing problem base which serves some centripetal function in the definition of the field and the validation of its activities. De Brigard's is a complementary approach. Though primarily descriptive, it is a significant attempt to treat historically a single investigative or methodological focus within the field. It points the way to historical analyses of other investigative emphases – personality and culture, for instance – within the context of the field as a whole. That all anthropologists are not of the same mold is obvious to anyone who has attended an anthropological meeting; that anthropology as a discipline has had, as a continuing theme in its history, the task of constantly reconciling differences of approach and intent, is one of its unique features. The emergence and resolution of differences, the passing of fads and the fixing of a shifting canon, are features of its history, and they raise interesting problems for the understanding of its past.

It is the understanding of that past which is the object of any history of anthropology. It is not an antiquarian's tale nor the creation of a folk-like myth. Its value lies in the present, for, as anthropologists should know more than any others, it is the patterns of the past which embrace the present.

REFERENCES

BENDYSHE, THOMAS
1865 "The history of anthropology," in *Memoirs of the Anthropological Society of London* 1:335–458.

CANNON, WALTER
1964 History in depth: the early victorian period. *History of Science* 3:20–38.

GRUBER, JACOB W.
1966 "In search of experience: biography as an instrument for the history of anthropology," in *Pioneers of American anthropology.* Edited by June Helm. Seattle: University of Washington Press.

HALLOWELL, A. IRVING
1965 The history of anthropology as an anthropological problem. *Journal of the History of the Behavioral Sciences* 1:24–38.

HARRIS, MARVIN
1968 *The rise of anthropological theory.* New York: Thomas Crowell.

KUHN, THOMAS S.
1962 *The structure of scientific revolutions.* Chicago: University of Chicago Press.

LÉVI-STRAUSS, CLAUDE
1967 [1963] *Structural analysis.* New York: Anchor-Doubleday.

MERTON, ROBERT K.
1973 *The sociology of science.* Chicago: University of Chicago Press.

STOCKING, GEORGE W., JR.
1965 On the limits of "presentism" and "historicism" in the historiography of the behavioral sciences. *Journal of the History of the Behavioral Sciences* 1:211–218.

THACKRAY, ARNOLD, ROBERT K. MERTON
1972 On discipline building: the paradoxes of George Sarton. *Isis* 63:473–495.

URRY, JAMES
1973 "*Notes and queries on anthropology* and the development of field method in British anthropology," in *Proceedings of the Royal Anthropological Institute of Great Britain and Ireland for 1972*, 45–57.

Notes on Inquiries in Anthropology: A Bibliographic Essay

DON D. FOWLER

One of the principal methodological aims of anthropology has been to achieve comparability of its data. The sheer volume of the data, their complexity and seeming randomness, have posed problems since the beginnings of the discipline. Efforts to achieve comparability of data have produced an extensive literature on field methods, data collection, and data processing: e.g. Jongmans and Gutkind (1967), Kroeber et al. (1953:3–76, 401–487), Naroll and Cohen (1970), and Richards (1939) and the sources therein.

The inherent difficulty in attempting to collect field data useful for comparative purposes is neatly summed up in a letter from L. Fison to A. W. Howitt in 1874: "In the bitterness of my soul I said Satan made a mistake in troubling Job with boils.... and showed only a superficial acquaintance with the stupidity of human nature — he should have set him to making ethnological enquiries" (quoted in Walker 1971:126; cf. Resek 1960:128).

One means of accumulating comparable data has been through the use of field manuals, guides, handbooks, and questionnaires. *Notes and queries* (Royal Anthropological Institute 1964) is perhaps the best known field manual currently in use, together with a variety of guides and manuals for specific world areas, or the cross-cultural study of specific topics: e.g.

This paper is extracted from a larger study currently underway (Fowler n.d.). I am indebted to William Fenton, Margaret Blaker, Margaret Hodgen, Warren d'Azevedo, John C. Ewers, Gordon Hewes, Dell Hymes, James Urry, and George W. Stocking, Jr. for aid and comments on an earlier draft. They are not, however, responsible for errors and omissions herein. Thanks are also due to the U.S. National Archives, the American Philosophical Society, the American Antiquarian Society, the New-York Historical Society, and the Capetown South Africa Library for providing information and copies of unpublished manuscript materials.

medicine, life histories, child care, folklore, socialization, art, proxemics, etc. (see Campbell and Levine 1970; Jongmans and Gutkind 1967; Paul 1953; Cooper 1931; Goldstein 1964; Lindgren 1939; and Bartlett et al. 1939 for reviews and bibliography).

Most anthropologists are aware that field manuals, guides, and circulars were used as early as the 1840's (Hodgkin, et al. 1841; Schoolcraft 1947; Morgan 1862). Few are aware, however, that the antecedents of these manuals and guides date to the 1500's and perhaps earlier, long before "anthropology" or "ethnology" crystallized as distinct scholarly disciplines. These early works were not "anthropological" in the strict sense but many contained questions designed to recover comparative data on race, culture, society, and ethnopsychology. To the historian of anthropology, these guides, manuals, and circulars provide a valuable source of information on the overt and covert conceptions of, and attitudes about, race, culture, society, language, and ethnopsychology, held by European and American scholars from the sixteenth to the twentieth centuries.

The present paper is essentially a bibliographic essay, designed to outline the early history of field manuals and guides and to suggest some contributions to the history of anthropology which a close study of them affords.

Many of the works with which we are concerned were called INQUIRIES, a usage adopted herein. Inquiries have been produced for all the sub-fields of anthropology. Herein our discussion is limited principally to ethnographic and linguistic inquiries. Those for other sub-fields have their own developmental histories and deserve separate treatment. Many inquiries must be classed as ephemera. In some cases they are listed or described in secondary literature, or, replies to them exist, but no copies of the original documents have turned up (e.g. Gallatin 1836).

For present purposes, inquiries are broadly defined to include the following:

1.   Inquiries designed by governmental agencies to collect data on colonial possessions or potential possesions. Included here are various MEMORANDA issued by the Spanish Council of the Indies between 1577 and 1792 which generated a large body of ethnohistorically useful data known as the *Relaciones geográficas* (Cline, et al. 1972:183–449). Also included are specific instructions or manuals issued to government sponsored parties of exploration, several of which will be noted below.

2.   TRAVELER'S GUIDES, pamphlets, or books sold commercially as guides for educated travelers in foreign countries.

3.   Inquiries produced by scholarly societies, either for general collection

of data or for specific countries. Often scholarly societies developed the inquiries for government expeditions.

4. Inquiries developed by individual scholars to guide their own research (e.g. Bourke 1881; Petty 1686) or circulated by them to specific persons who might provide information on particular topics. Most of these latter works were intended as field guides, but we would have to include here guides to library research, such as Herbert Spencer's guide (1904: II, 202) for the accumulation of data for the *Descriptive sociology* volumes (Spencer 1873–1881). Spencer's guide is regarded as a forerunner of the *Outline of cultural materials* (Murdock, et al. 1965) and the Human Relations Area Files (Murdock 1959:16; Carneiro 1968:123).

EARLY INQUIRIES

The date of the "first" or "earliest" inquiry is unknown. Hodgen (1964: 22–23) suggests that Herodotus may have used a fairly consistent set of questions, or at least categories, in discussing the peoples and cultures he visited or heard about. Hodgen (1964:91) also suggests that John of Pian de Carpini, who travelled in Mongol territory in the mid-1200's (Cameron 1970:31), laid out a "questionnaire" with ethnographic content in his *Historia Mongolorum*.

Curtin (1964:15) suggests that the Spanish Council of the Indies began issuing Memoranda in 1517, but most of the Memoranda produced by the Council were dated after 1577 (Cline, et al. 1972:183). As previously noted, these Memoranda were issued for administrative purposes, but they generated a large body of data on indigenous populations of New Spain including demography, toponyms, languages, former political institutions, warfare, dress, religion, etc. (Cline, et al. 1972:183–449).

Perhaps the first true anthropological inquiry was the set of MINUTAS on "all the topics referring to the material and mental culture of the Aztecs" (Nicolau d'Olwer 1952:136; cf. Bandelier 1932:12; Jiménez-Moreno 1938:xiv–xv) developed by Fray Bernardino de Sahagún after 1529 to guide his monumental study of Aztec languages and cultures embodied in his *General history of the things of New Spain* (Dibble and Anderson 1950–1969) and other works (García Icazbalceta 1886:247–323; Garibay 1971: 63–88).

Traveler's guides began to be published in the late 1500's in Europe (Howard 1914:205–209): e.g. Turler (1575), Lipsius (1592), Meier (1589), Palmer (1606), Goodall (1630), Neale (1643), Howell (1642), Woodward (1696), East Indies Company (1705), Tucker (1757), and Berchtold (1789).

Many such guides were written as aids to young English gentlemen making the Grand Tour of the Continent (Trease 1967:78). The number of questions with anthropological content varied but usually included queries on foods, habits, clothing of different occupations and social ranks, religious and social rites, and local laws.

In 1630 King Gustavus II Adolphus of Sweden issued a *Memorial* containing a program for extensive investigations into Swedish culture, society, folklore, material cultures, folk medicine, etc. (Lindgren 1939: 330).

Soon after the formation of the Royal Society of London in 1660, committees of the Society produced several inquiries or GENERAL HEADS on a variety of topics and specific countries including Turkey, the East Indies, Hungary and Transylvania, Egypt, Greenland, and Guinea (Royal Society 1665-1667, passim). One well known member of the Society, Robert Boyle (1692), also produced a *General heads for a natural history of a country* which includes questions on human physique, racial features, "inclinations and customs," the relative fruitfulness of the women, diseases, and "traditions concerning all particular things relating to that country, as either peculiar to it, or at least, uncommon elsewhere." William Robertson apparently circulated questions when compiling data for his (Robertson 1777) *History of America* (Hymes n.d.).

The Royal Society continued to produce inquiries in the eighteenth century, e.g. Hunter (1768). The society sponsored James Cook's first voyage of exploration to the South Seas in 1768-1771 (Cook 1771; Villiers 1967:77-163). Presumably Cook's instructions included ethnographic inquiries of some sort, but they are not recorded in Cook's *Journal* nor in the *Transactions* of the Society. A set of questions was prepared by the Society on the Eskimos for Banks' exploration of Newfoundland and Labrador in 1766 (Lysaght 1971:218-221).

A further impetus to the development of inquiries was the burgeoning interest in "antiquities," including folklore, in the seventeenth and eighteenth centuries, especially in the British Isles (Dorson 1968; Evans 1956). This interest led, for example, to Edward Lhwyd's (1697, in Jessup 1961: 178-179; cf. Campbell and Thomson 1963:3) inquiries on the geography and antiquities of Wales and Scotland.

During the eighteenth century a number of inquiries were apparently developed as part of the instructions for parties of exploration sent to Siberia and the North Pacific after 1719 by Peter the Great and his successors (de Grunwald 1956:179-180). For example, Gerhard Müller drew up ethnographic instructions for the Kamchatka expedition of 1733-1743, and later Russian expeditions carried inquiries developed by the Russian

Academy of Sciences (Academy of Sciences 1926:162–167; Müller 1761; Russov 1900).

Perhaps the most extensive eighteenth-century inquiry was that by Johann David Michaelis (1774) who proposed a scholarly expedition to the Red Sea and prepared a 500 page inquiry on biota, ethnography, medicine, linguistics, economics, etc. under the patronage of the Danish court (Hansen 1964).

Thus, by the end of the eighteenth century there had developed in Europe a practice of issuing inquiries on a variety of topics and in a variety of formats. None was strictly "anthropological" but they were part of a larger tradition of "compiling and collecting" information in many fields (Gruber 1970:1290). But the age of specialization in science was dawning and inquiries began to be produced for specific fields, increasing in length and detail as various disciplines developed.

THE NINETEENTH CENTURY

In 1799–1800 in France, the short-lived Society of the Observers of Man (Bouteiller 1956; Stocking 1968:13-41) developed two inquiries for the ill-fated Baudin expedition to Oceania, one on physical anthropology by Georges Cuvier (Hervé 1910) and a second on ethnography by Joseph-Marie Degérando (1800, 1883). The latter is notable for its insistence that observers should learn native languages and conduct extended periods of what today is called "participant observation." The Degérando inquiry was later used as the basis for an inquiry produced by the Ethnological Society of Paris (1841).

As the foregoing suggests, the development of anthropological inquiries in the nineteenth century was in part closely related to the development of scholarly societies devoted to anthropology and/or ethnology, a subject which cannot be treated here, but see Stocking (1971), Broca (1871), and Burrow (1966).

French efforts after 1841 include a series of ethnological instructions issued by the Anthropological Society of Paris for specific countries (e.g. Gosse, et al. 1861, 1862) and a general inquiry on sociology and ethnography (Anthropological Society of Paris 1860–1873, 1889). The French also issued a variety of traveler's guides, as did others e.g. Kaltbrunner (1881).

British anthropological efforts in the nineteenth century began with the development of inquiries designed to guide the collection of demographic, economic, and sociopolitical data on West Africa prior to colonization, e.g. that issued by the African Institution (1807–1824: IV, 75–82) in 1811. In 1849 the British Admiralty issued a general *Manual of scientific Enquiry* (Herschel 1849) which included a chapter on ethnology by J. C. Prichard.[1]

The British Association for the Advancement of Science issued its first anthropological inquiry in 1841 (Hodgkin, et al. 1841; Hodgkin and Cull 1852). In 1874 the Association collaborated with the Anthropological Institute of Great Britain and Ireland to produce the first edition of *Notes and queries* (British Association 1874). The full development of *Notes and queries* in relation to British anthropology is treated by Urry (1973) and will not be reiterated here. The British Association also developed several other specific inquiries: e.g. Lubbock, et al. (1873), Lane-Fox, et al. (1878–1880), Galton, et al. (1883, 1893–1895), Tylor, et al. (1885–1898), Dawson, et al. (1897). The Association also cooperated with the Anthropological Society of Bombay and other agencies in India in the development of inquiries for that country (Turner, et al. 1891; Risley 1893–1895; Risley, et al. 1885). The Anthropological Institute also circulated separately an inquiry on "racial" color perception (Allen 1877). Frazer also circulated his own inquiries in various editions, but with the questions relatively unchanged, between 1877 and 1916 (Frazer 1887, *et seq.*). Thomas (1900, 1906) developed questions on specific topics, and in 1867 Darwin circulated queries on the expression of emotions, the answers to which were incorporated in his study of expression of emotion in man and animal (Darwin 1872, 1873).

Other inquiries developed within the British Empire in the nineteenth century, including those for Australia by Fison and Howitt (1874, in Walker 1971: Appendix 4) and Taplin (1879), and a circular by W. H. I. Bleek, ca. 1870, in South Africa. A copy of the latter has not yet turned up.

AMERICAN INQUIRIES

Nineteenth-century inquiries in the United States include both vocabulary lists and ethnographic guides. Sometimes the two were combined, but often vocabulary lists were circulated separately.

Two factors stimulated the collection of vocabularies in the United States. One was the attempt, following European examples, e.g. those stimulated by Catherine of Russia (von Adelung 1815; Pallas 1786, 1786–

---

[1] Prichard's article appeared in the first three editions of the *Manual*. In the fourth edition, the article was revised by E. B. Tylor (1871). In the fifth edition, Tylor (1886) replaced Prichard's article with one of his own on "anthropology."

1789; Yankiewitch de Miriewo 1790–1791) and later Adelung and Vater (1806–1817), to compile standardized vocabulary lists as the basis for genetic classifications of languages (Bonfante 1954). The second, related, factor was the concern over the "origins" of the Amerindians (Allen 1963:113-137; Huddleston 1967). By the 1780's various scholars felt that if an adequate genetic classification of Amerindian languages could be achieved, and connections demonstrated with Eurasian languages, the "origins" problem might be resolved on a scientific basis. A principal proponent of this approach was Thomas Jefferson (Lipscomb, et al. 1903: II,110). Jefferson in fact collected Amerindian vocabularies for over thirty years, often using a list of "queries" which he sent to various people (Boyd 1950–1965:IX, 640–642, X, 240; XI, 414) and by circulating a printed vocabulary list (Jefferson n.d.). His "intension was to publish the whole [collection] and leave the world to search for affinities between these and the languages of Europe and Asia" (T. Jefferson to J. Correa de Serra, 26 April 1816, in Jackson 1962: 611–612).But his vocabularies were stolen and scattered in 1809, ending the project (Jackson 1962:611).

Benjamin Smith Barton also collected vocabularies, often through written queries (Pennell 1936), hoping to demonstrate connections between Asia and the New World (Barton 1797:80). Albert Gallatin also circulated vocabulary lists, the data from which were included in his initial classification of Amerindian languages (Gallatin to W. Marcy, 17 March 1841, in Adams 1960: II, 525–526; Gallatin 1826, 1836).

The use of inquiries for ethnographic purposes in the United States apparently began in 1798, with the production of a *Circular* developed by a committee of the American Philosophical Society chaired by Thomas Jefferson (Jefferson, et al. 1799) which requested information on a broad range of subjects, including "plans... of ancient Fortifications, Tumuli, and other Indian works of art,..." and inquiries "into the Customs, Manners, Languages and Character of the Indian nations, ancient and modern" (Jefferson, et al. 1799:xxxvii–xxxviii).

Jefferson's *Instructions* of exploration to Lewis and Clark, with additional inputs from Benjamin Rush and others (Jackson 1962:17–18), included inquiries on ethnography and linguistics. Jefferson's *Instructions* set a pattern for subsequent federally-sponsored expeditions to the West, e.g. the instructions produced by Du Ponceau, et al. (1819) for the Long expedition to the Rocky Mountains.

The first American inquiry to recognize the full complexity of Amerindian languages and cultures and the problems of studying them was produced by Lewis Cass (1823) and can rightfully be regarded as a landmark in the development of field methods in American anthropology.

The Cass inquiry contains sixteen major headings with over 350 detailed questions and an extensive vocabulary and grammatical section. The Cass inquiry was later used by Charles C. Trowbridge to collect data on several tribes in the Great Lakes and adjacent areas (Kinietz 1938, 1946; Kinietz and Voegelin 1939).

The Cass inquiry stimulated the work of Henry Rowe Schoolcraft, who served under Cass as an Indian agent (Freeman 1959). The inquiries developed by Schoolcraft (1847) brought in the data he compiled pell mell in his voluminous *Historical and statistical information...* (Schoolcraft 1851–1857).

The Smithsonian Institution began circulating anthropological inquiries in the 1860's (Gibbs 1862, 1863; Henry 1878; Mason 1875). Perhaps the best known Smithsonian-sponsored inquiry was the one circulated on behalf of Lewis Henry Morgan (1862) which brought him much of the data for his classic *Systems of consanguinity and affinity...* (Morgan 1871). It is interesting that Lewis Cass, then United States Secretary of State, acted to facilitate Morgan's work 1871:ix).

After John Wesley Powell formed the Bureau of Ethnology in 1879, he too saw the utility of inquiries. He laid out plans for a general Manual of Anthropology, but only three sections appeared, a linguistic inquiry (Powell 1877), a volume on sign language by Garrick Mallery (1880), and a volume on mortuary practices by H. C. Yarrow (1880). A draft manuscript by Powell on Indian medical practices remains unpublished (Fowler, ed. n.d.). The Bureau of Ethnology inquiries were used by John Gregory Bourke (Bourke 1881; Sutherland 1964:173) as the basis for his own inquiry.

Toward the turn of the century the Smithsonian also issued other inquiries to guide the collection of museum specimens (Holmes and Mason 1899).

SUMMARY

As anthropology became professionalized after ca. 1880 and fieldwork became the hallmark of the discipline (Urry 1973), inquiries became more detailed and sophisticated. In the twentieth century inquiries, though no longer so-called, have continued to be produced as anthropologists have developed new field methods and data processing techniques.

Our purpose in the present paper has been briefly to trace the history of some ancestors of modern anthropological field manuals by providing a preliminary bibliography, and to suggest the possible uses in the history of anthropology which a close study of inquiries affords.

REFERENCES

ACADEMY OF SCIENCES OF THE U.S.S.R.
1926   *The Pacific: Russian scientific investigations.* Leningrad: Publishing Office of the Academy of Science of the U.S.S.R.
ADAMS, HENRY, *editor*
1960   *The writings of Albert Gallatin,* three volumes. New York: Antiquarian Press. (Originally published in 1879.)
ADELUNG, JOHAN C., JOHAN S. VATER
1806–1807   *Mithridates oder allgemaine Sprachenkunde mit dem Vater Unser als Sprachprobe in bey nahe funfhundert Sprachen und Mundarten,* four volumes. Berlin: Vassische buchandlung.
AFRICAN INSTITUTION
1807–1824   *Queries relative to Africa.* Reports of the Committee of the African Institution, Report 4:75–82.
ALLEN, DON CAMERON
1963   *The legend of Noah: renaissance rationalism in art, science, and letters.* Urbana: University of Illinois Press.
ALLEN, GRANT
1877   Questionnaire on colour perception. *Journal of the Anthropological Institute of Great Britain and Ireland* 7:543.
ANTHROPOLOGICAL SOCIETY OF PARIS
1860–1873   *Bulletins 1–12.*
1889   *Questionnaire de sociologie et d'ethnographie* (second edition). Paris A Hennuyer. (First edition 1883.)
BANDELIER, FANNY R., *translator*
1932   *A history of ancient Mexico by Fray Bernardino de Sahagún,* two volumes. Nashville: Fisk University Press.
BARTLETT, F. C., *et al., editors*
1939   *The study of society: methods and problems.* New York: Macmillan.
BARTON, BENJAMIN SMITH
1797   *New views of the origin of the tribes and nations of America.* Philadelphia: printed for the author by John Bioren.
BERCHTOLD, COUNT LEOPOLD
1789   *An essay to direct and extend the inquiries of patriotic travelers with further observations...,* two volumes. London: privately printed.
BONFANTE, GIULIANO
1954   Ideas on the kinship of the European languages from 1200 to 1800. *Journal of World History* 1:679–699.
BOURKE, JOHN GREGORY
1881   *Memoranda for use in obtaining information concerning Indian tribes.* Fort Omaha, Nebraska: privately printed. (Reprinted 1964 in "The diaries of John Gregory Bourke" by Edwin V. Sutherland, 173–196.)
BOUTEILLER, M.
1956   La Société des Observateurs de l'Homme, ancêtre de la Société d'Anthropologie de Paris. *Anthropological Society of Paris, Bulletins and Memoirs,* tenth series, 8:448–465.

BOYD, JULIAN, *editor*
1950–1965   *The papers of Thomas Jefferson, 1760–1790*, seventeen volumes. Princeton: Princeton University Press.

BOYLE, ROBERT
1692   *General heads for the natural history of a country, great or small; drawn out for the use of travellers and navigators...* London: printed for John Taylor and S. Holford.

BRITISH ASSOCIATION FOR THE ADVANCEMENT OF SCIENCE
1874   *Notes and queries on anthropology, for use of travellers and residents in uncivilized lands.* London: Stanford.

BROCA, PAUL
1871   The progress of anthropology in Europe and America: an address before the Anthropological Society of Paris, 1869. Translated by W. Lea Roberts. *Journal of the Anthropological Institute of New York* 1: 22–42.

BURROW, J. W.
1966   *Evolution and society: a study in Victorian social theory.* Cambridge: Cambridge University Press.

CAMERON, NIGEL
1970   *Barbarians and Mandarins: thirteen centuries of western travelers in China.* New York and Tokyo: Walker/Weatherhill.

CAMPBELL, DONALD T., ROBERT A. LEVINE
1970   "Field-manual anthropology," in *A handbook of method in cultural anthropology.* Edited by R. Naroll and R. Cohen, 366–387. Garden City: Natural History Press.

CAMPBELL, J. L., D. THOMSON
1963   *Edward Lhwyd in the Scottish Highlands, 1699–1700.* Oxford: Clarendon.

CARNEIRO, ROBERT L.
1968   "Herbert Spencer," in *International encyclopedia of the social sciences,* volume fifteen, 121–128.

CASS, LEWIS
1823   *Inquiries, respecting the history, traditions, languages, manners, customs, religion, etc. of the Indians living within the United States.* Detroit: Sheldon and Reed.

CLINE, HOWARD F., *et al.*
1972   "The relaciones geográficas of the Spanish Indies and New Spain, 1577–1792," in *Guide to ethnohistorical sources,* part one. Handbook of Middle American Indians 12:183–449.

COOK, JAMES
1771   *A journal of a voyage round the world in his Majesty's Ship Endeavour, in the years 1768, 1769, 1770, and 1771....* London: printed for T. Becket and P. A. DeHondt. (Reprinted 1967 as Bibliotheca Australiana Series 14. Amsterdam: N. Israel.)

COOPER, JOHN M.
1931   Questionnaire on the relations between religion and morality. *Primitive Man* 4(4):61–63.

CURTIN, PHILIP D.
1964   *The image of Africa: British ideas and action, 1780–1850.* Madison: University of Wisconsin Press.

DARWIN, CHARLES
1872   "Queries about expression for anthropological inquiry," in *Smithsonian Institution Annual Report for 1867*, page 324.
1873   *The expression of the emotions in man and animals.* New York: D. Appleton.

DAWSON, GEORGE, et al.
1897   *An ethnological survey of Canada.* British Association for the Advancement of Science, Report 67:44–51. London

DEGÉRANDO, JOSEPH-MARIE
1800   *Considérations sur les diverses méthodes à suivre dans l'observation des peuples sauvages*, Paris. (Translated and edited 1969 by F. C. T. Moore, *The observation of savage peoples*. Berkeley and Los Angeles: University of California Press.)
1883   Documents anthropologiques: l'ethnographie en 1800. *Revue d'Anthropologie*, second series, 6:152–182.

DE GRUNWALD, CONSTANTIN
1956   *Peter the Great.* Translated by Viola Garvin. London: Douglas Saunders with Macgibbon and Kee.

DIBBLE, CHARLES, ARTHUR J. O. ANDERSON, editors and translators
1950–1969   *Florentine Codex: general history of the things of New Spain by Fray Bernardino de Sahagún*, books 1–12. Monographs of the School of American Research 14, parts 2–13.

DORSON, RICHARD
1968   *The British folklorists: a history.* Chicago: University of Chicago Press.

DU PONCEAU, PETER STEPHEN, et al.
1819   "Heads of enquiry and observation among each of the Indian tribes of the Missouri." Original manuscript in American Philosophical Society Library, Philadelphia.

EAST INDIES COMPANY
1705   *The agreement of the customs of the East Indians… to which are added instructions to young gentlemen that intend to travel.* London: W. Davis.

ETHNOLOGICAL SOCIETY OF PARIS
1841   *Instructions générales addressées aux voyageurs.* Ethnological Society of Paris, Memoirs 1.

EVANS, JOAN
1956   *A history of the society of antiquaries.* Oxford: Printed at the University Press by Charles Batey for the Society of Antiquaries.

FISON, LORIMER, ALFRED W. HOWITT
1874   "Instructions for ascertaining the terms of consanguinity and affinity in use among the Australian aborigines." Melbourne: Office of the Board for the Protection of Aborigines. (Reprinted 1971 in *Come wind, come weather, a biography of Alfred Howitt* by Mary Howitt Walker, Appendix 4.)

FOWLER, DON D.
n.d.   "Notes on *Inquiries* in Anthropology 1500–1900. Changing interpretations of man and culture." (In preparation.)

FOWLER, DON D., editor
n.d.   "John Wesley Powell's field manual for study of Indian medical practices, 1881." (In preparation.)

FRAZER, JAMES G.
1887   *Questions on the manners, customs, religions, superstitions, etc. of the uncivilized or semi-civilized peoples.* London. (Second revised edition 1889, reprinted in the *Journal of the Anthropological Institute of Great Britain and Ireland* 18:431–449.)

1907   *Question on the customs, beliefs and languages of savages.* Cambridge: Cambridge University Press. (Second edition 1910; third edition 1916.)

FREEMAN, JOHN FINLEY
1959   "Henry Rowe Schoolcraft." Unpublished doctoral dissertation, Harvard University.

GALLATIN, ALBERT
1826   *A table of Indian tribes of the United States, east of the Stony Mountains, arranged according to languages and Dialects.* Washington: Office of Indian Affairs. (Printed copy with: Albert Gallatin to Thomas L. McKenney, March 4, 1826. Letter book 125:731–735. Letters received. Office of Indian Affairs. Record group 75. National Archives, Washington.)

1836   *A synopsis of the Indian tribes of North America.... Archaeologica Americana: Transactions and Collections of the American Antiquarian Society* 2:1–422.

GALTON, FRANCIS, et al.
1883   *Final report of the Anthropometric Committee.* British Association for the Advancement of Science, Report 53:253–306.

1893–1895   *Ethnographical survey of the United Kingdom.* British Association for the Advancement of Science, Report 63:621–653; Report 64:419–431; Report 65:509–518. London. (*Heads* of *inquiry* issued separately, 1894, London: Spottiswoode.)

GARCIA ICAZBALCETA, JOAQUÍN
1886   *Bibliografía mexicana del siglo XVI, part one: Catalogo razonado de los libros impresos en Mexico de 1539 a 1600. Con biografías de autores y otras illustraciones*, 247–323. Mexico.

GARIBAY, ÁNGEL MARÍA
1971   *Historia de la literatura Nahuatl,* volume two: *El trauma de la Conquista (1521–1750).* Mexico: Editorial Ponua.

GIBBS, GEORGE
1862   "Instructions for archaeological investigations in the United States," in *Smithsonian Institution annual report for 1861,* 392–396.

1863   *Instructions for research relative to the ethnology and philology of America.* Smithsonian Miscellaneous Collections 7 (160).

GOLDSTEIN, KENNETH S.
1964   *A guide for field workers in folklore.* Hatboro, Pensylvania: Folklore Associates.

GOODALL, B.
1630   *The tryall of travell....* London: John Norton.

GOSSE, L. H., et al.
1861   Questions ethnologiques et médicales relatives au Pérou. *Anthropological Society of Paris, Bulletin,* first series, 2:86–137.

1862   Instructions ethnologiques pour le Mexique. *Anthropological Society of Paris, Bulletin,* first series, 3:112–237.

GRUBER, JACOB W.
1970   Ethnographic salvage and the shaping of anthropology. *American Anthropologist* 72:1289–1299.

HANSEN, THORKILD
1964   *Arabia Felix. The Danish Expedition of 1761–1767.* London: Wm. Collins Sons.

HENRY, JOSEPH
1878   *Circular in reference to American archaeology.* Smithsonian Miscellaneous Collections 15(316).

HERSCHEL, JOHN F. W., *editor*
1849   *A manual of scientific enquiry prepared for the use of Her Majesty's Navy and adapted for travellers in general.* London: J. Murray. (Second edition 1851; third edition 1859; Fourth edition 1871; fifth revised edition by J. Ball 1886, London: Eyre and Spottiswoode.)

HERVÉ, GEORGES
1910   Les instructions anthropologiques de G. Cuvier pour le voyage du "Géographe" et du "Naturaliste" aux Terres Australes. *School of Anthropology of Paris, Review* 20:289–302.

HODGEN, MARGARET T.
1964   *Early anthropology in the sixteenth and seventeenth centuries.* Philadelphia: University of Pennsylvania Press.

HODGKIN, THOMAS, RICHARD CULL
1852   *A manual of ethnological inquiry; being a series of questions concerning the human race.* British Association for the Advancement of Science, Report 22:243–252.

HODGKIN, THOMAS, *et al.*
1841   *Queries respecting the human race, to be addressed to travellers and others.* British Association for the Advancement of Science, Report 11: 332–339.

HOLMES, WILLIAM HENRY, OTIS TUFTON MASON
1899   *Instructions to collectors of historical and anthropological specimens.* U.S. National Museum, Bulletin 39, part N.

HOWARD, CLARE
1914   *English travellers of the Renaissance.* London: John Lane, The Bodley Head.

HOWELL, JAMES
1642   *Instructions for forriene travell; shewing by what cours, and in what compasse of time, one may take an exact survey of the kingdomes and states of Christendome...* London: Printed by T. B. for Humphrey Mosley.

HUDDLESTON, LEE E.
1967   *Origins of the American Indians, European concepts, 1492–1729.* Austin: University of Texas Press.

HUNTER, WILLIAM
1768   Observations on the bones, commonly supposed to be elephant bone, which have been found near the River Ohio in America. *Royal Society, Philosophical Transactions* 58:39–40.

HYMES, DELL
n.d.   "History of anthropology, bibliography." Mimeographed manuscript, University of Pennsylvania.

JACKSON, DONALD, editor
1962   Letters of the Lewis and Clark expedition with related documents, 1783–1854. Urbana: University of Illinois Press.

JEFFERSON, THOMAS
n.d.   "Vocabulary List of 276 words." Copy in American Philosophical Society Library, Philadelphia.

JEFFERSON, THOMAS, et al.
1799   Circular letter. American Philosophical Society, Transactions 4: xxxvii–xxxix. (Reprinted 1809 in Transactions 5.)

JESSUP, RONALD, compiler.
1961   Curiosities of British archaeology. London: Butterworths.

JIMÉNEZ-MORENO, WIGBERTO
1938   "Fray Bernardino de Sahagún y su obra," in Historia general de las cosas de Nueva Espana by Fray Bernardino de Sahagún, volume one, xiii–lxxxi.

JONGMANS, D. G., P. C. W. GUTKIND, editors
1967   Anthropologists in the field. New York: Humanities Press.

KALTBRUNNER, D.
1881   Aide-memoire de voyageur. Zurich: J. Wurster.

KINIETZ, VERNON
1946   Delaware culture chronology. Indiana Historical Society, Prehistory Research Series 3(1).

KINIETZ, VERNON, editor
1938   Meearmeear traditions by C. C. Trowbridge. University of Michigan Museum of Anthropology, Occasional Contributions 7.

KINIETZ, VERNON, ERMINIE W. VOEGELIN, editors
1939   Shawnese traditions: C. C. Trowbridge's account. University of Michigan Museum of Anthropology, Occasional Contributions 9.

KROEBER, A. L., et al.
1963   Anthropology today: an encyclopedia inventory. Chicago: University of Chicago Press.

LANE-FOX, A. L., et al.
1878–1880   Reports of the Anthropometric Committee. British Association for the Advancement of Science, Report 48:152–156; Report 49:175–210; Report 50:120–159.

LHWYD, EDWARD
1697   To promote the work; queries in order to the geography, and antiquities of the country. Oxford. (Reprinted 1961 in Curiosities of British archaeology. Compiled by Ronald Jessup, 178–179.)

LINDGREN, E. J.
1939   "The collection and analysis of folklore," in The study of society: methods and problems. Edited by F. C. Bartlett et al., 328–378. New York: Macmillan.

LIPSCOMB, A. A., et al., editors
1903   The writings of Thomas Jefferson, volume two: 1–247. Jefferson's notes on Virginia. Washington: Jefferson Memorial Society.

LIPSIUS, JUSTUS
1592   A direction for travailers. Taken out of Justus Lipsius [by Sir John Stradling] and enlarged for the behoofe of the right honorable Lord, the

young Earle of Bedford. London: Imprinted by R. B. for Cuthbert Burbie.

LUBBOCK, JOHN, *et al.*

1873   Report of the Arctic Committee of the Anthropological Institute. *Journal of the Anthropological Institute of Great Britain and Ireland* 2: 293–306.

LYSAGHT, A. M.

1971   *Joseph Banks in Newfoundland and Labrador, 1766*. London: Faber.

MALLERY, GARRICK

1880   *Introduction to the study of sign languages among the North American Indians as illustrating the gesture speech of mankind*. Washington: Government Printing Office.

MASON, OTIS T.

1875   *Circular relative to the Indian tribes of the United States*. Washington: U.S. Government Printing Office.

MEIER, ALBERT

1589   *Certaine briefe, and special instructions for gentlemen, merchants, students, souldiers, marriners, etc. Employed in services abrode, or in any way occasioned to converse in the kingdomes, and governments of foreign princes*. London: John Wolfe.

MICHAELIS, JOHANN DAVID

1774   *Recueil de questions proposées à une société des savants, qui par ordre de Sa Majesté Danoise font le voyage de l'Arabia; traduit de l'Allemand*. Amsterdam and Utrecht: J. B. Merian.

MORGAN, LEWIS HENRY

1862   *Circular in reference to the degrees of relationship among different nations*. Smithsonian Miscellaneous Collections 2(10).

1871   *Systems of coonssanguinity and affinity of the human family*. Smithsonian Contributions to Knowledge 17.

MÜLLER, GERHARD FRIEDRICH

1761   *Voyages from Asia to America for completing the discovery of the northwest coast of America*, London: T. Jefferys.

MURDOCK, GEORGE P.

1959   "Sociology and anthropology," in *For a science of social man*. Edited by J. P. Gillin, 14–31. New York: Macmillan.

MURDOCK, GEORGE P., *et al.*

1965   *Outline of cultural materials* (fourth revised edition). Behavior Science Outlines 1.

NAROLL, RAOUL, RONALD COHEN, *editors*

1970   *A handbook of method in cultural anthropology*. Garden City: Natural History Press.

NEALE, T.

1643   *A treatise of direction how to travell safely and profitably into forraigne countries*. London: H. Robinson.

NICOLAU D'OLWER, LUIS

1952   *Fray Bernardino de Sahagún (1499–1590)*. Panamerican Institute of Geography and History Publication 142.

PALLAS, SIMON PETER
1786   *Modele du vocabularie, qui doit servir à la comparaison de toutes les langues.* St. Petersberg.

PALLAS, SIMON PETER, *editor*
1786-1789   *Linguarum totius orbis vocabularia comparative; augustissimae cura collecta,* two volumes. St Petersberg and Leipzig: J. Z. Logan.

PALMER, THOMAS
1606   *An essay of the meanes how to make our trauiles into forraine countries, the more profitable and honourable.* London: Imprinted by H. L. for Matthew Lownes.

PAUL, BENJAMIN
1953   "Interview techniques and field relationship," in *Anthropology today: an encyclopedia inventory.* Edited by A. L. Kroeber, et al., 430–451. Chicago: University of Chicago Press.

PENNELL, FRANCIS W.
1936   Travels and scientific collections of Thomas Nuttall. *Bartonia* (18):1–51.

PETTY, WILLIAM
1686   "Quaeries concerning the nature of the natives of Pennsilvania." (Reprinted 1927 in *The Petty papers, some unpublished writings of Sir William Petty.* Edited by Marquis of Landsdowne, 115–118. London: Constable.)

POWELL, JOHN WESLEY
1877   Introduction to the study of Indian languages (Second revised edition, 1881.) Washington: Government Printing Office.

RESEK, CARL
1960   *Lewis Henry Morgan: American scholar.* Chicago: University of Chicago Press.

RICHARDS, AUDREY I.
1939   "The development of field work methods in social anthropology," in *The study of society: methods and problems.* Edited by F. C. Bartlett, et al., 272–316. New York: Macmillan.

RISLEY, H. H.
1893-1895   Progress of anthropology in India. *Journal of the Anthropological Society of Bombay* 6:88–93.

RISLEY, H. H., *et al.*
1885   Ethnographical questions. *Journal of the Anthropological Society of Bombay* 3:503–504. Bombay. (Also issued as a separate, 1885, Ethnological Survey of India, Poona.)

ROBERTSON, WILLIAM
1777   *The history of America,* two volumes. London: W. Strahan.

ROYAL ANTHROPOLOGICAL INSTITUTE OF GREAT BRITAIN AND IRELAND
1964   *Notes and queries on anthropology* (sixth revised edition). London: Routledge and Kegan Paul.

ROYAL SOCIETY OF LONDON
1665-1667   Philosophical Transactions.

RUSSOV, F., *editor*
1900   "G. F. Müller's Instruktion fur den Akademiker — Adjuncten, J. E. Fisher." *Sbovnick Muzeia po Antropologii i Etnografii pri Imperatorsko Akademii Nauk* 1(1):37–109.

SCHOOLCRAFT, HENRY ROWE
1847 *Inquiries, respecting the history, present condition and future prospects of the Indian tribes of the United States.* Washington: Office of Indian Affairs. (Reprinted 1851–1857 as Appendix I of Schoolcraft.)
1851–1857 *Historical and statistical information respecting the history, condition and prospects of the Indian tribes of the United States,* six volumes. (Various editions issued.)
SPENCER, HERBERT
1873–1881 *Descriptive sociology: or, groups of sociological facts classified and arranged...,* eight volumes. London: William and Norgate.
1904 *An autobiography,* two volumes. New York: D. Appleton.
STOCKING, GEORGE W., JR.
1968 *Race, culture and evolution: essays in the history of anthropology.* New York: The Free Press.
1971 What's in a name? The origins of the Royal Anthropological Institute (1837–1871). *Man, Journal of the Royal Anthropological Institute* 6: 369–390.
SUTHERLAND, EDWIN V.
1964 "The diaries of John Gregory Bourke: their anthropological and folklore content." Unpublished doctoral dissertation, University of Pennsylvania.
TAPLIN, GEORGE, *editor*
1879 *The folklore, manners, customs and languages of the South Australia aborigines: gathered from inquiries made by authority of the South Australian Government.* Adelaide: E. Spiller, Acting Government Printer. (Reprinted 1967. New York: Johnson Reprint.)
THOMAS, N. W.
1900 Questions on animal superstition. *Man, Journal of the Royal Anthropological Institute* 1:114–116.
1906 Questions on dolls. *Man, Journal of the Royal Anthropological Institute* 6(68):105–106.
TREASE, GEOFFREY
1967 *The grand tour.* New York: Holt, Rinehart, and Winston.
TUCKER, JOSIAH
1757 *Instructions for travellers.* London: privately printed.
TURLER, JEROME
1575 *The traveiler of Jerome Turler, divided into two bookes. The first conteining a notable discourse of the manner, and order of traveiling oversea, or into straunge and forrein countreys. The second comprehending an excellent description of the most delicious realme of Naples in Italy....* London: by William How, for Abraham Veale.
TURNER, WILLIAM, *et al.*
1891 *Report of the committee to investigate the habits, customs, physical characters, and religions of the natives of India.* British Association for the Advancement of Science, Report 60:547. London.
TYLOR, E. B.
1871 "Ethnology by the late J. C. Prichard" (revised), in *A manual of scientific enquiry* (fourth edition). Edited by J. Herschel. London: J. Murray.

1886   "Anthropology," in *A manual of scientific enquiry* (fifth edition). Edited by R. S. Ball, 225–238. London: Eyre and Spottiswoode.

TYLOR, E. B., *et al.*
1885–1898   *Reports of the Committee... [on] the Northwestern tribes of the Dominion of Canada.* British Association for the Advancement of Science, Report 55:696–707; Report 58:233–254; Report 60:553–715; Report 68:628–697.

URRY, JAMES
1973   "Notes and queries on anthropology and the development of field methods in British anthropology, 1870–1920," in *Proceedings of the Royal Anthropological Institute of Great Britain and Ireland for 1972*, 45–57.

VILLIERS, ALAN
1967   *Captain James Cook.* New York: Charles Scribner's Sons.

VON ADELUNG, FREDERICH
1815   *Catherinens der Grossen Verdienste um die vergleichende Sprachunkunde.* St Petersberg: F. Drechsler.

WALKER, MARY HOWITT
1971   *Come wind, come weather, a biography of Alfred Howitt.* Melbourne: Melbourne University Press.

WOODWARD, J.
1696   *Brief instructions for making observations in all parts of the world....* London: Rich. Wilkin.

YANKIEWITCH DE MIRIEWO, FEODOR, *editor*
1790–1791   *Comparative dictionary of all languages and dialects in alphabetical order arranged.* St. Petersberg. (Published in Russian, translated title cited 1891 by Pilling in *Bibliography of the Algonquian languages.* Bureau of American Ethnology, Bulletin 13:541.)

YARROW, HENRY C.
1880   *Introduction to the study of mortuary customs among the North American Indians.* Washington: U.S. Government Printing Office.

The History of Ethnographic Film

EMILIE DE BRIGARD

Ethnographic films have been produced ever since the technological inventions of nineteenth-century industrial society made possible the visual recording of encounters with other societies. Since its beginning, ethnographic film has been burdened with the expectation that it will reveal something about primitive cultures – and ultimately, all of culture – which can be grasped in no other way. The fulfillment of this expectation is what concerns us here. It is usual to define ethnographic film as film that reveals cultural patterning. From this definition it follows that all films are ethnographic, by reason of their content or form or both. Some films, however, are clearly more revealing than others.

Since the simultaneous inventions in Europe and America of motion pictures, shortly before the turn of the century, almost every people in the

I am indebted for information about Haddon to Peter Gathercole and James Woodburn. Many others have generously helped me in countless ways. Among those not named in the text are: Charles Weaver and the staff of the American Museum of Natural History; Jacques Ledoux and the staff of the Cinémathèque Royale de Belgique; Ernest Lindgren and the staff of the British Film Institute; and Tahar Sheriaa, Executive Secretary of the Journées Internationales Cinématographiques de Carthage. This paper has benefited from discussions with Erik Barnouw, Jean Rouch, and Richard Sorenson, who called certain inaccuracies to my attention; and from the editorial scrutiny of Paul Hockings and Timothy Thoresen, the chairmen of the sessions on Visual Anthropology and the History of Anthropology. I alone am responsible for the views expressed, and for errors of fact and omission. I am especially grateful to the Wenner-Gren Foundation for Anthropological Research, The Museum of Modern Art, the Smithsonian Institution, and the Choreometrics Project of Columbia University for support, and to the Directors of these bodies for their encouragement.

This paper is a précis of the forthcoming illustrated volume, *Anthropological cinema*, to be published by the Museum of Modern Art (New York). Copyright © 1973 by Emilie Rahman de Brigard.

world has been filmed in one way or another, and a few groups have been filmed repeatedly, intensively, and brilliantly.[1] Examination of the corpus of ethnographic film and its literature shows that filmmakers have been guided (and also limited) by the technical means available to them, by the theoretical formulations of anthropology and cinematic art and by the intended and actual uses of their films. The history of technical progress, theoretical advance, and increasing sophistication in the use of film runs counter to a long-standing reluctance on the part of social scientists to take film seriously. The overwhelmingly verbal bias of anthropology was naively, and ineffectually, challenged by the innovators of ethnographic film in the years before World War I. The period between the wars saw solid if isolated achievements in theory and application, and, outside the academic sphere, the creation of an audience for social documentary films; but ethnographic film became an institutionalized scientific field, with recognized specialists and a body of criticism, only during the 1950's. In 1973, on the twenty-first anniversary of the formation of the International Committee on Ethnographic and Sociological Film, its members recognized that their discipline was in process of reinterpretation and unprecedented growth.

It is no accident that respect for film in the scientific community in recent years has been equaled by interest in the concerns of anthropology among the viewing public. The postwar revolution in communications technology is responsible for this. Today's young citizens have grown up with the new freedom of 16-mm synchronous sound filming, the impact of television transmission, and the possibility of computerized videotape storage of records. This technological revolution has facilitated development of ethnographic film from the fragmentary and idiosyncratic to the systematic and thorough; it has also caused the disappearance of much of its traditional subject matter. But the irony of the situation is superficial. Although the inclination to capture "the conspicuous, the traditional and the bizarre" is still present, both in scientific and in commercial films, it has gradually been giving way to a more thoughtful tendency to try to record, as coherently as possible, items of unspectacular but significant behavior. We now turn our cameras on ourselves for a good hard look at our own societies, thus redressing an imbalance which the "native" subjects of ethnographic films have found highly offensive.

[1] A definitive filmography of ethnographic films, invaluable for determination of filming priorities, has not yet been published. The International Committee on Ethnographic and Sociological Film has to date completed catalogues of ethnographic films of Subsaharan Africa (1967), the Pacific (1970), Asia and the Middle East (in press), and is assembling material on films of Latin America.

Ethnographic film began as a phenomenon of colonialism, and has flourished in periods of political change: socialist revolution, democratic reform, independence for developing nations. Its problems bear comparison with those of the new cinemas in former colonies: like these it enjoys an essential seriousness (sometimes ideologically tinged) and suffers from technical and financial handicaps by comparison with the established film industry. Like these it struggles to overcome Hollywood conventions; and it does without mass acceptance. But a few ethnographic filmmakers have influenced important movements in the cinema, and thus shaped the way in which generations of viewers saw life on the screen. Moreover, there are indications that some films have aided cultural renewal. The most exciting possibility of ethnographic films is to enable many who would not otherwise do so – amongst them, those whose specialized knowledge directs man's affairs – TO SEE, newly and richly, the range of patters in the behavior of man. Its essential function, however, was stated by its very first practitioner and remains unchanged today. Film "preserves forever all human behaviors for the needs of our studies" (Regnault 1931:306).

The first person to make an ethnographic film was Félix-Louis Regnault, a physician specializing in pathological anatomy who became interested in anthropology around 1888, the year in which Jules-Étienne Marey, the inventor of "chronophotography," demonstrated his new camera, using celluloid roll film, to the French Académie des Sciences. In the spring of 1895, Regnault, aided by Marey's associate, Charles Comte, filmed a Wolof woman making pots at the Exposition Ethnographique de l'Afrique Occidentale. The film showed the Wolof method of making pottery, using a shallow concave base which is turned with one hand while the clay is shaped with the other. Regnault claimed that he was the first to note this method, which, he said, illustrates the transition from pottery made without any wheel at all to that made on the primitive horizontal wheel used in ancient Egypt, India, and Greece. He wrote up his experiment, including several line drawings taken from the film, and published it in December, 1895; the same month that the Lumières gave the first public projection of "cinématographe" films, a successful commercial experiment which launched the motion picture industry (Lajard and Regnault 1895; Sadoul 1966: 11).

Regnault's subsequent films were devoted to the cross-cultural study of movement: climbing a tree, squatting, walking, by Wolof, Fulani, and Diola men and women (Regnault 1896a, 1896b, 1897). He championed the systematic use of motion pictures in anthropology, and proposed the formation of anthropological film archives (Regnault 1912, 1923a,

1923b). Toward the end of his life he seems to have felt that his urgings had not been effective. In fact the Anglo-Saxons and Germans soon overtook the French in ethnographic filming; nonetheless, Marey's countrymen continued to excel in filming physiology (Michaelis 1955: 87).

One of the events marking the transformation of nineteenth-century speculative anthropology into a discipline with standards of evidence comparable to those of natural science was the Cambridge Anthropological Expedition to the Torres Straits, which Alfred Cort Haddon, a former zoologist, mounted in 1898. The expedition was conceived as a team effort of systematic salvage ethnography covering all aspects of Torres Straits life, including physical anthropology, psychology, material culture, social organization, and religion. A whole battery of recording methods was used, some of them new, such as W. H. R. Rivers' genealogical method, which has since become standard, and photography, together with wax-cylinder sound recording and motion pictures. Haddon's ethnographic films, for which a Lumière camera was used, are the earliest known to have been made in the field. What remains of them (several minutes' worth) shows three men's dances and an attempt at firemaking.

Haddon encouraged his colleagues to array themselves for fieldwork with photographic equipment. In 1901 he wrote about filming in a letter to Baldwin Spencer, who was about to undertake an expedition to Central Australia. Spencer and his associate, F. J. Gillen, spent the next thirty years studying the Australian Aborigines, and they produced monumental ethnographies copiously illustrated with photographs, but Spencer filmed on only two occasions, in 1901, and in Northern Australia in 1912. Despite flies, difficulties of transport, and the shyness of the Aranda, he collected over 7,000 feet of film, chiefly of ceremonies, and a number of wax cylinders. The scale of this effort (running time more than an hour) was large for its time, and the films are still legible enough to be used in research today. One long sequence of a Bugamani ceremony on Bathurst Island is even eerily beautiful. Notwithstanding the merit of what had been done, Spencer apparently made no further use of his films once they were housed in the National Museum at Victoria. Another colleague of Haddon's, Rudolf Pöch of Vienna, saw the Torres Straits films at Cambridge in 1902, and then took motion picture and stereoscopic cameras on his field trips to New Guinea and Southwest Africa in 1904 and 1907. Pöch's attempts at filming met with mechanical snags – underexposure and loosening of the lens through rough handling. Nearly half of the footage exposed in New Guinea failed to come out. Pöch ruefully advised developing film in the field whenever possible, or at least testing a strip from each roll, in order to catch and correct technical problems as they came up. He managed to film dance in Cape Nelson, girls carrying water and children playing in Hanuabada (Port Moresby), and a man being shaved with an obsidion razor (Pöch 1907: 395 ff.).

Pöch's films were restored and published by the University of Vienna in 1960, and Spencer's were shown in a retrospective of Australian ethnographic films which attracted world-wide attention in 1967. To be unused and unknown has been the fate of all too many ethnographic films stored in the vaults of museums or in the garages of anthropologists' families. Many were destroyed as fire hazards, and others will soon be beyond saving, unless the programs of restoration which have been carried out on an *ad hoc* basis since the 1950's are rationalized, centralized, and well funded.

Of the pioneers of ethnographic film, only Regnault is known to have made use of it over a period of years. Why were the efforts of others without a sequel? Filming has always been far more expensive than writing, and it was, relatively speaking, even more so in the early years of the century.[2] There was real danger in working with highly inflammable nitrate film; gruesome fatalities occurred as late as the 1950's, and taking the necessary precautions, for example building a fireproof projection booth, added expense and inconvenience. Filming in the field resembled a wrestling match with protean equipment: cumbersome cameras fixed on tripods, with or without panning heads, viewfinders, or extra lenses, and using film whose low exposure index demanded shooting in broad daylight. These technical difficulties were serious enough; when problems of theory were also taken into account, the prospects for ethnographic film seemed bleak indeed.

Regnault had a theoretical focus for his filming: "the study of physiology proper to each ethnic group" (Regnault 1931: 306). Haddon's motive was apparently the urgent one of salvage, and cannot be faulted as such; but ethnographic salvage, however valuable, is not a substitute for a program of scientific inquiry. Moreover, interest in the material expressions of culture, which occupied Haddon's generation, began to be supplanted, early in this century, by emphasis on psychologistic traits and the intangibles of social structure. For many years it was beyond the technical capabilities of cinematography to follow this shift.

Up to this point the exposition has been concerned with ethnographic research films, which were made by scientists and were not intended to be

[2] For examples of budgets, see Hilton-Simpson and Haeseler (1925: 330) and Collier (1967: 127-135).

seen by laymen. But if we were to limit ourselves to what has been filmed by scientists, our history would appear poorer than it is. Comparative study of human behavior on a global scale, by means of the World Ethnographic Film Sample, would be severely hampered if all commercial and sponsored films were excluded.

Edgar Morin (1956) has described the transformation of motion pictures, the plaything of inspired *bricoleurs*, into the cinema, the dream machine of the masses. From its earliest days, two tendencies in the cinema can be made out: the documentary or *actualité* film, originated by the Lumières, and the fiction film, invented by Méliès in 1897 to win back to the box office a public which had speedily become bored by motion pictures (Sadoul 1966: 32). Actuality is generally less expensive to film than fiction. At various times and places, producers and public have preferred one of these tendencies to the other, but the distinction is often blurred to take advantage of both. The hybrid *documentaire romancé* – the story film set in a genuine exotic background – made its appearance by 1914.

Among the earliest commercial films were some autobiographical documentaries of the Lumière family: *Le déjeuner de Bébé, La partie d'écarté, La pêche à la crevette*, etc. (1895).[3] In 1896–1897, their *opérateurs* fanned out across the globe, showing films to curious crowds on all continents and shooting items to be sent back to Lyon for the Lumière catalogue (Sadoul 1964). The American firm of Edison sent cameramen to film Samoan dancers at Barnum and Bailey's Circus, Walapai snake dancers in the pueblo, and Jewish dancers in the Holy Land. From 1905, Pathé Frères produced and distributed 35-mm *actualités* with an average length of 300 feet on a variety of subjects in Europe and abroad; other firms engaged in this activity were Warwick, Urban, Kineto, and Gaumont.[4]

Georges Méliès' firm, Star Film, which was known for its fantastic productions (as a trip to the moon was then considered), suffered chronic financial difficulty after an initial period of success. In 1912, Gaston Méliès, a brother, sought to cash in on the vogue for films of faraway places by producing melodramas in the South Seas. He assembled cameras, film, and a troupe of actors, and took ship for Tahiti and New Zealand. On his return to New York in 1913, Star Film released five two-reel *documentaires romancés*, none of which has survived. The best of

---

[3] For further information on the films cited, see the item on "Filmography" in Hockings (1975).
[4] The national archives of many countries contain film catalogues which repay close study.

them, from the point of view of ethnographic production values, was probably *Loved by a Maori Chieftainess*, in which an English explorer of the 1870's, about to be killed by a headhunter, escapes to an island with the help of a beautiful princess, marries her, and is accepted as her husband by the Maori. The action took place against a background of genuine village life, dancing, and war canoes (O'Reilly 1970: 289–290). Méliès planned to distribute a whole series of these tropical entertainments, but he discovered that most of his film had been ruined by a year of South Seas humidity. Star Film never recovered from the blow. Georges Méliès sold his company and eventually died a pauper (Sadoul 1966: 39).

Apart from entertainment, what is the value of nonscientific films of peoples and customs? Availability of information supplementing the film is of critical importance. *Actualités* and newsreels, often short and sometimes falsified, seldom give a systematic view of anything, although dance fares better than most categories. Human behavior in documentary and fiction films is subject to directorial distortion to such an extent that the film may be scientifically worthless. However, authenticity can be found on levels untouched by dramatic action.

A case in point is Edward Curtis' remarkable 1914 film, *In the Land of the Head-Hunters*. (The beginnings of visual ethnography of the American Indian, incidentally, are not in the films of Edison or Thomas Ince, but in still photography [Taft 1938: 249 ff.][5] The photographers of the Indians were not trained anthropologists, but the best of them did their work with enthusiasm, extraordinary dedication, and sensitivity.) Curtis, a prolific still photographer, spent three seasons with the Kwakiutl filming a drama of love and war in settings painstakingly reconstructed for precontact authenticity. Curtis had learned the same lessons as D.W. Griffith, and he handled suspense well. What gives his film its lasting appeal is the way in which Indian elements are used to tell the story visually. Its plot, which concerns a wicked sorcerer, a hero, and their respective factions battling for a girl, was to recur twenty-five years later, in H. P. Carver's Ojibwa melodrama, *The Silent Enemy*.

Toward the end of the pioneer period of ethnographic film came the first use of film in applied anthropology, the origin of the colonial cinema. By 1912, it had occurred to the Americans who administered the Philippines that films might serve a purpose in native education: where a -anguage barrier prevented giving lessons successfully by word of mouth,

---

[5] For surveys of photography in anthropology, see Rowe (1953); Mead (1963); and Collier (1967).

films would convey the message. Worcester, the Secretary of the Interior for the Philippines, devised a program of sanitary education for the provinces. To hold the interest of the Bontoc Igorot, Ifugao, and Kalinga between health films, Worcester's subordinates projected scenes of native and foreign life. The program achieved the desired result; when shown moving pictures of better conditions, the people showed a disposition to change. Moreover, Worcester reported, "the old sharply drawn tribal lines are disappearing... At the same time that all of this has been accomplished, the goodwill of the people has been secured" (Donaldson 1912: 41–42).

The generation before World War I was a time of innovation; the period between the wars was a time of popularization. In 1931, Regnault surveyed the status of film in anthropology, formulated a typology of film according to its use for entertainment, education, or research, and asserted that the importance of film in scientific research had been forgotten (Regnault 1931: 306). In fact, this was not the case; film had an established place in the laboratory (Michaelis 1955). But until Mead and Bateson's work of 1936–1938, the films made by anthropologists in the field, though intrinsically valuable, were not original in conception. What was new was the spread of film in anthropological teaching, fostered by museums and universities. Alongside the development of the teaching film, educational motion pictures, in the broadest sense, found a new dimension in the documentary. The technical advance of miniaturization of the 16-mm teaching film made possible the unprecedented fluency of Mead and Bateson's visual research. The aesthetic development of the documentary profoundly influenced the shape of the ethnographic film when it came into its own after World War II.

The history of the teaching film can be traced from the origins of motion pictures, but its great spurts occurred during the World Wars and in the periods following them, when film equipment and personnel were diverted to civilian life (Anderson 1968). By the mid-1920's, the anthropological teaching film evolved its canonical forms: the single-concept film of ceremonial, crafts, and the like; and the filmed cultural inventory, more or less complete. Another form, the comparison film (of houses of the Arctic and the tropics, for example) was less common. In format the anthropological teaching film was from ten minutes to over an hour long, silent, with intertitles which sometimes took up more than half of the film. After the adoption of sound in 1927, voice-over narration gradually replaced titles.

Museums were well-suited to produce films on anthropological subjects, since they had the possibility both of sending cameramen on their expeditions and of attracting steady audiences to their programs. An excellent series about the Zuñi was made in 1923 by F. W. Hodge, ethnologist, and Owen Cattell, cameraman, for the Heye Foundation-Museum of the American Indian. An overview film, *Land of the Zuñi and Community Work*, shows planting, threshing, water carrying, children at play, and gambling, by men, women, and children who appear to be going about their daily occupations with complete absorption, oblivious of the camera. Three films of ceremonials show dancing and the planting of sacred wands. The rest of the series covers hairdressing, housebuilding, baking bread, and tanning and wrapping deerskin leggings. Despite occasional awkwardness in the technical process films, these compare favorably with the series directed by Samuel Barrett at the University of California more than thirty years later.

Sensing the possibility of profit, commercial film producers entered into association with museums and universities; the Harvard-Pathé project produced a number of short, straightforward films on the *Battacks of Sumatra, Mongols of Central Asia, Wanderers of the Arabian Desert'* etc. (1928), before the relationship was dissolved. Nordisk Films Kompagni and Svensk Filmindustri coproduced the Svarta Horisonter (Black Horizons) series (1935–1936) directed in Madagascar by Paul Fejos, the Hungarian director. Later, as Director of Research of the Wenner-Gren Foundation, Fejos trained film crews in anthropology (*Nomads of the Jungle*, 1952) and anthropologists in filming (at Yale and Columbia Universities), but his excellent anthropological documentaries (*A Handful of Rice*, 1938; *Yagua*, 1941) are not as well known as his theatrical films, *Lonesome* (1928) and *Légende hongroise* (1932) (Bidney 1964; Dodds 1973).

Eastman Kodak developed the 16-mm format (1923) expressly for the school market, but by the 1950's most educational films were still being filmed in 35-mm and reduced for distribution. A certain stiffness marred even the best of these films. And the format of the visual lecture, now in color, is with us still.

However successful teaching films might be (and it should be remembered that Eastman Teaching Films was a subsidized operation, designed to bolster the parent firm's sales of film stock), they were surpassed in visibility and profitability by explorer films and by fiction films set in exotic locations, which enjoyed great popularity between the wars. Among explorers, Martin Johnson was the durable producer of *On the Borderland of Civilization* (1920), *Simba, Congorilla, Baboona,* and *Borneo* (1937). Frank Hurley's *Pearls and Savages* (1924) was probably the first film made in New Guinea. The makers of *Grass* (1925), Merian Cooper and Ernest Schoedsack, went on to film Lao villagers and elephants in

Chang (1927), before their greatest success, *King Kong* (1933). Léon Poirier's *Croisière noire* (1926), the first feature-length French film made in Africa, did its job (advertising Citroën trucks) so well that it was released in a sound version in 1933. The Marquis de Wavrin's *Au pays du scalp*, record of an Amazon expedition edited by Cavalcanti and with music by Maurice Jaubert, appeared in 1934. Fiction films of the period include episodes of the *Perils of Pauline*, filmed in the Philippines in the 1920's, and Cecil B. de Mille's remake of *Squaw Man* (1931), which is all the more poignant since it is unclear which locale is meant to be more exotic, the studio interior of an English country house or the Wild West. W. S. Van Dyke directed the singularly offensive *Trader Horn* (1930), which was partly filmed in Africa, and *Tarzan, the Ape Man* (1932). Jean Mugeli's *Rapt dans la jungle* (1932) was the first Melanesian talking picture. And André-Paul Antoine and Robert Lugeon produced what was to become the first publicly exposed ethnographic film hoax, *Les mangeurs d'hommes* (1930). Antoine and Lugeon engaged a village of Christianized Small Namba to enact a terrifying drama of cannibalism, supposedly set in the "unknown region" of the interior of Malekula, where the authority of the white man was "entirely nominal." The deception was unmasked by their host in the field, the Bishop of Port Vila, but not before a celebrity-studded première had taken place in Paris (Leprohon 1960).

Although he transcended these genres, Robert Flaherty began his film-making career as an explorer, and he continued by directing a South Seas love story for Hollywood. *Nanook* (1922) was described by a spokesman for the Asia Society as "drama, education, and inspiration combined"; and of *Moana* (1926) John Grierson wrote: "*Moana*, being a visual account of events in the life of a Polynesian youth, has documentary value." Both films were technically innovative. For *Nanook*, Flaherty used a tripod with gyro-movement, which allowed him to follow and anticipate his subjects with the delicacy which became his trademark; and while filming *Moana* he discovered that the panchromatic film intended for his special color camera gave excellent skin tones in black and white, and his improvement became industry standard. (Unfortunately, Flaherty's interest in the problems of sound did not equal his visual gifts.) As an artist, Flaherty is of the first rank; as an anthropologist (which in any case he did not pretend to be) he leaves much to be desired. Iris Barry's attack on the authenticity of *Nanook* can never be well answered, since Flaherty, always the raconteur, did not leave a systematic record of its making. Mrs Flaherty's 1925 account of the conditions under which *Moana* was filmed is sufficient to dismiss its value as a record of interpersonal behavior, although its sequences of crafts are acceptable. Alas for Flaherty! *Man of Aran* (1934) was denounced for being escapist, for ignoring the political realities of the tenant system; *The Land* (1942) was shelved because it was considered too pessemistic, too grimly realistic to be circulated in wartime. Flaherty's gift was not that of a reporter or recorder, but rather that of a revealer.

The social documentary film, which came into being in the 1920's and flourished in the 1930's, was a mass education medium sensitive to the needs of government policy or of opposition politics in various countries. "Of all the arts," Lenin told his Commissar of Education, Lunacharsky, "for us the cinema is the most important" (Leyda 1960: 161). "I consider *Las Hurdes* one of my surrealist films," remarked Buñuel (Taylor 1964: 90). Scientific data are to be found amidst the actuality, but they are clothed in argument more subtle than fiction. If the explorer film cannot escape its exploitative nature, neither can the documentary desist from visionary exhortation.

Concern with the transformations in society is a trait common to Soviet anthropologists and filmmakers; as Marxists, they have tried not only to describe social change, but also to cause it to happen (Debets 1957; Krupianskaya, *et al.* 1960). What is striking about the first generation of Soviet filmmakers is the closeness of their ties to science, as well as to the *avant-garde* in art. Theoretical explicitness and candor about how they produced their effects distinguished Eisenstein, Pudovkin, and other Soviet filmmakers from their Western contemporaries, from whom they had learned much. Dziga Vertov, the pioneer of Soviet documentary, directed the *Kino-pravda* series (i.e. "cinema truth"; *"cinéma vérité"*) (1922) and expressed the following theory of montage, or "the organization of the seen world":

1. Montage during the observation period (immediate orientation of the naked eye at all times and places).
2. Montage after observation (logical organization of vision into one or another definite direction).
3. Montage at the time of filming (orientation of the ARMED eye — the moving picture camera — during the search for the appropriate camera position, and adjustment to the several changing conditions of filming).
4. Montage after filming (rough organization of the filmed material according to main indications, and ascertaining what necessary shots are missing).
5. Judgment of the montage pieces (immediate orientation to link certain juxtapositions, employing exceptional alertness and these military rules: judgment – speed – attack).
6. Final montage (exposition of larger themes through a series of smaller

subtler themes; reorganization of all material while keeping the rounded sequence in mind; exposure of the very heart of all your film-objects) (Belenson [1925] quoted in Leyda [1960:178-179]).

Three Songs of Lenin (1934) is considered to be Vertov's best film. It ends with a lyric section on the progress "from past to future, from slavery to freedom" of the Soviet Union's Central Asian ethnic minorities. The Soviets encouraged the development of regional filmmaking in Uzbekistan, Armenia, Georgia, and elsewhere. Mikhail Kalatozov's *Salt for Svanetia* (1930) shows past hardships of life in the Caucasus ("tormenting hunger for salt") overcome by Soviet technical aid (tractors construct an all-weather road). The Svans took offense at the film, and denied that the old customs portrayed in it had ever existed. Another "before and after" film, Viktor Turin's *Turksib* (1928), shows the building of the Turkestan-Siberian railway and the reactions of people along its path.

In Eastern and Central Europe, documentary filmmakers approached traditional life with a reverential attitude. Karel Plicka directed *Za Slovensky ludem* [Games of Slovak Youth, 1931], *Večna piseň* [The Eternal Song, 1941], and *Zem spieva* [Earth in Song, 1933], which he considered to be his "hymn to the Slovak people." Drago Chloupek and A. Gerasimov filmed a Croation *zadruga* in 1933 (*Dan u jednoj velikoj hrvatskoj porodici* [A day in a large Croatian family], anticipating later peasant symphonies by Henri Storck in Belgium and Georges Rouquier in France. German filmmakers were also attracted by folklore and ethnographic subjects, which they fashioned into *Kulturfilme*. The more ambitious of these trace the development of a trait from primitive beginnings to its advanced form. Wilhelm Prager's *Wege zu Kraft und Schönheit* (1925) compares Greco-Roman with modern German athletics, and illustrates the development of dance from Hawaiian and Burmese, through Spanish and Japanese, to Russian ballet and the dance dramas of Rudolf Laban. It concludes with shots of famous sportsmen, including Lloyd George golfing and Mussolini on horseback. The UFA publicist claimed that this film would promote "the regeneration of the human race" (Kracauer 1947:143).

French documentary, unlike Soviet and German documentary, was individualist, largely anti-establishment, and undeveloped (cf. Rotha *et al.* 1963:268). Noteworthy, even brilliant beginnings were made, but they were to mature later or elsewhere. In 1926, Alberto Cavalcanti made *Rien que les heures*, the first of the city symphonies. In 1929, Georges Rouquier made *Vendanges*, forerunner of *Farrebique* (1946) and his other films of peasant life. An obscure film, *Coulibaly à l'aventure* (1936), made by G.

H. Blanchon in French West Africa, preceded Rouch's *Jaguar* by twenty years, both in theme (migrant labor) and treatment (improvised acting). Documentary techniques found their way into fiction films, such as Jean Renoir's *Toni* (1934).

In Spain, Luis Buñuel used money won in a syndicalist lottery to produce that succinct masterpiece of dreamy outrage, *Las Hurdes* (1932). The stuff of Buñuel's argument is not only the misery of the inhabitants of Cáceres, but also our curiosity, never innocent, because human.

No such dark scruples are to be found in British and American documentaries, which were meliorist in tone and popular in scope.[6] A film of North Sea herring fisheries, John Grierson's *Drifters* (1929), was the beginning of the British documentary movement, which had as its purpose the formation of a more aware citizenry by means of the "creative treatment of actuality" (Hardy 1966). Production was supported by government and industry, and dealt with the broad topics of Empire capitalism, domestic social reform, and (with the coming of war) colonial propaganda. Rotha (1936) describes two stages of British documentary: the first, "impressionistic" stage peaked with Basil Wright's exquisite *Song of Ceylon* (made for the Ceylon Tea Propagation Board in 1935), with its symphonic structure and Eisensteinian views of Sinhalese working the fields. The second, or "realist," stage quietly anticipated the social reporting of the 1960's, by making use of spontaneous, unrehearsed speech, filmed with synchronous sound. In *Housing Problems* (produced for the British Commercial Gas Association in 1935), Edgar Anstey and Arthur Elton took camera and microphone into the working-class districts of South London. The residents pointed out the vermin and other signs of dilapidation "without prompting" (Rotha 1936: 255). In this way the film not only gained credibility but disarmed potential criticism of the makers' motives: "When the subjects raised more obvious social issues, facts and people were made to speak for themselves" (Broderick 1947: 50). To Rotha's stages must be added a third, beginning with the formation, in 1939, of the National Film Board of Canada, under Grierson, and the Colonial Film Unit (CFU), directed by William Sellers. Both were propaganda organizations, concerned with the war effort, Grierson from a stance inside European culture, Sellers from the outside. The CFU, for example, made a film designed to present the British way of life to Africans, *Mister English at Home* (1940). In the decade after the war,

---

[6] Until McCann (1973), the British movement was the better documented, thanks to John Grierson and his editor, Forsyth Hardy. Grierson's writings, when collated with an account of Britain's domestic situation between the wars, constitute a primer on the politics of film.

Sellers and his group were instrumental in developing television in Anglophone Africa.

Whatever the ideological angle of filmmakers in the 1920's and 1930's, their films share a new quality: for the first time since the Lumières, ordinary people in their everyday surroundings were seen on the screen. At the same time, the mass medium of cinema was becoming demystified through technology. Amateur filming in 16-mm was no longer an oddity. Armed with the ciné-Kodak, Major P. H. G. Powell-Cotton and his family filmed systematically in Africa during the 1930's and 1940's. In a single year, 1937–1938, the impresario, Rolf de Maré, collected an estimated 49,000 feet of 16-mm film of dance, in Sumatra, Java, Bali, and the Celebes. Film, the toy of scientists and the instrument of fantasists, was coming of age.

In anthropology, the middle of the 1930's was the watershed between film's unimportance and its acceptability. To W. D. Hambly, Melville Herskovits, Patrick O'Reilly, and Marcel Griaule, film was an illustration, not an integral part of research to be used in understanding and cited in publication. Quality, in this kind of filming, still meant 35-mm and, if possible, a trained cameraman. (But Norman Tindale, in Australia, and Franz Boas, in British Columbia, took their own 16-mm films.) By contrast, Gregory Bateson and Margaret Mead's decision to use cameras in Bali and New Guinea, in 1936–1938, was dictated by the needs of their research. They innovated both in the scale of their filming and photography (22,000 feet of 16-mm film, 25,000 stills) and in its aim, the description of the "ethos" of a people.

The shift in scale was directed primarily at recording the types of non-verbal behavior for which there existed neither vocabulary nor conceptualized methods of observation, in which the observation had to precede the codification (Mead 1963:174).

Harris states that Mead turned to photography as a direct result of criticism of her previous works, challenged over their "soft" unverifiable data (Harris 1968:417). Mead's own account of the events leading to the "quantum leap" of research in Bali and Iatmul emphasizes personal and intellectual factors (Mead 1972). Whatever its causes, the effect of methodological originality in *Balinese Character* was to make photography a respected tool in anthropological research (Bateson and Mead 1942).

The expedition to Bali was financed by the Committee for the Study of Dementia Praecox, who recognized an opportunity to cast some light upon the etiology of schizophrenia. The anthropologists brought complementary abilities to the project: Mead's unsurpassed note-taking skill and her interest in babies and family life, Bateson's grounding in natural science (he had been a student of Haddon, another former zoologist) and interest in communication and context. His was the task of taking pictures, while Mead and a Balinese secretary, equipped with chronometers, recorded events verbally, and carefully cross-referenced the pictures and notes. They were without means of recording sound.

We tried to use the still and the moving picture cameras to get a record of Balinese behavior, and this is a very different matter from the preparation of a "documentary" film or photographs. We tried to shoot what happened normally and spontaneously, rather than to decide upon the norms and then get the Balinese to go through these behaviors in suitable lighting (Bateson and Mead 1942:49).

For the greater part of their two years' stay, Mead and Bateson lived in the mountains at Bajoeng Gede, where "everything went on in a kind of simplified slow motion," owing to the poverty and hypothyroidism of the villagers. Bateson took pictures "as a matter of routine," without asking special permission. Habitually he directed attention to his photography of small babies, and the parents came to overlook the fact that they were included in the frame as well, so that the angular viewfinder, for photographing sensitive subjects, was seldom needed or used. Some theatrical performances were specially staged in daylight, as a concession to the camera. As the corpus of photographed data grew, it "was used consciously to compensate for the changing sophistication of the viewer" (Mead 1963:174), by comparing photographs taken before a hypothesis was formulated with those made afterwards.

On their way home from the field, Bateson and Mead spent six months in New Guinea, collecting comparative data among the Iatmul. Then World War II made fieldwork impossible, and other urgent research priorities demanded attention. Despite these, Bateson and Mead prepared *Balinese Character* and edited several films, which were released, after the war, in the Character Formation in Different Cultures Series (1952). In discussions of film, Mead often fails to distinguish it from still photography, a usage which reflects her method in dealing with both (Mead 1963). After viewing the 25,000 stills sequentially, Bateson and Mead chose and arranged 759 of them in 100 plates, thematically juxtaposing related details without "violating the context and the integrity of any one event" (Mead 1972:235). The films were edited chronologically (*Trance and Dance in Bali*) or by presenting contrasting items of behavior (*Childhood Rivalry in Bali and New Guinea*).

While Bateson and Mead were in Bali, Jean Rouch was in Paris, studying engineering and forming the associations which would lead to his be-

coming a leader of the ethnographic film wave in Europe, and an indefati-
gable producer and popularizer. At the Musée de l'Homme, Rouch heard
the lectures of Marcel Mauss and Marcel Griaule. He encountered Henri
Langlois, now the director of the Cinémathèque française. His decision
to study anthropology seriously was made during the war, which he spent
in French West Africa supervising the construction of roads and bridges.
"Culture conflict struck me from the start," he said (Desanti and Decock
1968:37). Rouch was not among those chosen, in 1946, for the Ogooué-
Congo Expedition, a well-equipped (in 35-mm) group of explorer-film-
makers (Francis Mazières, Edmond Séchan, and Pierre Gaisseau) and
anthropologists (Raoul Hartweg, Guy de Beauchêne, and Gilbert Rouget).
Instead he floated down the Niger with two friends, making films by trial
and error with a 16-mm Bell and Howell from the flea market. The tripod
soon fell overboard, and necessity nudged Rouch toward an original
shooting style (Rouch 1955). In order to film a hippopotamus hunt on the
river, he enlisted the help of Damouré Zika, a Sorko who was to collab-
orate with Rouch in research and filming (*Les maîtres fous*, 1953), as did
Oumarou Ganda (star of *Moi, un noir*, 1957; director of *Le wazou poly-
game*, 1971) at a later date. Rouch's career has been described as one of
"inveterate amateurism" and "incurable dilettantism" (Marcorelles
1963: 18). Rouch is, in fact, the first full-time ethnographic film professional.

The only film that Rouch had to show for those months on the Niger
was sufficiently well done to be bought by Actualités Françaises, blown up
to 35-mm, embellished with narration and shown as *Au pays des mages
noirs*, on the same bill as Rossellini's *Stromboli*. There was a grander
sequel in 1955, when a number of Rouch's short films in color were enlarged, combined, and released as a feature, *Les fils de l'eau*. This was
rapturously reviewed in *Cahiers du cinéma* by Claude Beylie, who compared Dogon cosmogony to the philosophy of Thales, Empedocles, and
Timaeus, and asserted: "WE are the monsters" (Beylie 1959). Rouch by
this time was Executive Secretary of the International Committee on
Ethnographic Films (CIFE), which had been formed in 1952 at the International Congress of Anthropological and Ethnological Sciences at
Vienna, to further preservation, production and distribution. The French
section of this organization prepared analyses and critiques of 106 films,
and in 1955 UNESCO published this catalogue as part of its series on
Mass Communication. Thus, under Rouch's care, the genre of ethnographic film acquired scientific and political as well as artistic stature in
the postwar decade.

Others besides Rouch were active in this transformation (or, as Rouch called it, "renaissance"), and there were other conceptions besides that of CIFE as to what an ethnographic film should be. In Germany, the Institut für den Wissenschaftlichen Film was reorganized immediately after the war, and soon German anthropologists were again filming in Melanesia, Africa and Europe. The Institute's approach to anthropological film was characterized by emphasis on scientific purity (Spannaus 1961:73–79). Subjects and treatments that might have ideological significance were to be avoided, along with the tendency to admit laymen to the field. The Institute conducted intensive courses in film technique for anthropologists preparing to do fieldwork, and supplied equipment for expeditions supported by the Deutsche Forschungsgemeinschaft, provided the applicants had taken the course. On the basis of this program, the Institute published its "Rules for film documentation in ethnology and folklore" in 1959. These require that filmmaking be done by persons with sound anthropological training or supervision, and that an exact log be kept; that the events recorded be authentic (technical processes can be staged for the camera, but not ceremonies), filmed without dramatic camera angles or movement, and edited for representativeness.

In 1952, the Institute's director, Gotthard Wolf, was the first to implement what had repeatedly been proposed, by establishing at Göttingen the first systematic anthropological film archive. Films meeting the Institute's scientific criteria were first solicited from anthropologists in Germany and then, with growing success, from abroad. At the start, Konrad Lorenz worked on assembling and arranging the *Encyclopaedia cinematographica* and others have added several thousand films on anthropological and biological subjects. To facilitate comparative research, each film consists of a single "thematic unit," such as dance, work, or ritual, and the films are arranged in natural science categories, biological subjects by phylum, genus, and species, ethnological ones by geographical location and social grouping, e.g.:

SOUTH AMERICA
BRAZIL
E75 Tukurina (Brazil, Upper Purus River) — Curing the sick by medicine men. 1950 (Color, 2½ minutes) H. Schultz, São Paulo.

This natural science treatment of ethnographic film contrasts with and complements CIFES' social science orientation. (The Committee added the *"Sociologique"* to its name in 1959.) Several countries have institutional affiliations with both CIFES and the *Encyclopaedia cinematographica;* CIFES has been less active than its counterpart, however, in making films routinely available to scholars. Wolf's efforts in this regard have been major and prescient. Since 1966, an American archive of the

Encyclopaedia cinematographica has been housed at Pennsylvania State University; and in 1970, a Japanese archive was established at Tokyo.

As ethnographic film became institutionalized, it quickly accumulated a literature. Definitions and typologies of ethnographic film were devised. Griaule sustained Regnault's conception of ethnographic filming as a scientific activity concerned with traditional ethnographic subjects. He distinguished three film types: archive footage for research, training films for anthropology courses, and public education films (including, occasionally, "works of art") (Griaule 1957). (Although Griaule was hardly a film enthusiast, he became in death the subject of a "public education" film — of his own Dogon funeral.) André Leroi-Gourhan expressed a more original view of things in an article, "Le film ethnologique existe-t-il?", in which he applied the term "ethnological" to another tripartite classification: the research film, the "exotic" travel film (to be abhorred as superficial and exploitative), and the "film of environment... produced with no scientific aim but deriving an ethnological value from its exportation" (Leroi-Gourhan 1948). These contrasting typologies of ethnographic film, one exclusive in tendency and the other inclusive, survive to this day. Griaule's view has been echoed by many who differ among themselves chiefly as to the degree of prophylaxis necessary against the "contamination" of the commercial cinema. On the other hand, it has been pointed out by Sol Worth that definitions of ethnographic film are tautological, since no film can be called ethnographic in and of itself (Worth 1969). Much depends upon the uses to which a film is put, regardless of the intentions of its author. A single film can be used in a variety of ways. It's a simple matter, when film represents the confrontation between "us" and "them" (Europeans and natives; scientists and laymen), for the filmmaker and the viewer to negotiate the conventions. But especially since World War II (though even long before it), neither "we" nor "they" have ceased to change.

The "steady inertia" *vis-à-vis* new technical devices in anthropology, of which Rowe complained in 1952, has since been supplanted by steadily accelerating activity, heightened, in recent years, by the availability to anthropologists of videotape. We are now waiting for videotape storage of data, in a central location servicing far-flung terminals, to be implemented (Ekman *et al.* 1969). But the existence of technology has never been a sufficient condition of scientific advance.

Although Kuhn (1962) has questioned the existence of paradigms in the social sciences, a fair degree of consensus exists as to what constitutes normal anthropological research using film. The state of the field a decade ago can be glimpsed in Michaelis (1955), Spannaus (1961), and Mead

(1963); today's situation is exposed in the paper in Hockings (1975), and, often more revealing, in their overlapping bibliographies. New uses of film, and refinements of old ones, are constantly occurring. Semiotic analysis and evocative techniques have joined the following long-established uses of film by anthropologists: as a note-taking tool for events which are too complex, too rapid, or too small to be grasped with the naked eye or recorded in writing; as a means of salvaging data for future generations of researchers, either because the behavior is about to disappear, or because the theoretical equipment to deal with it does not yet exist; and for comparisons. These may be either synchronic (cross-cultural emic-etic, macro-micro) or diachronic (individual maturation or cultural change).

The use of film to elicit responses, which occurred in psychological research as early as 1909, became fairly common in psychiatry during World War II (Moreno 1944; Saul 1945; Prados 1951), and was adapted to sociological research by Rouch and Morin in the early 1960's. (In 1925, Mead used still photos taken during the filming of *Moana* to elicit responses from Samoan children.) Rouch not only recorded his actors' comments and exclamations at seeing themselves on the screen (in *Jaguar*), but also used the presence of cameras and cameramen to provoke psychodramas in *La pyramide humaine* (1959) and *La punition* (1962). Worth and Adair carried the process still further in 1966, when they experimented with eliciting films AS RESPONSES. They undertook to teach a group of Navaho men and women to make their own motion pictures, on any subject they wanted, in order to elicit a "visual flow" that could be analyzed semiotically, i.e. "in terms of the structure of images and the cognitive processes or rules used in making those images."

A working hypothesis for our study was that motion picture film, conceived, photographed, and sequentially arranged by a people such as the Navajo, would reveal aspects of coding, cognition, and values that may be inhibited, not observable, or not analyzable when the investigation is totally dependent on verbal exchange – especially when such research must be done in the language of the investigator (Worth and Adair 1972:27–28).

The Navaho filmmakers learned to use 16-mm Bell and Howell cameras with amazing rapidity, and within two months produced short exercises and seven silent films. These were shown to the Navaho community, analyzed by the researchers (who compared them with films made by Philadelphia teenagers), and eventually placed in distribution, where they have acquired a renown in experimental film circles.

The use of videotape as an experimental agent in urban anthropology, by George Stoney, the Rundstroms, the Videograph project and others, has added synchronous sound (namely, speech) to the resources available to informants for their productions.

Reinterpretation of "ethnographic film" as a process of communication between filmers and filmed is among chief developments in this kind of filming since the war. The Balinese experience has never been replicated, but it served to open up the whole communication field, which has been so fertile that only a few of its works can be mentioned in this short account. When war and cold war destroyed some cultures outright and made others inaccessible, Columbia University's Research in Contemporary Cultures Project, directed by Ruth Benedict, gathered together a team from various disciplines to study cultures "at a distance," by means of interviews, films (preferably Grade B films, less idiosyncratic), literature, art, and other types of material. During the war, Bateson worked at the Museum of Modern Art on an analysis of the UFA film, *Hitlerjunge Quex* (1933), in order to derive some of the "psychological implications of Nazism." Martha Wolfenstein went on to apply the principles of thematic analysis to the content of films made in Western nations (England, France, Italy, and the United States), and discovered national patterns in fantasy. These studies gave rise to others dealing with personal and formal levels of filmic communication, exemplified in the "*politique des auteurs*" expounded in *Cahiers du cinéma* from 1950, and the anthropology and semiology of the cinema (Powdermaker 1950; Morin 1956; Metz 1974.

One would assume that the study of nonverbal communication would demand the use of film, and the members of the American linguistic school have used not only film but also videotape in their research. But Ray L. Birdwhistell, who adapted the methods of descriptive linguistics to the study of culture, at first used film less to study communication than to communicate about it; he mapped the kinesics of American English by eye, using a written notation system (Birdwhistell 1952). Other researchers in choreometrics have from the start depended upon rater consensus and successive refinements of parameters discovered by repeated inspection of a large sample of dance films. The musician and folklorist, Alan Lomax, has since 1961 directed a cross-cultural study of expressive style, of global proportions, involving song, dance, and speech; his Choreometrics Project, which is concerned with movement style, has collected for analysis films of dance and work from nearly two hundred cultures. Most of the footage analyzed by Lomax and his collaborators was filmed by others, both scientists and laymen, for a variety of reasons. Each extract found to be acceptable for research was coded, using a descriptive system based on the Laban Effort-Shape theory. The ratings thus obtained were computerized for multifactor analysis, into summaries identifying the most "potent classifiers" of cultural style. The aim of Lomax's research is the development of an evolutionary taxonomy of culture (Lomax 1968; Lomax, Bartenieff, and Paulay 1969; Lomax and Berkowitz 1972). In applied terms, it is also the renewal and revitalization of cultures, threatened by mass media "greyout," which spring to life again when confronted with self-expression (Lomax 1973).

The method of the research film can be summarized by the statement that the ratio of analysis to observation is high at this end of a continuum which extends, at the other extreme, to the purest, most uninterpretable aesthetic experiences. Research film technique is expected to behave with a modesty befitting the handmaid of the mind. Where research use of film involves production, the technology is in general that which can be mastered by a nonprofessional cameraman. Film costs in research budgets are modest compared with documentary or theatrical production, and the proportion of usable footage is greater. Videotape, in use since the late 1960's, offers advantages of easy handling, immediacy, and economy (the tape is reusable). If an image of high quality is required, conventional filming is called for. At present, this means shooting 16-mm with or without the recording of synchronous sound on quarter-inch tape. It's possible, though unusual, for a single person to be a complete film crew, by using, for example, a zoom-equipped Beaulieu connected to a Nagra (Polunin 1970).

In the course of research into ecology, epidemiology, and child development in New Guinea and elsewhere, E. Richard Sorenson has developed a conception of the "research cinema film" which is, together with the *Encyclopaedia cinematographica*, a leading attempt at rationalization of ethnographic film archives. Such systematization is essential if future research involving film is to be carried out efficiently — or at all (Sorenson and Gajdusek 1966; Sorenson 1967).

The uses of ethnographic film in education range from scholarly communication, such as Birdwhistell's *Lecture on Kinesics* (1964), to elementary-school social studies, for which the multi-media *Man, a Course of Study: the Netsilik Eskimos* was designed. Since World War II, the social sciences have received an increasing share of academic importance, and markets for textbooks and educational films have grown enormous. Until the mid-1960's, the bread-and-butter of ethnographic film in education was the descriptive documentary, used as an adjunct to lectures and "relevant readings" in college courses on ethnology. The best of these filmed ethnographies are very good indeed: Robert and Monique Gessain's *Obashior endaon* (1964) and William Geddes' *Miao Year* (1968) spring immediately to mind. Both films were by-products of the fieldwork of their authors.

The most spectacular and influential of all visual ethnographies is John Marshall's record of the Bushmen, filmed on several expeditions to the Kalahari desert in the 1950's and still being edited. After collaborating with Robert Gardner to produce *The Hunters* (1958), Marshall photographed the celebrated *Titicut Follies* (directed by Fred Wiseman), and filmed the activities of the Pittsburgh police for the Lemberg Center for the Study of Violence. Concurrently, he was developing a theory of reportage and pedagogy as he structured the Bushman material (over 500,000 feet in all) into short sequences. He became dissatisfied with *The Hunters*: it had not been filmed with synchronous sound, and its synthetic story depends heavily on narration; furthermore, it gives undue importance to hunting in Bushman subsistence, which is in fact more dependent upon gathering. *Men Bathing*, *A Joking Relationship*, and *An Argument about a Marriage* concentrate, instead, on the details of interpersonal interaction during a short time span; the dialogue was hand-synched and translated by means of subtitles. These film episodes were shown in the introductory anthropology course at Harvard to illustrate concepts such as avoidance and reciprocity. The police series (*Three Domestics*, *Investigation of a Hit and Run*, etc.) was filmed in long uninterrupted shots with synchronous sound, representing virtuoso camera performances under difficult conditions for which Marshall's work in the Bridgewater State Hospital had prepared him. They have been used for police training and in law school and junior high school discussions. With Timothy Asch, Marshall in 1968 formed the Center for Documentary Anthropology, where Asch and Napoleon Chagnon, using the "sequence concept" which they had developed, are collaborating on a series of more than forty films of the Yąnomamö (*The Feast*, *Magical Death*, and others). The films are being subjected to curriculum experimentation during the editing process.

Instruction in ethnographic filming, initiated by Mead at Columbia in the 1940's has of late become extremely popular with undergraduates, many of whom have used home movie cameras since childhood. Rouch and Gardner have trained individually a number of filmmakers. In Rouch's words, only "one in a hundred" turns out to have the capacity for combining scientific rigor with cinema fluency. How can this capacity be developed? A "how-to" literature exists (Dyhrenfurth 1952; Collier 1967; sections in *Research Film* and the *Program in Ethnographic Film Newsletter*). Gatherings such as the International Film Seminars (from 1955), the Festival dei Popoli (from 1959), the Conferences on Visual Anthropology organized by Jay Ruby (from 1968), Venezia Genti (1971–

1972), several UNESCO round tables, and the UCLA colloquium (1968), provide opportunities to learn from new films. University programs are effective in teaching film strategies, but much work remains to be done on the theoretical underpinning of ethnographic film, beginning with the problem of reconciling often rivalrous systems of science and art. Too many social scientists still feel uncomfortable about following the advice of Luc de Heusch, the anthropologist-filmmaker:

Ethnographers should make themselves familiar with contemporary film theories and abandon the notion that the camera purely and simply shows reality (de Heusch 1962:25).

Finally, accessible film collections (such as the Museum of Modern Art's and the Royal Anthropological Institute's) are essential if students are to profit fully from accumulated experience.

Unlike the specialized uses of film in research, where conclusions are expressed verbally, and unlike the uses of film in education, where effectiveness is dependent upon context, the use of ethnographic film as public information depends upon the presence, in self-contained form, of visual attractiveness and intellectual substance — a most demanding format. But this use, by making it possible for many to view the richness of human resources, makes it slightly more possible that we will preserve and encourage them in the years to come.

The personal film statement on a universal theme is a durable public information format. Robert Gardner, whose film *Dead Birds* (1963) was praised by *Variety* and Robert Lowell, first expressed his theory of film while he was engaged in producing *The Hunters* at the Film Study Center at Harvard. Gardner's cinematography is conservative (he filmed *Dead Birds* using a battery-driven Arriflex, without synchronous sound), and much of the expressive power of his films is produced by editing of images and by the commentary. Gardner's binnacle has been his own sensibility, applied to universal themes such as the relationship of men and women, and death.

I saw the Dani people, feathered and fluttering men and women, as enjoying the fate of all men and women. They dressed their lives with plumage, but faced as certain death as the rest of us drabber souls. The film attempts to say something about how we all, as humans, meet our animal fate (Gardner 1972:35).

Other nonintrusive sensibilities have produced anthropological documentaries with forms recognizable by those steeped in European tradition, hence readily accepted by lay audiences. Jorge Preloran's *Imaginero/Hermógenes Cayo* (1970) and *Araucanians of Ruca Choroy* (1971) employ a biographical model. Of Cayo, Preloran remarked, "I was not interested in the details of his situation, but rather in the image of his soul" (Suber 1971:48). Although the audience for these films may feel that "its humanity is confirmed" (in Gardner's words) by viewing them, the films can also be employed to reaffirm and reinforce European cultural hegemony.

A film which caused a scandal when shown to African students in Paris marked Rouch's turning from conventional documentary to what he and Edgar Morin, resurrecting Vertov's title, were to call *cinéma vérité*. ("Vertov and Flaherty are my masters," Rouch declared in 1963). While studying Songhay religion in Accra in 1953, Rouch was invited by the priests of the Hauka sect to document sequences of a possession cult. The result was *Les maîtres fous*, a short film showing Hauka adepts, possessed by spirits of generals, doctors, and truck drivers from the British power structure, as they slaughter a dog, cook and eat it, march back and forth, dance violently and foam at the mouth. By including shots of the Hauka going about their menial daily work in the city, Rouch implies that the cult helps its members to cope with the strains of everyday life, particularly in the colonial situation (cf. Muller 1971:1473). The film is not fully comprehensible without Rouch's written treatise on the subject (Rouch 1960); nonetheless it excited such strong reactions that both Europeans and Africans urged him to destroy it. He demurred, and *Les maîtres fous* went on to win a prize at Venice. However, after this experience Rouch began the "cinema of collective improvisation" with *Jaguar*, his "ethnographic science fiction" collaboration with Damouré, Lam, and Illo playing three young migrant workers in search of fortune on the Ghana coast. By the time the film was completed, Rouch sensed that the period of freedom of movement between the newly independent West African nations was over, and that the experience could never be duplicated. In a sense, what Rouch and Morin accomplished in 1960 with *Chronique d'un été* was a condensation of the *Jaguar* process: instead of planning a dramatic improvisation before shooting, and recording the dialogue and comments of the actors afterward, the characters in *Chronique d'un été* were instantly created, with the help of the prototype Éclair camera, the Nagra recorder, and the question "Are you happy?"

Well might one ask such a question. While *Chronique d'un été* was being filmed in Paris, France was undergoing the painful disengagement from Algeria. Much has been made of the new portable synchronous sound filming rig, which enabled cameraman Michel Brault to follow the subject for ten minutes or more without stopping the camera, as if this hardware in itself had caused *cinéma vérité* to happen; but the motivations of the filmmakers are at least as important in its history. In addition to the leftist political message of much of *cinéma vérité*, the films of Rouch, Ruspoli, and Marker demanded renegotiation of the existing conventions governing the roles of filmmaker, subject, and audience: the filmmaker appeared to become a transmitter of "truth," the subject would henceforth be judged by his own words and actions, and a heavy burden of interpretation was now placed on the viewer. It is no coincidence that the other home of *cinéma vérité* — the place, in fact, where it all began, according to one critic, with Brault's photography of *Les raquetteurs* (1958) (Madsen 1967) — was Québec, where cultural and political differences are still a problem. In the 1960's the superpowers, after more than a decade of colonial crisis, were redefining their stance *vis-à-vis* the minorities. Culture contact was implicit in *cinéma vérité*; and the function of *cinéma vérité* was politicization.

This use of film encountered opposition, and long before it arrived in Hollywood, *cinéma vérité* had gone on the defensive. Financing was hard to come by (Marcorelles 1963). Rouch has known the discomfort of being ridiculed by Europeans and shut out by Africans. The "new kind of journalism" which Richard Leacock and his colleague D. A. Pennebaker developed for television in 1960 was resisted by critics (Bluem 1965) and sponsors. *Cuba si! Yanki no!* was withdrawn from circulation in 1961, and *Happy Mother's Day*, a report of the commercial pressures to which the parents of quintuplets were subjected, was broadcast by ABC television in an altered version.

Even traditional ethnography has had a hard time getting on television in an intellectually reputable form. Thanks to an unusual decision of the head of programming at CBS television, the Netsilik became known to millions who saw *Fight for Life!*, a specially edited presentation of the material embellished with narration and background music. In television the Europeans and Japanese seem to be far in advance of the United States.

One of the major changes in motion pictures since World War II has been decentralization of production, as professional equipment became available on an unprecedented scale. Georges Sadoul's *Histoire du cinéma mondial* gives an account of the development of national cinemas. When Sadoul laid down his pen in 1966, after writing, "in fifty countries, the nation and its people became, in all their diversity, the material for ever more numerous films," only Africa remained without a cinema. This is no longer the case. Senegal's Ousmane Sembene, known to American audiences for *Mandabi, Tauw,* and *Emitai*, is one of a growing number of artists who are gaining fluency in all film genres (Hennebelle 1972). The effect of African production has not yet been felt outside, and until it is, returnees from the festivals at Tunis and Ouagadougou can only try to describe what Europe and the United States are missing — what Rouch has labelled with justice "spiritual assistance for the overdeveloped countries" (Desanti and Decock 1968).

Film is such a rich trove of data that its usefulness depends upon a happy choice of level of analysis. The retrospective significance of a film often differs from the prospective significance intended by its maker. Films can be put to more than one use and should thus be preserved with written records. The most striking change in ethnographic film since its beginnings, and especially since World War II, has been the shift in the orientation of the camera, which no longer looks out at the world, but rather inside one's world. In Mali, Cisse has made *Cinq jours d'une vie*, a film of boys growing up, learning the Koran, migrating to the city, and returning to the village. In the United States and elsewhere, filmmakers are hard at work filming cultural enclaves, family life, and even their own biographies; autobiography, veiled in Flaherty's *Louisiana Story*, is now explicit. Recently some scholars in the field of semiotics have rediscovered Eisenstein's fascination with Freud and Malinowski, and his interest in myth which he planned to express in *Que viva México!* A flowering of ethnographic films fulfilling Eisenstein's promise would indeed be as important as drama or the novel have been in the past in helping people understand themselves. The history of ethnographic film is rich in examples of film's unique capacity to record the multileveled nature of events, of its usefulness in teaching new ways of seeing, and of its power to evoke deeply positive feelings about mankind by communicating the essence of a people.

REFERENCES

ANDERSON, JOSEPH L.
  1968   "The development of the single-concept film in a context of a general history of educational motion pictures and innovation in instructional media." Unpublished master's thesis, Ohio State University.
BALIKCI, ASEN, QUENTIN BROWN
  1966   Ethnographic filming and the Netsilik Eskimos. *Educational Services Incorporated Quarterly Report* (Spring-Summer): 19-33.
BATESON, GREGORY
  1943   "An analysis of the film *Hitlerjunge Quex* (1933)." New York: Museum of Modern Art Film Library, and Institute for Intercultural Studies (typescript).
BATESON, GREGORY, MARGARET MEAD
  1942   *Balinese character: a photographic analysis.* New York Academy of Sciences, Special Publications 2.

BEYLIE, CLAUDE
1959   Review of Rouch: *Les fils de l'eau. Cahiers du Cinéma* 91:66-67.
BIDNEY, DAVID
1964   Paul Fejos 1897-1963. *American Anthropologist* 66:110-115.
BIRDWHISTELL, RAY L.
1952   *Introduction to kinesics.* Louisville: University of Louisville Press.
BLUEM, A. WILLIAM
1965   *Documentary in American television.* New York: Hastings.
BRODERICK, A.
1947   *The factual film: a survey sponsored by the Dartington Hall Trustees.* London: Oxford University Press.
COLLIER, JOHN, JR.
1967   *Visual anthropology: photography as a research method.* New York: Holt, Rinehart and Winston.
COMITÉ DU FILM ETHNOGRAPHIQUE
1955   *Catalogue of French ethnographical films.* Reports and Papers on Mass Communication 15. Paris: UNESCO.
COMITÉ INTERNATIONAL DU FILM ETHNOGRAPHIQUE ET SOCIOLOGIQUE
1967   *Premier catalogue sélectif international de films ethnographiques sur l'Afrique noire.* Paris: UNESCO.
1970   *Premier catalogue sélectif international de films ethnographiques sur la région du Pacifique.* Paris: UNESCO.
DEBETS, G. F.
1957   Forty years of Soviet anthropology. Washington: National Science Foundation / Smithsonian Institution. (Originally Sorok let sovetskoi antropologii. *Sovetskaya Antropologia* 1:7-30.)
DE BRIGARD, EMILIE
i.p.   *Anthropological cinema.* New York: Museum of Modern Art.
DE HEUSCH, LUC
1962   *The cinema and social science: a survey of ethnographic and sociological films.* Reports and Papers in the Social Sciences 16. Paris: UNESCO.
DESANTI, DOMINIQUE, JEAN DECOCK
1968   Cinéma et ethnographie. *Arts d'Afrique* 1:37-39, 76-80.
DODDS, JOHN W.
1973   *The several lives of Paul Fejos.* New York: Wenner-Gren Foundation.
DONALDSON, LEONARD
1912   *The cinematograph and natural science.* London: Ganes.
DYHRENFURTH, NORMAN G.
1952   Film making for scientific field workers. *American Anthropologist* 54:147–152.
EKMAN, PAUL, W. FRIESEN, T. TAUSSIG
1969   "VID–R and SCAN: tools and methods for the automated analysis of visual records," in *Content analysis.* Edited by G. Gerbner *et al.* New York: Wiley and Sons.
FLAHERTY, DAVID
1925   Serpents in Eden. *Asia* 25: 858-869, 895-898.
FLAHERTY, FRANCES HUBBARD
1925a   Setting up house and shop in Samoa. *Asia* 25: 638-651, 709-711.
1925b   Behind the scenes with our Samoan stars. *Asia* 25: 746-753, 795-796.

1925c   A search for animal and sea sequences. *Asia* 25: 954-963, 1000-1004.
1925d   Fa'a-Samoa. *Asia* 25: 1084-1090, 1096-1100.

GARDNER, ROBERT G.
1957   Anthropology and film. *Daedalus* 86:344-350.
1972   "On the making of *Dead Birds*," in *The Dani of West Irian*. Edited by Karl G. Heider. Andover, Mass.: Warner Modular Publications 2.

GRIAULE, MARCEL
1957   *Méthode de l'ethnographie*. Paris: Presses Universitaires de France.

HARDY, FORSYTH
1966   *Grierson on documentary* (second edition). Berkeley: University of California Press. (Originally published 1947.)

HARRIS, MARVIN
1968   *The rise of anthropological theory*. New York: Crowell.

HEIDER, KARL G.
1972   *Films for anthropological teaching* (fifth edition). Washington: American Anthropological Association.

HENNEBELLE, GUY
1972   *Les cinémas africains en 1972*. L'Afrique Littéraire et Artistique 20. Paris and Dakar: Société Africaine d'Édition.

HILTON-SIMPSON, M. W., J. A. HAESELER
1925   Cinema and ethnology. *Discovery* 6:325-330.

HOCKINGS, PAUL, editor
1975   *Principles of Visual Anthropology*. World Anthropology. The Hague: Mouton.

INTERNATIONAL SCIENTIFIC FILM ASSOCIATION
1959   Rules for film documentation in ethnology and folklore. *Research Film* 3:238-240.

KRACAUER, SIEGFRIED
1947   *From Caligari to Hitler: a psychological history of the German film*. Princeton: Princeton University Press.

KRUPIANSKAYA, V., L. POTAPOV, L. TERENTIEVA
1960   "Essential problems in the ethnographic study of peoples of the USSR." Paper presented at the Sixth International Congress of Anthropological and Ethnological Sciences, Paris.

KUHN, THOMAS S.
1962   *The structure of scientific revolutions*. Chicago: University of Chicago Press.

LAJARD, J., FÉLIX REGNAULT
1895   Poterie crue et origine du tour. *Bulletin de la Société d'Anthropologie de Paris* 6:734-739.

LEPROHON, PIERRE
1960   *Chasseurs d'images*. Paris: Éditions André Bonne.

LEROI-GOURHAN, ANDRÉ
1948   Cinéma et sciences humaines – le film ethnologique existe-t-il? *Revue de Géographie Humaine et d'Ethnologie* 3:42-51.

LEYDA, JAY
1960   *Kino*. New York: Macmillan.

LOMAX, ALAN
1968   *Folk song style and culture: a staff report on cantometrics.* Washington: American Association for the Advancement of Science. Publication 88.
1973   Cinema, science, and culture renewal. *Current Anthropology* 14: 474–480.
LOMAX, ALAN, IRMGARD BARTENIEFF, FORRESTINE PAULAY
1969   Choreometrics: a method for the study of cross-cultural pattern in film. *Research Film/Le Film de Recherche/Forschungsfilm* 6:505–517.
LOMAX, ALAN, NORMAN BERKOWITZ
1972   The evolutionary taxonomy of culture. *Science* 177:228–239.
MCCANN, RICHARD DYER
1973   *The people's films.* New York: Hastings House.
MADSEN, AXEL
1967   Pour la suite du Canada. *Sight and Sound* 36 (2):68–69.
MARCORELLES, LOUIS
1963   *Une Esthétique du réel, le cinéma direct.* Paris: UNESCO.
MEAD, MARGARET
1963   "Anthropology and the camera," in *Encyclopedia of photography.* Edited by W. D. Morgan. New York: National Educational Alliance.
1972   *Blackberry winter: my earlier years.* New York: Morrow.
MEAD, MARGARET, RHODA MÉTRAUX
1953   *The study of culture at a distance.* Chicago: University of Chicago Press.
METZ, CHRISTIAN
1974   *Language and cinema.* The Hague: Mouton.
MICHAELIS, ANTHONY R.
1955   *Research films in biology, anthropology, psychology and medicine.* New York: Academic Press.
MORENO, J. L.
1944   Psychodrama and therapeutic motion pictures. *Sociometry* 7:230-244.
MORIN, EDGAR
1956   *Le cinéma ou l'homme imaginaire.* Paris: Les Editions de Minuit.
MULLER, JEAN CLAUDE
1971   Review of *Les maîtres fous. American Anthropologist* 73:1471–1473.
O'REILLY, PATRICK
1970   (orig. 1949). "Le 'documentaire' ethnographique en Océanie." In *Premier cataloque sélectif international de films ethnographiques sur la région du Pacifique.* Edited by Comité International du Film Ethnographique et Sociologique, pp. 281–305. Paris: UNESCO.
PÖCH, RUDOLF
1907   Reisen in Neu-Guinea in den Jahren 1904–1906. *Zeitschrift für Ethnologie* 39:382–400.
POLUNIN, IVAN
1970   Visual and sound recording apparatus. *Current Anthropology* 11: 3-22.
POWDERMAKER, HORTENSE
1950   *Hollywood, the dream factory.* Boston: Little, Brown.

PRADOS, MIGUEL
1951   The use of films in psychotherapy. *American Journal of Orthopsychiatry* 21:36-46.
REGNAULT, FÉLIX-LOUIS
1896a   Les attitudes du repos dans les races humaines. *Revue Encyclopédique* 1896:9–12.
1896b   La locomotion chez l'homme. *Cahiers de Recherche de l'Académie* 122:401; Archives de Physiologie, de Pathologie et de Génétique 8:381.
1897   Le grimper. *Revue Encyclopédique* 1897:904–905.
1912   Les musées des films. *Biologica* 2 (16) (Supplement 20).
1923a   Films et musées d'ethnographie. *Comptes Rendus de l'Association Française pour l'Avancement des Sciences* 11:880–881.
1923b   L'histoire du cinéma, son rôle en anthropologie. *Bulletins et Mémoires de la Société d'Anthropologie de Paris* 7-8: 61-65.
1931   Le rôle du cinéma en ethnographie. *La Nature* 59:304-306.
ROTHA, PAUL
1936   *Documentary film*. London: Faber and Faber.
ROTHA, PAUL, SINCLAIR ROAD, RICHARD GRIFFITH
1963   *Documentary film* (third edition). London: Faber and Faber.
ROUCH, JEAN
1953   Renaissance du film ethnographique. *Geographica Helvetica* 8:55.
1955   Cinéma d'exploration et ethnographie. *Connaissance du Monde* 1:69–78.
1960   *Essai sur la religion songhay*. Paris: Presses Universitaires de France.
ROWE, JOHN HOWLAND
1953   "Technical aids in anthropology: a historical survey," in *Anthropology Today*. Edited by A. L. Kroeber, 895–940. Chicago: University of Chicago Press.
SADOUL, GEORGES
1964   *Louis Lumière*. Paris: Seghers.
1966   *Histoire du cinéma mondial des origines à nos jours* (eighth edition). Paris: Flammarion.
SAUL, LEON S., HOWARD ROME, EDWIN LEUSER
1945   Desensitization of combat fatigue patients. *American Journal of Psychiatry* 102:476–478.
SORENSON, E. RICHARD
1967   A research film program in the study of changing man. *Current Anthropology* 8:443-469.
SORENSON, E. RICHARD, D. CARLETON GAJDUSEK
1966   The study of child behavior and development in primitive cultures. *Pediatrics* 37 (1), part 2, Supplement.
SPANNAUS, GUNTHER
1961   "Der wissenschaftliche Film als Forschungsmittel in der Völkerkunde," In *Der Film im Dienste der Wissenschaft*, 67–82. Göttingen: Institut für den Wissenschaftlichen Film.
SUBER, HOWARD
1971   Jorge Preloran. *Film Comment* 7 (1):43–51.
TAFT, ROBERT
1938   *Photography and the American scene: a social history, 1839–1889*. New York: Macmillan.

TAYLOR, JOHN RUSSELL
1964   Cinema eye, cinema ear. New York: Hill and Wang.
WOLF, GOTTHARD
1972   Encyclopaedia Cinematographica 1972. Göttingen: Institut für den Wissenschaftlichen Film.
WOLLEN, PETER
1969   Signs and meaning in the cinema. London: Thames and Hudson.
WORTH, SOL
1969   The development of a semiotic of film. Semiotica 1:282–321.
WORTH, SOL, JOHN ADAIR
1972   Through Navajo eyes: an exploration in film communication and anthropology. Bloomington: Indiana University Press.

Scotland as the Model of Mankind: Lord Kames' Philosophical View of Civilization

GEORGE W. STOCKING, JR.

Adam Smith once said that "we must every one of us acknowledge Kames for our master"; and his biographer suggested that Kames was "intimately connected with every species of improvement, whether of an intellectual or a political nature, that took place in Scotland during his age." Yet of that small (and often face-to-face) group of landed advocates, university professors, "Moderate" clergy, and literary men whose collective brilliance may almost be equated with the Enlightenment in Scotland, Kames was until very recently among the least appreciated. Perhaps this was because Boswell's projected life of Kames was never completed. Or perhaps it was because — Smith to the contrary nothwithstanding — Kames was less the architect than the embodiment of his age. Certainly, his life reads like a social history of Scotland during the eighteenth century.[1]

---

[1]   Smith as quoted in Alexander Tytler, Lord Woodhouselee, *Memoirs of the life and writings of the Honourable Henry Home of Kames*, two volumes (Edinburgh, 1807):I, 160; cf. v. — on which I have relied most heavily for biographical material on Kames. Boswell's unpublished materials were included in *Private papers from Malahide Castle*, edited by G. Scott and F. Pottle (Mount Vernon, New York 1928–1934): XV, 260–316; Tytler, however, drew on them in his supplement of 1809. The recent interest in Kames has come primarily from scholars in English literature, beginning with H. W. Randall, *The critical theory of Lord Kames*, Smith College Studies in Modern Languages 28(1941), and most recently evident in Arthur E. McGuinness, *Henry Home, Lord Kames* (New York, 1970), which includes references to the intervening literature. See also W. C. Lehmann, *Henry Home, Lord Kames, and the Scottish Enlightenment* (The Hague, 1971), which came to my attention after the present essay was written. In Germany, where Kames' esthetic theories influenced Lessing, Herder, and Schiller, there has been a longer tradition of Kames studies, including Joseph Martin, *Die Psychologie Henry Homes* (Halle, 1911); Wilhelm Neumann, *Die Bedeutung Homes für die Asthetik und sein Einfluss auf die deutschen Asthetiker* (Halle, 1894); Joseph Norden, *Die Ethik Henry Homes* (Halle, 1895); and Joseph Wohlgemuth, *Henry Homes Asthetik und ihr Einfluss auf deutsche Asthetiker* (Berlin, 1893).

Henry Home was the name to which he was born in 1696 on the family estate of Kames in the Lowland county of Berwick. His father was "a country gentleman of small fortune," whose reduced circumstances and large progeny forced his son to rely on "his own abilities and exertions" to achieve his fortune. Although young Home received the rudiments of a classical education under a household tutor, his father — like many of the Scottish gentry in the period of aroused commercial expectations following the Union with England in 1707 — "saw no necessity for... the tedious and expensive discipline of the University." Instead young Home was indentured to a Writer to the Signet (or solicitor) in Edinburgh. However, an early glimpse of the elegant home life of the President of the Court of Session inspired Home to abandon the lesser branch of the Scottish legal profession and embark on an arduous program of self-study, not only of "the sciences of the Roman law, and the municipal law of Scotland," but of the whole range of liberal studies which the status and the profession of barrister required. Eventually, Home succeeded in attaching himself to a prominent Advocate, and in 1723 he was himself called to the bar.[2]

Home's progress to legal eminence was not a quick or easy one. Law was a favored career of the sons of landed gentry, and at its upper levels the competition was keen. Furthermore, Home's energy seems for a while to have been distracted by the company of some young blades, and it was not until he woke up one day to a debt of £300 that he turned again with diligence to the law. By 1732, however, he had published two legal volumes which established his reputation, and from the late 30's on he was involved in most of the important cases before the Court of Session.[3]

In 1741, Home finally married at the age of 45. Though at first his circumstances were still such as to make economy "a necessary duty" for his wife, their life together was always "consistent with every rational enjoyment of social and polished life." The evenings were filled with whist, the theatre, the concert, and the assembly-room — often closing with a "small domestic party" where a few intimate friends found "a plain but elegant supper" and savored "sensible and spirited conversation" until after midnight. But Home's daytime hours were as rigorously allotted as those of Benjamin Franklin (who was later his friend), and his legal career prospered accordingly. In 1752 he achieved his life's ambition when he was appointed — under the title Lord Kames — to a judgeship on the

[2] Tytler, Memoirs, I, 1–2, 8–10, 14, 30.
[3] Randall, Critical theory, 6–7; H. G. Graham, The social life of Scotland in the eighteenth century, reprinted edition (London, 1969), 32–33; Tytler, Memoirs, I, 56; Kames, Remarkable decisions of the Court of Session, from 1716–1728 (Edinburgh, 1728); and Essays upon several subjects in law (Edinburgh, 1732).

Court of Session. For the next thirty years Kames enjoyed the life of affluent eminence which had inspired his decision to train himself as Advocate — in Edinburgh during judicial sessions, and during vacations at his paternal estate in Berwick, and later at the estate of Blair-Drummond in Kincardine, which descended to his wife by entail upon the death of her brother in 1766. His activity continued virtually without let up until his death at 86, and throughout this period he was centrally involved in the political, religious, social, economic, and intellectual developments which sustained the Scottish Enlightenment.[4]

By the time that Home became Lord Kames, Scotland had already changed considerably since his childhood. In 1700, the Scottish gentry — save for its highest ranks — lived in relatively rude conditions, and the peasantry generally existed "in misery, hunger, and in the shadow of death." The recently re-established Presbyterian Church waxed grimly dogmatic and fanatically pious, and its outlook was not quickly softened by the policy of Toleration which the terms of the Union necessitated. When the Scots Parliament ceased to exist, the dignity and trade of Edinburgh declined, and the city was left to stagnate in a pious, squalid post-medieval gloom. As far as the life of the mind was concerned, the period between 1690 and 1725 has been characterized as one of "dreary stagnation of all intellectual life and destitution of scholarship in Scotland." To visitors from below the Tweed, it was a dark undeveloped land — so dismaying that "Had Cain been Scot, God had ne'er changed his doom, Not made him wander, but confined him home."[5]

By the beginning of the second quarter of the century, however, all this had begun to change. Commercial life had quickened, especially in Glasgow, and linen manufacture had been introduced in twenty-five counties. The last executions for witchcraft occurred in 1727, by which time a so called "Moderate" party was beginning to grow within the Scottish Kirk. University life had begun to shake "the dry bones of medievalism," and Edinburgh was beginning to provide those social graces which Kames savored, although not without constant friction with the more austere sections of the Scottish clergy.[6] With the failure of the Jacobite Rebellion of 1745, Scottish development entered a new and much more dynamic phase, the various aspects of which are reflected directly in Kames' biography.[7]

4   Tytler, *Memoirs*, I, 57, 107–110, 151, II, 27.
5   Graham, *Social life*, 2, 5ff., 81ff., 146ff., 276–277, 508, cf. W. L. Mathieson, *Scotland and the Union; a history from 1695–1747* (Glasgow, 1910b), 218ff.
6   Mathieson, *Scotland*, 251ff., 347; Graham, *Social life*, 92ff., 348ff., 487, 515.
7   Mathieson, *The awakening of Scotland: a history from 1747–1797* (Glasgow, 1910a);

Kames had inherited Jacobite opinions from his family, and it was only in the 1720's that he adopted what his biographer called "the rational persuasion" that "the foundation of all regular government is the free consent of the people governed." When the Court of Sessions ceased to function during the Rebellion, he spent his time writing a small volume on "British Antiquities" in which he argued that Scottish feudal institutions had been borrowed from England, that the English bicameral Parliament was superior to the Scottish, and that the divine right of kings was based on the foolish assumption that God in this area required direct intermediaries "when in other matters he chooses to govern the world by second causes and ordinary means." But although Kames' biographer — writing in the context of the French Revolution — found Kames' political opinions embarrassingly radical, in his own time they were never such as to seriously disturb the peace of mind of any loyal Englishman. Despite his acquaintance with Franklin and his prediction that the American colonies would ultimately gain their freedom, Kames repudiated the Lockean doctrine of taxation as "totally subversive of government" and described American revolutionaries as men "pampered with prosperity" who were "sacrificing their native country to a feverish desire of power and opulence."[8]

Perhaps the soundness of Kames' politics in 1745 helped remove lingering doubts about his early Jacobitism, which may have been a factor in slowing his career. In any case, after winning his judgeship he played an important role in activities designed to solidify the Union with England and to reconstruct the social order of the Highlands, where the clan system had broken down in the aftermath of defeated rebellion and in the face of measures to end the feudal power of the chiefs who had supported the Pretender. In 1755, Kames was appointed to the Board of Trustees for the Encouragement of the Fisheries, Arts and Manufactures of Scotland, as well as Commissioner of the forfeited Jacobite estates, whose rents were now to be applied to the special purpose "of civilizing the inhabitants on the said estates, and those of the other parts of the Highlands and Islands of Scotland, [and] the promoting among them of the Protestant religion, good government, industry and manufactures, and the principles of loyalty." That what was involved was in effect an attempt to change both High-

---

Graham, *Social life*, 205, 210, 496; cf. David Kettler, *The social and political thought of Adam Ferguson* (Columbus, Ohio, 1965), 15–32 ("The transformation of Scotland").
8   Tytler, *Memoirs*, I, 117–122; Kames, *Essays upon several subjects concerning British antiquities* (Edinburgh, 1747); *Sketches of the history of man*, second edition, four volumes (Edinburgh. 1778), II, 273, 341, 363, 412.

land culture and the personality of Highland Scots, is evident in a letter
Kames wrote to the Duchess of Gordon:

Travelling through the counties of Aberdeen and Banff,... it is pleasant to see
the young creatures turning out everywhere from their little cottages, full of
curiosity, but no less full of industry; for every one of them is employed; and in
knitting stockings, they lose not all the while a single motion of their fingers....
There is the same curiosity to be observed upon your banks of the Spey, and
through the county of Moray; but alas! the industry is wanting; for the young
people go about there perfectly idle.... The part I allot for the Dutchess of
Gordon, is to train the young creatures about her to industry; ...for in the tender
years the strongest impressions are made, and once giving children the habit of
industry, it will last them for life. What I would therefore propose... is to introduce the knitting of stockings among the young folk of both sexes.... Our
Trustees for the Manufactures... will most cordially second your operations. In
the meantime, you may order a fit person to be secured for teaching the children
to spin and knit, and the only thing that will be expected from your Grace... is
to encourage the children to exert themselves, by some small premiums to those
who are the most deserving.[9]

In addition to his extensive correspondence with influential landholders,
Kames pushed this policy of economic development and cultural change
through the medium of his several publications on agriculture; and his
own estates were a practical model of the "rational principles" he preached.
To encourage a more progressive agricultural style, he spent hours in the
fields directing his farm servants during vacations. And when he came into
control of his wife's estate, he undertook one of the century's most ambitious schemes of agricultural improvement — the reclamation of five
hundred acres of the Moss of Kincardine, whose rich soil had for centuries
lain idle under an eight-foot stratum of moss.[10]

The mixture of benevolence and self-interest which impelled Kames'
various improving activities is evident in the same letter to Lady Gordon
quoted above:

In point of morality, I consider, that the people upon our estates are trusted by
Providence to our care, and that we are accountable for our management of
them, to the Great God, their Creator, as well as ours. But observe and admire the
benevolence of Providence. What else does it require of us, but to introduce
industry among our people, the sure way to make them virtuous and happy,
and the way not less sure of improving our estates, and increasing our revenues?[11]

[9] Randall, *Critical theory*, 7–9, 10; Mathieson, *Awakening*, 370ff.; Tytler, *Memoirs*, I,
202–204, II, 65–66.
[10] Kames, *Progress of flax-husbandry in Scotland* (Edinburgh, 1766); *The gentleman
farmer; being an attempt to improve agriculture by subjecting it to the test of rational
principles* (Edinburgh, 1776); Tytler, *Memoirs*, I, 111–112, II, 28–30.
[11] Tytler, *Memoirs*, II, 64–65.

By a happy providential dispensation, benevolence to one's dependents was also the road to personal prosperity.

The same providential optimism characterized Kames' general religious views, which, although in some respects advanced, were not inconsistent with his identification with the Moderate party in the Scottish Church. In his youth he had been Episcopalian as well as Jacobite, and his intellectual reorientation in the 1720's seems to have been religious as well as political. For seven years, he studied the work of the liberal English theologian Samuel Clarke, debating the issues of free will, the unity of God, and the bases of morality. For more than twenty years, beginning in 1737, he corresponded with David Hume, whose sceptical opinions were a stimulus to so much Scottish thought. But as his biographer suggests, Kames was by nature more inclined to dogmatism than to scepticism, and he responded to Hume's doubt by searching for principles of certainty.[12]

There were two aspects of Hume's argument which greatly disturbed Kames. On the one hand, he felt that by founding morals on the principle of "utility" — with pleasure and pain determining our perception of virtue and vice — Hume threatened to undercut the basis of human social order, since this "seems to annihilate all real distinction of right and wrong in human actions, and to make the preference depend on the fluctuating opinions of men with respect to the general good." On the other hand, Kames felt that Hume's scepticism as to the "reality of the connection between cause and effect" threatened "to invalidate every argument for the existence of God, drawn from the works of Nature, as the effects of a designing cause." To answer Hume, Kames published in 1751 a volume on the principles of "natural religion."[13]

Kames' argument followed along lines similar to other Scottish philosophers of the "common sense" school. Reacting against the subjectivist and sceptical arguments Berkeley and Hume had derived from the thought of Locke, refusing to accept sensationalism or associationism as the primary principle of human thought, they argued that the activities of the human mind were guided by certain innate principles. Prior to and ultimately independent of experience, these principles provided a sure foundation for morality, religion and reason. Following Francis Hutcheson, the first of the Scottish school, Kames argued that there was implanted in all men a "moral sense" (analogous to the five external senses) which gave

[12]   Randall, *Critical theory*, 5–6; Mathieson, *Awakening*, 123; Tytler, *Memoirs*, I, 26–29, 86, "Appendix", 15–17.
[13]   Tytler, *Memoirs*, I, 133–134; Kames, *Essays on the principles of morality and natural religion* (Edinburgh, 1751).

men an instinctive sense of what was right and wrong. Similarly, there was an instinctive sense of deity which was the basis of natural religion. And although there was no single sense which underlay reason, it too was founded on innate principles, including "an intuitive perception of the connexion of causes and effects." Kames appealed to observation and experience to establish these innate principles, but much of his argument for them was posed in terms of "final causes" — IF we had no inner moral sense, THEN society would be impossible. Indeed, he stood out from the other Scots both in the extent to which he relied on the argument from final causes and in the number of innate principles he postulated — although many of them were simply "branches of the moral sense."[14]

The difference between Kames and Hume on religious issues may be posed another way. Whereas Kames wrote of "the history of natural religion," Hume wrote a *Natural history of religion* in which he denied the innateness of the idea of God and treated human religious sentiment as a secondary phenomenon based on feelings of fear and hope in the face of an unpredictable future. But if Kames required a more certain basis for religious belief than Hume would allow, his religious views were nevertheless on the whole quite "enlightened." Revealed religion had little place in his intellectual system, and he treated the Bible quite casually as an historical document depicting the life of primitive peoples, its present text certainly a corruption of the original versions. Much Catholic belief and practice he of course dismissed as absurd superstition — especially such prayers and penances which contravened the notion that God governed the world by "inflexible laws" from which "he can never swerve in any case." And although his views on fore-ordination and necessity were rather Calvinist, he felt that God ruled "with equity and mildness" a world populated by men whose basic natures were on the whole good — as indeed they must be if created by a wholly beneficent Deity. On the whole Kames' religious views were little different from those of eighteenth-century English Deists in general.[15]

Such a viewpoint was quite acceptable to the "Moderates" in the Scottish Church, but there were traditionalists who found Kames' thinking disturbing. In discussing free will, he argued that although man's actions were in fact determined, he nevertheless acted with a delusory conviction

---

[14]   James Bonar, *Moral sense* (New York, 1930); Gladys Bryson, *Man and society: the Scottish Inquiry of the eighteenth century* (Princeton, 1945); S. A. Grave, *The Scottish philosophy of common sense* (Oxford, 1960); James McCosh, *The Scottish philosophy* (New York, 1875); Kames, *Sketches*, IV, passim; Tytler, *Memoirs*, I, 135.
[15]   Hume, *Four dissertations: I — the natural history of religion....* (London, 1757); Kames, *Sketches*, IV, 244, 277, III, 188; McGuinness, *Henry Home*, 28–57; Basil Willey, *The eighteenth century background* (London, 1940).

that he was a free agent. The notion that God would thus delude mankind as to His governance was attacked as unworthy of the Divine Nature, and in 1756 an attempt was made in the General Assembly to censure the authors of certain "infidel writings" — among whom Hume was named, and Kames included by implication. Although Kames later modified the offending passages, the power of the Moderates by this time was such that the censure was defeated.[16]

In this more liberal context, Scottish intellectual life flowered in the years after 1760, and despite his advancing years and his duties as judge, Kames continued to contribute. In 1758, he published a volume tracing the "progressive stages of improvement" of criminal law and the law of property from barbarous to civilized times, suggesting ways in which by comparing the laws of England and Scotland, both could be made more "rational." (Kames was particularly concerned with the elimination of Scottish entails, which by restricting the transfer of land seemed to him a serious bar to Scottish commercial development.) In 1760 he published *The principles of equity*, in which he tried to reduce to a science "founded in the human constitution" that large area of legal disputation outside the common law which was traditionally seen as lying largely within the discretionary power of the judge.[17]

In 1762, Kames turned from law to aesthetics, tracing "the rules of criticism to their true principles in the constitution of the human mind" — rather than founding them on the authority of other writers or the past practice of poets and painters. Just as man was constituted with a moral sense by which he could judge right and wrong, so he was constituted with a sense of beauty by which to judge works of art. From here, Kames went on to define the specific principles and rules which elicited Voltaire's ironic comment that it was "an admirable result of the progress of the human spirit that at the present time it is from Scotland we receive rules of taste in all the arts — from the epic poem to gardening."[18]

In 1760, the idea that notions of civilization and refinement might emanate from Scotland could still provoke smiles of amusement in Paris and in London. For Scots, the assumption of cultural inferiority to the English was of course a particularly sensitive issue, in view of Scotland's

---

[16]   Tytler, *Memoirs*, I, 139–140, 142–146; Mathieson, *Awakening*, 222–223.

[17]   Tytler, *Memoirs*, I, 215ff., 230ff.; Kames, *Historical law tracts* (Edinburgh, 1758); *Principles of equity* (Edinburgh, 1760).

[18]   Tytler, *Memoirs*, I, 273, 293; Kames, *Elements of criticism*, three volumes (Edinburgh, 1762); Mathieson, *Awakening*, 204; Randall, *Critical theory*, passim; McGuinness, *Henry Home*, 58–118.

political subordination and economic backwardness — and of the fact that Scotsmen did not speak acceptable English. One of the goals of the Select Society, which the Edinburgh intellectuals formed in 1754, was in fact to "promote the reading and speaking of the English language." In this context, that a Scotsman should attempt to define the *Elements of criticism* was perhaps more a mark of the progress of the human spirit than Voltaire's irony intended. In any case, Kames had no doubt that Scotsmen were fit to lay down rules for its cultivation — two of the works of his last twenty years were intended to guide the education of the young.[19]

First published in 1774, the *Sketches of the history of man* was the culmination of Kames' varied literary labors. Although for thirty years he had collected material for a systematic natural history of man, in the end Kames felt that all he had produced were "a few imperfect sketches." Rambling and unsystematic, even self-contradictory at points, the work is clearly amateurish in certain areas — although always with a conviction of authority befitting a jurist of rather stern reputation. Kames apparently worked up his subjecits as he went along, as a judge might work up the materials a specific case required, and composed in the same way he wrote his legal opinions, by dictating to an amanuensis. Indeed, the style is conversational, and at times even earthy; Kames was not above telling us, as a Victorian evolutionist never would have done, that the Kamchatkans believed that rain was made by "some deity pissing upon them."[20]

The subject matter of Kames' *Sketches* is reflected in its major divisions: the "Progress of men as individuals" (or, in the second edition, "of men independent of society"); the "Progress of men in society"; and the "Progress of sciences." It is customary to treat this sort of account in terms of "conjectural history" and "the comparative method." The former phrase was introduced by the last of the great Scottish "moral philosophers," Dugald Stewart, who suggested that in "examining the history of mankind as well as in examining the phenomena of the material world, when we cannot trace the process by which an event HAS BEEN produced, it is often of importance to be able to show how it MAY HAVE BEEN produced by natural causes." Although the "comparative method" was not spoken of as such until the nineteenth century, its basic assumption was taken for granted by many eighteenth-century French and Scottish writers. Adam Ferguson had stated it concisely a few years before Kames wrote: "It is in

---

[19]   Mathieson, *Awakening*, 202; Tytler, *Memoirs*, I, 128; Kames, *Introduction to the art of thinking* (Edinburgh, 1761); *Loose hints upon education, chiefly concerning the culture of the heart* (Edinburgh, 1781).
[20]   Tytler, *Memoirs*, II, 163; Kames, *Sketches*, IV, 252.

[the] present condition [of the American Indians] that we behold, as in a mirrour, the features of our own progenitors; and from thence we are to draw our conclusions with respect to the influence of situations, in which, we have reason to believe, our fathers were placed." Assuming that human nature was everywhere the same, and developed everywhere in a gradual and uniform progress, one could use the data of contemporary savagery to construct a "reasoned" or "conjectural" history of the development of human activities, social institutions, and mental faculties — in short, of the whole process of human refinement, or to use a term just coming into use, of human "civilization." In contrast to the sacred history of the Bible, such reasoned history would explain how these phenomena might have been produced naturally by a Deity who since creation had operated only through "fixed laws," "second causes," and "ordinary means." In contrast to traditional secular histories, it focused on the major movements in the progress of mankind rather than on particular events in the lives of kings or of nations.[21]

Kames' *Sketches* fits into this framework. He took for granted the notion that contemporary savages represent the earliest stages in the development of human nature, and he traced that development through various sequences. Thus from the point of view of subsistence, Kames saw man developing from the hunter or savage state to the shepherd state, and thence to the agricultural, the dynamic being provided by the pressure of population on available food, with "necessity, the mother of invention" stimulating the movement from one stage to the next. Similarly, religion moved through six stages from primitive belief in numerous malevolent deities to refined belief in one benevolent one. Although the stages are not always so well-marked, Kames traced similar progressions in morality, reason, government, property, commerce, useful arts, fine arts, manners, and the treatment of the female sex. He did not subsume all of these sequences within the processual dynamic of population pressure. Indeed, there was no overriding explanatory framework, save that of providential design and final causes, unless it be a generalized metaphor of growth from infancy to maturity. Nor was Kames systematic in developing correlations between the sequences. On the whole, however, they were each assumed to be uniform for all of mankind.[22]

However, if it is true that Kames' argument fits within a framework of "conjectural history," this is hardly the whole story, or even the most in-

[21]   Stewart as quoted in Bryson, *Man and society*, 88; Ferguson, *An essay on the history of civil society* (1767), edited by Duncan Forbes (Edinburgh, 1966), 80; Kenneth Bock, *The acceptance of histories* (Berkeley, 1956).
[22]   Kames, *Sketches*, I, 93, 99, 424, II, 226, IV, 250.

teresting thing about the *Sketches*. Although Kames did draw on travel
accounts to define his picture of original human nature, in sheer quantitative terms the data of contemporary savagery did not bulk very large in
his argument. He was more likely to refer to Old Testament peoples, or
to Greek myth and epic, or to Roman and Medieval history. One is also
struck by the weight he gave to quite recent and in many cases dated events.
Many of his examples of the ways of "savage" or "barbarous" or "un-
polished" men — especially when he documented the cruelty of savages —
were drawn from European history up to a period quite close to his own
time. He was still fighting the intellectual battles of the early modern age:
arguing the savagery of the Greeks and Romans to show the inferiority
of the "ancients" to the "moderns"; offering examples of pre-reformation
barbarism to show the superiority of Protestantism to Catholicism. Another way of looking at this is to suggest that the process of civilization
was for Kames a very recent one, by no means yet complete in all of
Europe. Indeed, he felt that it was even then going on in Russia, where if
"the present Empress" were "to enjoy a long and prosperous reign, she
may possibly accomplish the most difficult of all undertakings, that of
polishing a barbarous people." [23]

Not only do the data of contemporary savagery bulk surprisingly
small, but Kames' two extensive accounts of "savage" peoples are quite
anomalous from the point of view of his conjectured normal sequences of
development, and in each case, he had difficulty explaining the anomaly.
At a slightly later date, the voyages of Captain Cook were to make the
South Sea Islanders the savages par excellence, and during the nineteenth-century debates over slavery, that role would be given to the black
African. But for Kames, it was still played by the American Indian, who
had already held the center of the stage for several centuries. Kames devoted a separate sketch to "The origin and progress of the American
nations." Their "progress" presented certain serious problems. Despite
the fact that there were domesticable animals in North America, the North
American tribes were in general remarkable for having failed ever to
progress from the hunter to the shepherd state. Paradoxically, however,
some of them had "advanced to some degree of agriculture." Even more
anomalous were the "political wonders" of the Mexicans and the Peru-
vians. Despite the fact that "with respect to religion," the Mexicans were
"no better than savages," they were "highly polished in the arts of society
and government." Following Buffon, Kames tried to explain the failure
to leave the hunter state by arguing that American Indian males were

[23] *Ibid.*, I, 365.

"feeble in their organs of generation": their relative "infecundity" fore-stalled the population pressures which might have advanced them to the shepherd stage. But for other departures from the uniform stages of human progress, he could do no more than profess his frank amazement.[24]

The second anomalous case was that of the Caledonians — the ancient inhabitants of Scotland and the ancestors of the present Scots. Kames' account of the Caledonians relied heavily on the recently "discovered" poems of Ossian. Ostensibly direct translations from the ancient Erse language by a young Highlander named James Macpherson, the Ossianic poems had a tremendous vogue in the later eighteenth century. From their first appearance in 1760, there was debate as to their authenticity, and they were eventually dismissed as largely fraudulent. But at least two of the Scottish conjectural historians felt otherwise. Adam Ferguson helped raise money to enable Macpherson to make trips to the Highlands and the Islands of Western Scotland to collect more material. And Kames had such "zeal for Ossian" that he was willing in this case to set aside his whole argument on the progress of manners. Primitive in every other respect, the ancient Caledonians were nevertheless courageous, humane, gentle to their women, and in general endowed with "manners so pure and refined as scarce to be paralleled in the most cultivated nations." They were, in short, the perfect embodiment of the "Noble Savage" convention which flourished in the literature of Western Europe in the latter half of the eighteenth century. Nor was Kames selfish with this heritage of savage nobility. Arguing that all the early inhabitants of Britain were of Celtic extraction, he extended the Ossianic dispensation to "every part of the island" in the period before the Roman conquest, and foreshadowing certain later currents of racial thought, found a similar pattern in the north of Europe generally.[25]

If the Ossianic episode stood alone in the *Sketches*, we might simply treat it as a compensatory assertion of cultural nationalism on the part of a Scotsman who was at one and the same time systematically emulating English models and being patronized by Englishmen. Perhaps most notably by Dr. Johnson, who felt that "the noblest prospect which a Scotsman ever sees is the high road that leads him to England." But there is evidence to suggest that Kames' idealization of the Scottish past was part of a larger ambivalence about the progress of civilization.

---

24   *Ibid.*, III, 138, 149, 152, 159, 161, 173.
25   E. D. Snyder, *The Celtic revival in English literature, 1760–1800* (Cambridge, Massachusetts, 1923), 69–86; McGuinness, *Henry Home*, 130–141; Kames, *Sketches*, I, 424–425, 494; Tytler, *Memoirs*, II, 88, 99; cf. Hoxie Fairchild, *The noble savage* (New York, 1961).

Let us consider Kames' picture of the savage in more general terms. There is much in it that is negative in the extreme. Deficient in reason and memory, dominated by their senses, and lacking foresight, savages were governed by passion, by imitation, and by habit. Like dogs, they were active when hunting, but extremely indolent and lazy at home. Treating their women like slaves, they gratified "animal love with as little ceremony as they do hunger or thirst." Timid by nature, but hardened to cruelty by the hunt, their punishments were sanguinary, because only their bodies, not their minds, were "sensible of pain."[26] And yet savages — even when they were not Gaelic — were not ALL bad. They were basically chaste and clean, and adultery was unknown among them. The simplicity of their wants, which were easily gratified, curbed their natural selfishness, and they never thought of "coveting what belongs to another." They expressed their "dissocial passions" only toward strangers — among their own tribe they seldom transgressed "the rules of morality." Savages outside Britain were in many respects quite unpleasant creatures, but were not entirely lacking in nobility.[27]

Kames' ambivalent view of savagery is better understood in the light of a similarly ambivalent view of the progress of mankind. True, he argued that there was a progress toward the "perfection" of human nature in each of its aspects — reason, the sense of deity, the sense of taste, and each of the "branches of the moral sense" — from "its infancy among savages to its maturity among polished nations." Just as human nature gradually matured in the human individual, so did it in mankind as a whole — through "experience," "education," "ripening," and "culture" — which it is worth noting was very little removed from its metaphorical roots in agriculture.[28] But with the dynamic of perfection so closely tied to a metaphor of growth, one immediately thinks of its antithesis: degeneration and decay. And surely enough, these figure rather largely in Kames' scheme.

Although the "useful arts" once gained were seldom lost, since they were "in constant practice," there was little else in the progress of civilization that was not subject to degeneration. Indeed, there is implicit in Kames a kind of general progress of corruption that paralleled the progress of civilization. As man moved from the hunting to the agricultural life, his manners softened, his faculties were refined, and he acquired a much greater pleasure in benevolence and generosity than he had in selfishness. But unfortunately, this "agreeable scene" could not last: "here the hoarding

---

[26] Kames, *Sketches*, I, 86, 259, 332, 341–342, 361, III, 222, IV, 130.
[27] *Ibid.*, I, 321–323, II, 21, 204, IV, 132.
[28] *Ibid.*, IV, 127–128.

appetite starts up to disturb that auspicious commencement of civilization." Skillful husbandry supplied a surfeit of necessaries, and paved the
way for arts and manufactures. Driven now by an "unwearied appetite"
for comfort, men were led from "simple necessaries" to "conveniences"
and thence "to every sort of luxury." Once again, "selfishness becomes
the ruling passion," and "opulence and sensual pleasure are idols wor-
shipped by all." Thus, "in the progress of manners, men end as they began;
selfishness is no less eminent in the last and most polished state of society
than in the first and most rude state." In a book which professed itself a
history of the human species "in its progress from the savage state to its
highest civilization and improvement," this progress of corruption seems
more than a bit anomalous.[29]

Perhaps we can begin to resolve the anomaly by approaching the matter
from another direction, and considering Kames' *Sketches* not as a natural
history of man but rather as an attempt to create a rational science of
progress on the basis of a study of human nature in a variety of social
contexts. From this point of view, one of the more important passages in
the book is a footnote in the first volume in which Kames attacked "certain philosophers" who would "boldly undertake to derive even the noblest principles from external circumstances relative to the body only,"
and who like "the celebrated Montesquieu" would argue that "courage
and cowardice" were simply dependent on climate. Kames himself did not
completely deny the indirect influence of climate on human culture. Indeed, he argued that the sequence of subsistence stages was only uniform
in temperate climes. But at several points he differentiated between "permanent manners," which were the result of external environment, and
those manners which were of interest to him. Thus the "stupidity" of the
New Hollanders was the product of their barren soil, which would never
allow them to progress beyond the hunter state: "people in that condition
must ever remain ignorant and brutish." What Kames was interested in,
on the other hand, was "such manners only as appear to proceed from
from the nature and character of a people, whether influenced by the form
of government, or depending on the degree of civilization."[30] The last
two phrases suggest a way of viewing Kames' *Sketches* as a whole: it was
not simply a reconstruction of the progress of the human species from
savagery to "its highest civilization." It was also a study of the effect of
social variables — of different forms of government and different degrees
or states of civilization — upon the generic aspects of human nature.

29   *Ibid.*, I, 191, 343–345, 347–348, 399–401, cf. 1.
30   *Ibid.*, I, 342, 99, 497, 315.

At this point, the mixed character of savages again becomes relevant. Savages had positive characteristics because they shared the same moral sense that all men have. That moral sense impelled them, as it did all men, toward cleanliness. If some savages were notoriously dirty, if "the nastiness of North American savages passes all conception," there were ways of explaining this. On the one hand, no "branch of the moral sense" was "equally distributed among all men" — just as some men have better eyesight, some had better moral senses. On the other hand, the moral sense — born weak, and developed only by culture — differed in its expressions in different stages of development, degrees of civilization, or different social contexts. The indolence of savages, which was a correlate of their hunter-state, had a further correlate in the tendency to dirtiness. But cleanliness was positively correlated with industry, and "industrious nations, accordingly, all the world over, are the most cleanly." The two virtues had progressed hand in hand in England since the mid-sixteenth century; but the Spaniards, "who are indolent to a degree, are to this day as dirty as the English were three centuries ago."[31]

There was no moral relativism in all this. Cleanliness was in all times and all places an absolute virtue. Indeed the whole point of the moral sense was to establish an absolute basis for human morals. But to say this does not mean Kames saw no tensions or ambiguities arising from the original nature of man. The sense of property was as much a part of human nature as the moral sense, and as necessary to the perfection of mankind. Without it, "there would be no industry; and without industry men would remain savages forever." And yet "affection for property" was a "Janus double-faced": "In thy right hand, Industry, a cornucopia OF PLENTY; in thy left, Avarice, a Pandora's box OF DEADLY POISON.[32]

Human nature was not built on any single principle. Man was a "compound of principles and passions, some social, some dissocial." Each had its final cause, each was a necessary part of the providential design, each contributed to the progress of the human species — nor could the perfection of mankind be based on the elimination of any element of the compound. It is in this context that Kames expostulated against "the supposed perfection of society" in a "golden age." Man's natural state was one of agitation and activity. Without the stimulation of opposite motives he "would rival no being above an oister or a sensitive plant." Nature had, "for wise purposes, impressed upon us a taste for variety." Constant repetition of "the same pleasures would render even a golden age tasteless, like an Italian sky during a long summer." On the whole, "the present

---

[31] *Ibid.*, I, 322–323, 327–328.
[32] *Ibid.*, I, 123, 126.

state of things, in which evils both natural and moral make a part, con-
tributes more to the enjoyment of life, as well as to the improvement of
our faculties and passions, than a uniform state, without variety, without
hopes and fears." Better therefore "to submit humbly to whatever befals,
and to rest satisfied, that the world is governed by wisdom, not by
chance." [33]

Did this mean that human development must always end where it
began, that growth and decay must repeat themselves in different nations
in an endless cycle? Some passages suggest this, but Kames also held out
the hope that a nation once ruined by opulence could be stimulated to a
"second progress" by "pinching poverty," and "thus go round in a circle"
— though he argued that "the world has not yet subsisted long enough to
afford any clear instance" of this cyclical recovery. And elsewhere there is
in fact evidence to suggest that Kames felt the degeneration of nations
might be avoided. The analogy of growth was only partial: "in the progress
from maturity to a declining state, a nation differs widely from an individual." The decline of individuals resulted from "old age"; that of nations,
from "disease." The former is unavoidable, but the latter suggests the
possibility of cure or perhaps even prevention. [34]

Certainly, Kames himself was not always inclined to "submit humbly to
whatever befals." He had little tolerance for irrational social policy, and
if he was neither radical in criticism nor revolutionary in prescription, he
did nevertheless have a great deal to say about how existing society might
be made to function more rationally. His discussion of "the progress of
man in society" included lengthy disquisitions on fiscal policy, the organization of the military, and "public police with respect to the poor"; and
in each case he offered detailed plans for their reform. [35]

Here, then, was the underlying purpose of Kames' study of human
nature in social context. "Of all the sciences, that of politics is the most
intricate; and its progress toward maturity is slow in proportion." But
Kames refused to believe that there was "some inherent vice in the nature
of government, that counteracts every effort of genius to produce a more
perfect mode." By understanding the way different aspects of human nature were affected by different forms of government and different degrees
of civilization, one could perhaps hope to create a rational science of
progress. By identifying oneself with "the necessary chain of [social]
causes and effects," rather than ignorantly struggling against it, one could
hope to counteract the progress of corruption, to prevent or cure the dis-

[33] *Ibid.*, II, 203, 209–210, 217, 221.
[34] *Ibid.*, II, 345–346, IV, 131–132.
[35] *Ibid.*, II, 354ff., III, 30ff., 82ff.

eases the body politic had always been heir to. Such a science would not eventuate in utopia. The stabilization of human progress was not to be achieved in a golden age, but by the golden mean — by maintaining in balance the opposing forces of human nature. Basically, what Kames hoped to do was recreate that "middle state, more suitable than either extreme to the dignity of human nature," when the appetite for property and the impulse of benevolence were somehow in balance, before the corruption began, when men still eschewed luxury and were both manly and industrious, and when all men were imbued with patriotism, the "cornerstone of civil society." [36]

Not all men could expect to achieve "the middle state." Kames took for granted that there would always be "inequalities of riches" in a commercial society. And his attitude toward the lower ranks of men was often quite harsh. To educate them too much would be dangerous; to allow them to vote for parliament would be a source of "idleness, corruption, and poverty." If in the administration of his welfare policy any of the poor "by neglect or oversight" happened to die of want, the example would "tend more to reformation, than the most pathetic discourse from the pulpit." On the other hand, Kames' social policies and moral injunctions were intended to soften the divisions within society. If the moral sense instructed us to be "submissive to our masters," it also instructed us to be "kind to our servants." If inequalities of riches would always exist, taxation would smooth them out somewhat, and in any case, they need not be the basis of "inequalities of privilege." [37]

To maintain a balanced social order, government must also reflect the golden mean. Nature had fitted a small portion of men to lead, and a greater portion to follow. The ideal form of government was therefore intermediate between democracy and despotism — a republic, or a limited monarchy, in which "every man has an opportunity to act the part that nature destined him for." For Kames, a "free state" was not one in which people were "governed by laws of their own making," but one in which "the laws of nature are strictly adhered to, and where every municipal regulation is contrived to improve society, and to promote honesty and industry." [38]

On the whole, it would seem that the social and political order Kames envisioned was very little different from that he saw around him in Scotland. The most important change had to do with national character. History was full of instances of the sapping of "manhood." Indeed, the

[36]   *Ibid.*, II, 409, III, 24, I, 152, I, 122, II, 155.
[37]   *Ibid.*, III, 94, 96, 107, IV, 32, II, 233.
[38]   *Ibid.*, II, 236, 247.

progress of arts and manufactures was in general linked with the weaken-
ing of the military spirit and the "manly" virtues. Witness the experience
of highland Scotland since the suppression of the clans: "The mildness with
which the highlanders have been treated of late, and the pains that have
been taken to introduce industry among them, have totally extirpated
depredations and reprisals, and have rendered them the most peaceable
people in Scotland; but have at the same time reduced their military spirit
to a low ebb." Firmly convinced that "a military and an industrious spirit
are of equal importance to Britain; and that if either of them be lost, we
are undone," Kames offered his plan for the organization of militia in
order "to reconcile these seeming antagonists," to "unite the spirit of
industry with that of war, and to form the same man to be an industrious
labourer, and a good soldier."[39]

At this point we are in a position to place the ambiguities and ambivalences of Kames' *Sketches* in a broader social and intellectual context.
On the one hand, there was Kames' experience of Scotland's progress and
improvement in his own lifetime. In discussing factors which affect the
rapidity of progress, Kames suggested that it was always rapid "when a
people happen to be roused out of a torpid state by some fortunate change
of circumstances: prosperity contrasted with former abasement, gives to
the mind a spring, which is vigorously exerted in every new pursuit."
There had been five such moments of flowering in human history, and the
last of them had been going on in Scotland since 1744. On the other hand,
there was the recurring refrain that this flowering was somehow a very
fragile thing: "Tremble, O Britain, on the brink of a precipice! How little
distant in rapacity from Roman Senators are the leaders of thy people!"[40]
Like Adam Smith, Kames was writing a history of how "from being a
savage, man rose to be a Scotchman." But in rising from savagery, he had
not ceased to be a man, and subject to all the frailties of his compound
nature. History — not CONJECTURAL history, but REAL history — contained
plenty of evidence of decline. Gibbon wrote at the same time as Kames,
and the fate of Rome was a major preoccupation of their age. Closer to
the present were the examples of Spain and Portugal, to which Kames
devoted considerable attention. But there were no actual historical models
of indefinite progress.

Furthermore, the dominant intellectual models were of a quite different
sort. Until the eighteenth century, the prevailing model — whether based
upon Biblical notions of the fall and flood, or upon classical notions of a

[39] *Ibid.*, III, 5, 24, 41.
[40] *Ibid.*, I, 186, 412.

primitive golden age — was one of a world in decay. Basil Willey has suggested that in the eighteenth century the prevailing tone was one of "cosmic optimism." But this optimism was not at first generally based upon the notion of progress. It was rather based on the ancient idea of the Great Chain of Being, and it was a rather static view, a complacent acceptance of this "best of all possible worlds," in which all possible beings were ranked hierarchically from the lowest to the highest in unbroken chain, with man placed in the middle ranges between animal and angel. As A. O. Lovejoy has suggested, it was only gradually that the Chain was "temporalized," or seen as being achieved in time. Similarly, it was only in the course of the eighteenth century that the idea of progress developed its characteristic modern meaning. In Kames there was still sometimes an ambiguity in the term: it was not, as we primarily think of it today, essentially unidirectional; there could be a progress of decay and corruption as well.[41]

Finally, in addition to the lack of historical and intellectual models, there was the ambiguity of Kames' own experience — the sense of loss as well as profit involved in the progress Scotland had experienced in Kames' lifetime. This was stronger perhaps in Ferguson, who had a Highland background and still spoke Erse as well as the Scottish English vernacular. But Kames resonates to many of Ferguson's themes. They both accepted Ossian; they both emphasized the corruption of polished nations; they both lamented the loss of manhood; and they both appealed for a revitalized civil virtue. Both felt that Scotland's commercial and intellectual progress had been won to some extent at the expense of the manly virtues they identified with the clan system.[42]

In this context, it is hardly surprising that there should have been ambiguities and ambivalences in Kames' notion of the progress of human civilization. Civilization has often been perceived as problematic; but it was problematic for Kames and his contemporaries in a somewhat special way. The fact that the word itself only at this time achieved a substantive (as opposed to a verbal) form suggests that the historical experience it encapsulated was a very recent one in the European consciousness.[43] Civilization did not yet have that ring of teleological inevitability that it was to convey in the nineteenth century, when the experience of European

---

[41] Willey, *Background*, 48; Lovejoy, *The great chain of being* (Cambridge, Massachusetts, 1936), 242–287; J. B. Bury, *The idea of progress* (New York, 1932); Lois Whitney, *Primitivism and the idea of progress* (Baltimore, 1934); cf. Lovejoy, *Essays in the history of ideas* (New York, 1960).
[42] Cf. Forbes, "Introduction," in Ferguson, *Civil society*, xxxi–xl.
[43] L. Febvre, et al., *Civilisation: le mot et l'idée* (Paris, 1930), 3–6.

civilization had a longer time dimension, and when Europeans were aggressively imposing their civilization on the rest of mankind.

Turning finally to the inheritance the Scots left behind them, what can we say about Kames and the later development of anthropology? As far as the early nineteenth century is concerned, the tendency of recent scholarship has been to minimize the influence of the Scots, at least in Britain. It has been argued that the interest in conjectural history and the comparative method went out of fashion, as the dominant utilitarian tradition focused on the factors affecting human behavior in the present, in terms of a straightforward pleasure/pain associationism which rejected the intuitionist arguments of the Scots. And yet there is a particular aspect of Kames' thought (which he did not share with his compatriots) which was very influential in the early nineteenth century, if only in a negative way. Anthropological debate in this period was dominated by a problem which, though not central to Kames' argument, was nevertheless one which engaged his attention, and on which he held rather unorthodox views.[44]

For Kames, this problem arose especially in connection with the American Indian. It was not simply the irregularities in their "progress" which troubled Kames; he also had his difficulties in treating their "origin." "As there has not been discovered any passage by land to America from the old world, no problem has more embarrassed the learned, than to account for the origin of American nations." True, Kamchatka was close by, but the Kamchatkans and the Americans spoke very different languages. More than that, a European or Asian origin would suggest that the extreme north of America was the first area populated, and it should therefore be well-populated today. But in fact it was not. Judging from the present distribution of population, one would have to conclude that America was first settled in Mexico and Peru, and the height of their civilization seemed to confirm this. On this basis, and on the basis of the physical appearance of American Indians, Kames decided that the only explanation of their origin was to assume that they were the product of a "local creation" — that is to say, that they were not descendants of Adam and Eve. Buttressing his suggestion with arguments from Buffon on the late emergence of the New World from the sea and the uniqueness of American land animals, he argued that this "local creation" need not contravene the Biblical account, since Adam and Eve might still be the

[44]   J. W. Burrow, *Evolution and society* (Cambridge, 1966), 10–16; cf. George W. Stocking, Jr., "From chronology to ethnology: James Cowles Prichard and British anthropology, 1800–1860," introduction to J. C. Prichard, *Researches into the physical history of man* (Chicago, 1973).

first parents of mankind — "i.e., of all who at that time existed, without being the first parents of the Americans."[45]

What Kames was arguing was later to be called polygenism — as opposed to monogenism — that is to say, the idea that there were many species of man, and that they did not all derive from the same parents. The first sketch of his book (or the "preliminary discourse" in the second edition) was in fact an argument that "God created many pairs of the human race, differing from each other both externally and internally; that he fitted these pairs for different climates, and placed each pair in the proper climate; that the peculiarities of the original pairs were preserved entire in their descendants." The argument leading to this conclusion was an extended treatment of the varieties of external appearance, internal disposition, and customary behavior among different groups of men, along with a refutation of alternative explanations in terms of climate. Kames no sooner presented this conclusion, however, than he backed off, suggesting that the Bible would not permit us to accept this point of view. But it is clear that he himself regarded it as "beyond any rational doubt," and his treatment of American Indians confirms that he actually accepted it.[46]

Kames did not see any contradiction between arguing on the one hand that men were not all members of the same species, and on the other, that they were all equal and shared a common human nature, "allowing for slight differences occasioned by culture and other accidental circumstances." Nor did he share the customary ninteeenth-century racist view of black Africans, though he thought them also to be a distinct species. He had once thought their "intellectual inferiority" was evidence of this species difference, but had decided that it was more likely the product of their social circumstances. And he in fact offered a glowing description of the town life of Guinea as an example of progress in the arts, and a moving story of the Foulah Prince Sambaboa as a "modern" illustration of the virtue of patriotism.[47]

Kames was not the first to suggest the polygenist viewpoint as to human origins. But his argument — hedged around as it was with accommodations to the Bible — was an influential one, and stimulated a number of counterattacks in defense of monogenism. Indeed, the question of the monogenetic or polygenetic origin of man was to become the central focus of early nineteenth-century anthropology; and in the context of debates on slavery and the slave trade, the polygenist argument was to assume a much less benign character. It was not until a decade after the publication of the

[45]   Kames, *Sketches*, III, 138, 146.
[46]   *Ibid.*, I, 76.
[47]   *Ibid.*, II, 53; IV, 22, 437, I, 64–65, 179, III, 347.

Origin of species that the debate between the monogenists and the polygenists came to end, and the ghosts of the dispute were not laid for long
after that.[48]

Apart from Kames' polygenism — in which he was not in any case
representative of the Scots as a group — what can we say about the heritage that the Scottish moral philosophers represent? The term itself suggests something of that heritage. These men wrote within a framework inherited from the ancients, in which philosophy was divided into three
large fields; the rational or logical, the natural, and the moral. Moral
philosophy was posed thus against natural philosophy (or natural science),
and was in a sense equivalent to the sciences of man, the behavioral
sciences, or the social sciences we know today. In this context, the historian of the Scots, Gladys Bryson, suggested that "no other group of thinkers
before the twentieth century so self-consciously set about encompassing
the whole range of discussion which now has become highly elaborated
and parceled out among the several social sciences." Elsewhere Bryson
argued that the individual modern social sciences developed out of the
generalized Scottish moral philosophy by a process of differentiation,
which she traced in the catalogues of American colleges in the nineteenth
century. Traditionally, the fourth year was devoted to the course in moral
philosophy taught by the college president. Gradually specific areas
branched off and were given separate treatment — first political economy,
then political science, with sociology emerging at the end of the century as
a kind of residual legatee of the moral philosophical tradition. In this
context, the heritage of the Scots is continuous and quite direct — so that
early twentieth-century American sociologists like Charles Horton Cooley
borrowed directly from Adam Smith's *Theory of the moral sentiments*
without acknowledging the source.[49]

Bryson's filiation doubtless reflects the particular influence of the
Scottish philosophy in the United States, where it was the dominant philosophical tradition in the nineteenth century. We have already suggested
that its fate in Britain was quite different, and it has been argued that
the re-emergence of social evolutionary thinking in Britain around 1860
was less a reflection of the continuity of Scottish influence than a response
to specific problems which had arisen in the utilitarian tradition. Be that
as it may, it is nevertheless a fact that when modern British social anthro-

[48]   Stocking, "From chronology to ethnology," in *Race, culture and evolution* (New
York, 1968), 42–68; William Stanton, *The leopard's spots* (Chicago, 1960).
[49]   Bryson, *Man and society*, 161, 176, 239; Bryson, The emergence of the social sciences from moral philosophy, '*International Journal of Ethics* (1932), 42: 304–322; W. C.
Lehmann, *Adam Ferguson and the beginnings of modern sociology* (New York, 1930).

pologists began to look for ancestors, it was to the Scots that they turned. The origin myths of both Radcliffe-Brown and Evans-Pritchard go back to the eighteenth-century moral philosophers:

We have already in the speculations of these 18th century writers all the ingredients of anthropological theory in the following century, and even at the present day: the emphasis on institutions, the assumption that human societies are natural systems, the insistence that the study of them must be empirical and inductive, that its purpose is the discovery and formulation of universal principles or laws, particularly in terms of stages of development revealed by the use of the comparative method of conjectural history, and that its ultimate purpose is the scientific determination of ethics.[50]

Doubtless there is something lost (or better, added) in this translation. Kames certainly was not, as Evans-Pritchard suggests of the Scots in general, a "firm believer in limitless progress," and his notion of society as "a natural system" was to say the least undeveloped. But there is no doubt that he believed that human actions were confined "within the great chain of causes and effects." He did upon occasion indicate a feeling for the functional interrelation of human customs. And while the ideas of "moral sense" and "final cause" do not seem in some respects too propitious a basis for a social science, there is nonetheless a clear analogy between analysis in terms of final causes and Radcliffe-Brown's notion of function as the correspondence between a social institution and the "necessary conditions of existence of the social organism." It is one of the characteristics of intellectual history (as acted, rather than as written), that men are able to choose their own ancestors, and it is by no means inappropriate for modern British social anthropologists to have chosen the Scots.[51]

REFERENCES

BOCK, KENNETH
1956 *The acceptance of histories.* Berkeley.
BONAR, JAMES
1930 *Moral sense.* New York.
BOSWELL, JAMES
1928–1934 *Private papers from Malahide Castle.* Edited by G. Scott and F. Pottle, 15:260–316. Mount Vernon, New York.

[50] Burrow, *Evolution and society*, passim.; E. E. Evans-Pritchard, *Social anthropology and other essays* (Glencoe, Illinois, 1962), 25; A. R. Radcliffe-Brown, *Method in social anthropology* (Chicago, 1958), 149–152.
[51] Evans-Pritchard, *Social anthropology*, 23–24; Radcliffe-Brown, *Structure and function in primitive society* (New York, 1965), 178.

BRYSON, GLADYS
1932   The emergence of the social sciences from moral philosophy. *International Journal of Ethics* 42:304–322.
1945   *Man and society: the Scottish Inquiry of the eighteenth century.* Princeton.

BURROW, J. W.
1966   *Evolution and society.* Cambridge.

BURY, J. B.
1932   *The idea of progress,* New York.

EVANS-PRITCHARD, E. E.
1962   *Social anthropology and other essays.* Glencoe, Illinois.

FAIRCHILD, HOXIE
1961   *The noble savage.* New York.

FEBVRE, L., *et al.*
1930   *Civilisation: le mot et l'idée.* Paris.

FERGUSON, ADAM
1966 [1767]   *An essay on the history of civil society.* Edited and with an introduction by Duncan Forbes. Edinburgh.

GRAHAM, H. G.
1969   *The social life of Scotland in the eighteenth century* (reprinted edition). London.

GRAVE, S. A.
1960   *The Scottish philosophy of common sense.* Oxford.

HUME, DAVID
1757   *Four dissertations: I — the natural history of religion....* London.

KAMES, LORD (HENRY HOME)
1728   *Remarkable decisions of the Court of Session, from 1716–1728.* Edinburgh.
1732   *Essays upon several subjects in law.* Edinburgh.
1747   *Essays upon several subjects concerning British antiquities.* Edinburgh.
1751   *Essays on the principles of morality and natural religion.* Edinburgh.
1758   *Historical law tracts.* Edinburgh.
1760   *Principles of equity.* Edinburgh.
1761   *Introduction to the art of thinking.* Edinburgh.
1762   *Elements of criticism,* three volumes. Edinburgh.
1766   *Progress of flax-husbandry in Scotland.* Edinburgh.
1776   *The gentleman farmer; being an attempt to improve agriculture by subjecting it to the test of rational principles.* Edinburgh.
1778   *Sketches of the history of man,* four volumes (second edition). Edinburgh.
1781   *Loose hints upon education, chiefly concerning the culture of the heart.* Edinburgh.

KETTLER, DAVID
1965   "The transformation of Scotland," in *The social and political thought of Adam Ferguson.* Columbus, Ohio.

LEHMANN, W. C.
1930   *Adam Ferguson and the beginnings of modern sociology.* New York.
1971   *Henry Homes, Lord Kames, and the Scottish Enlightenment.* The Hague.
LOVEJOY, A. O.
1936   *The great chain of being.* Cambridge, Massachusetts.
1960   *Essays in the history of ideas.* New York.
MARTIN, JOSEPH
1911   *Die Psychologie Henry Homes.* Halle.
MATHIESON, W. L.
1910a   *The awakening of Scotland: a history from 1747–1797.* Glasgow
1910b   *Scotland and the Union: a history from 1695–1747.* Glasgow.
MCCOSH, JAMES
1875   *The Scottish philosophy.* New York.
MCGUINNESS, ARTHUR E.
1970   *Henry Home, Lord Kames.* New York.
NEUMANN, WILHELM
1894   *Die Bedeutung Homes für die Asthetik und sein Einfluss auf die deutschen Asthetiker.* Halle.
NORDEN, JOSEPH
1895   *Die Ethik Henry Homes.* Halle.
RADCLIFFE-BROWN, A. R.
1958   *Method in social anthropology.* Chicago.
1965   *Structure and function in primitive society.* New York.
RANDALL, H. W.
1941   *The critical theory of Lord Kames.* Smith College Studies in Modern Languages 28.
SNYDER, E. D.
1923   *The Celtic revival in English literature, 1760–1800.* Cambridge, Massachusetts.
STANTON, WILLIAM
1960   *The leopard's spots.* Chicago.
STOCKING, GEORGE W., JR.
1968   *Race, culture, and evolution.* New York.
1973   "From chronology to ethnology: James Cowles Prichard and British anthropology, 1800–1860," introduction in *Researches into the physical history of man.* By J. C. Prichard. Chicago.
TYTLER, ALEXANDER (LORD WOODHOUSELEE)
1807   *Memoirs of the life and writings of the Honourable Henry Home of Kames,* two volumes, appendix and supplement. Edinburgh.
WHITNEY, LOIS
1934   *Primitivism and the idea of progress.* Baltimore.
WILLEY, BASIL
1940   *The eighteenth century background.* London.
WOHLGEMUTH, JOSEPH
1893   *Henry Homes Asthetik und ihr Einfluss auf deutsche Asthetiker.* Berlin.

Albert Gallatin and the Survival of Enlightenment Thought in Nineteenth-Century American Anthropology

ROBERT E. BIEDER

Most works on the history of anthropology deal with the Enlightenment influences, especially the belief in social evolutionism that shaped the study of man, and then leap to the post-Darwinian nineteenth-century thinkers in whose works evolutionism again forms the keystone. In so doing, scholars neglect a significant period, when changing social currents produced major shifts in the sciences of man that are important to the understanding of post-Darwinian anthropology. In the brief scope of this paper it is impossible to deal adequately with all of these influences, but by examining the works of Albert Gallatin it is possible to bring into focus some of the anthropological concerns of early nineteenth-century America. Through his writings and as president of the American Ethnological Society, which he founded, Gallatin played a major role in the study of ethnology.

In his ethnological works Gallatin sought to uphold the ideals of the Enlightenment. The values to which he subscribed were those that had emerged in the early eighteenth century: unity of mankind, progress, advancement of science, and freedom from tyranny. In his writings he repeatedly emphasized these points. Gallatin believed he could see general laws of development that stretched back into the dim past of man, and he believed that the study of ethnology would flesh out these laws.

The descendant of minor Swiss nobility, Gallatin was born in 1761 in Geneva, a city which at the time ranked as one of the more enlightened and sophisticated in Europe, renowned for its famous academy. At this aca-

Some of the data upon which this paper is based were collected with the support of grants from the Phillips Fund of the American Philosophical Society and from the Ford Foundation.

demy Gallatin acquired a solid background in languages, geography, and mathematics, and came to realize the importance of a career in science. Later in life he recalled that in Geneva, "To all those who were ambitious of renown, fame, [and] consideration, scientific pursuits were the only road that could lead to distinction, and to these, or other literary branches, all those who had talent and energy devoted themselves" (quoted in Adams 1879 [1943]:14). This quotation takes on further significance in the light of a note Gallatin once sent to a friend in which he claimed that his public writings, that is, those concerned with government and econom-ics, were of little account; rather it was his scientific work in the area of philology and ethnology that would cause his name to be remembered (Hall 1931:109).

Gallatin came to America in 1780, and in subsequent years was elected or appointed to various offices in the new government. While it is not clear just when he first became interested in philology and ethnology, Gallatin may have developed this interest when, while serving in the Jefferson administration, he had the opportunity to observe the American Indians who visited Washington, D.C. (Bartlett n.d.: Frame 755). It is known, however, that in 1823 while Gallatin was the United States' Minister to France, Alexander von Humboldt requested him to prepare a memoir on the Indian languages of North America. Though the essay was never published, it received mention in Adriano Balbi's *Atlas ethnographique du globe* (A. Gallatin 1836:1). Gallatin returned to the United States in 1823 and from then until 1826 found time to do further work on Indian languages which resulted in the completion of a map and a brief classification of North American tribes by language groupings. Late 1826 found him again in government service as Minister to England, an appointment he accepted regretfully, since it took him away from the ethnological pursuits which greatly interested him and because government service increasingly proved onerous to him. Indeed, he found the drift of American and even world civilization displeasing. Gallatin's son recorded in his diary in 1827 that "Father has little dinners of his beloved cronies, Humboldt, Pozzo di Borgo, Baring, etc. I really enjoy their conversation – their contempt for the world amuses me" (J. Gallatin 1916:268). By his son's description, Gallatin preferred the in-tellectual atmosphere of Europe over that of America, evincing "a strong belief in the superiority of European intellect" (J. Gallatin 1916:192-193).

Observing the changing political life in America, Gallatin felt it would be "most distasteful to him" (J. Gallatin 1916:191). Thus upon returning from England in 1827, Gallatin left government service definitively and turned again to ethnological study. One senses that in his retreat from public life into scholarly study, Gallatin took refuge in ethnology. The old excitement and idealism of founding a new nation had dissipated; the government "no longer represented a single great political conception" (Adams 1879 [1943]:635). By 1830, the age of "Jacksonian Democracy," both government and society had become corrupt and "in such a spectacle there was to Mr. Gallatin no pleasure and deep pain" (Adams 1879 [1943]:635–636).

In Gallatin's dismay one recognizes a mental outlook that could find immense comfort in drawing upon the philosophical assumptions of his youth for shedding light upon investigations in his later years. One of these philosophical assumptions, social evolutionism (or developmentalism as it was then generally termed), became basic to Gallatin's ethnology. It assumed the progressive nature of man, that while all mankind had started in the primitive state, through one influence or another certain groups progressed to civilization. Further, the stages of this progression could be delineated, and by utilizing comparative history all known societies could be placed on a scale ranging from savagism to civilization. Inherent in developmentalism was the idea of history as progress which embodied the belief that what came earlier was necessarily inferior. For those who held these tenets of Enlightenment thought, the problem was how to raise man from the lower stages of civilization; as such, the problem became the "grand object" of civilized nations (Berkhofer 1962: 11–14). For these theorists the concept of culture did not exist; they believed in a human nature governed by reason and everywhere the same. Developmentalism, while attractive to many as a persuasive theory for explaining the relationship between Indian and European-American, failed to answer what caused the Indian's lack of progress, or even, why his numbers decreased in the face of civilization.

Gallatin's avowed purpose in his first major work, *A synopsis of the Indian tribes of North America*, was to answer these questions (A. Gallatin 1836:7). While the sections of *Synopsis* seem only vaguely connected, each being an essay in itself, there is a definite organization. Both the division into sections and the exposition of topics indicate that Gallatin sought to place the Indian in a developmental framework. His first four sections located the Indian geographically, generally moving from east to west in his summation, while section five demonstrated his conceptual approach. He began by linking geography and climate and then proceeded to demonstrate how these were further linked to the Indian's level of subsistence. In one sense, Gallatin provided "scientific proof" for the then currently held belief that as natural men Indians lived in harmony with nature (Levin 1959:127–129). The model Gallatin employed resembles a ladder with hunters at the bottom, agriculturalists halfway up and civilized man at the top. To Gallatin, agricultural life best indicated incipient civilization. While he recognized that it would take a long time to progress from the bottom step of the ladder to the agricultural level, when reached "it appears extremely improbable that...a people become agricultural should take such a retrograde step, as to degenerate again into the hunting or savage state" (A. Gallatin 1836:149). In Gallatin's view, such a step was unreasonable and hence unnatural.

Not choosing to rely wholly on subsistence patterns to demonstrate the developmental model, Gallatin set out in the last section of his essay to establish that languages developed according to certain laws. Here he took issue with those who believed that Indian languages are complex because of the preponderance of inflections. The misconception arose, he thought, because people erroneously considered the inflected Greek and Latin languages as somehow more advanced than the less inflected modern languages. Actually, he claimed, the reverse is true; classical languages were not as advanced as modern languages. Retaining his developmental scale, Gallatin posited the highly inflected languages at the bottom, claiming that inflected languages were probably the earliest languages of mankind; next higher up on the scale he placed Greek and Latin, locating modern languages at the top. Indian languages were primitive, their form resulting from natural causes, and afforded "no proof of their being derived from a nation in a more advanced state of civilization" (A. Gallatin 1836:6). Thus Gallatin controverted those who believed such languages to be survivals of a more advanced stage of civilization.

Gallatin's *Synopsis* must be seen as more than an essay on the classification of Indian tribes. Looked at in a broader context, it spoke to the ideological concerns of the day and constituted an important defense of Enlightenment social evolutionism.

In 1842, Gallatin founded the American Ethnological Society with the purpose of further documenting man's rise to civilization. Regardless of what others in the Society believed "ethnology" to be, for him ethnology was the study of man in a developmental framework. He saw no differences between the work of ethnologist and that of antiquarian. As defined by the American Antiquarian Society, the antiquarian's task consisted of "collecting and preserving such materials as may be useful in MARKING THE PROGRESS, not only of the United States but in OTHER PARTS OF THE GLOBE..." (Thomas 1820:17. Emphasis added.) Implicit in "marking the progress" was an assumed scale from primitivism to civilization. Explicating the progress of mankind was the goal of both societies; as Gallatin wrote in 1846 to the Secretary of War, W. L. Marcy, in reference to the American Ethnological Society: "The modern appellation of 'Ethnology' has been substituted for that of 'Antiquarian.' Its seat is at New York; that of the American Antiquarian Society is at Worcester, Massachusetts; the object of both is the same" (A. Gallatin 1879 [1960]:625).

Regardless of the intent of its founder, the American Ethnological Society functioned to stir up ethnological controversy. For some, such as Henry Rowe Schoolcraft, the accumulation of ethnological data seemed to offer further evidence in favor of the theory of degeneration which postulated that primitive peoples were not at an early stage of development but rather had fallen away from a higher civilization (Freeman 1965:306). Another member, Alexander Bradford, argued that the civilizations of the New World, that is, those of Central and South America, did not result from man's slowly raising himself up, but rather from the progress achieved by the diffusion of civilization from the Old World (Bradford 1841). Another Society member, Samuel G. Morton, whom the phrenologists hailed as one of the most outstanding scientists in America, engaged in the science of craniology. Morton believed that his findings denied the validity of philological conclusions supporting monogenism; his investigations pointed to the polygenetic origins of man (Stanton 1960:97–98). Polygenism explained primitivism as innate inferiority rather than as a lack of progress. Gallatin sought to refute these theories in writing his next essay.

Gallatin's emphasis upon developmentalism determined the structure of his essay, *Notes on the semi-civilized nations of Mexico, Yucatan, and Central America*. As in *Synopsis*, he constructed his argument in segmented fashion, massing the accumulated evidence in the concluding chapter. He posed two important questions concerning the history of man: "that of the presumed inferiority of some races; and whether savage tribes can, of themselves, and without foreign assistance, emerge from the rudest and lowest social state, and gradually attain even the highest degree of civilization known to us" (A. Gallatin 1845:181). Marshalling his evidence from languages, calendars, astronomy, and agriculture, Gallatin set forth his case. In response to the first question, he argued against the inherent inferiority of primitive races. More directly he attacked polygenism by pointing to evidence substantiating Indian migration from the Old World, contending that, "unless we suppose that which we have no right to do, a second miraculous interposition of Providence in America...," one must conclude that the Indians emerged from Asia at a very remote time (A. Gallatin 1845:179). He next turned to confront the issue of diffusion and degeneration. In his thinking, diffusion did not mean solely the transferral of traits from one cultural area to another, but meant rather a transferral of such traits from the Old World to the New. The implications of such a theory were repugnant for Gallatin, the social evolutionist. He did not deny that some cultural traits could be spread over adjacent areas; he held only that from earliest times "it is most certain that man has in the main been left to his own resources, and that the whole mass of his present knowledge and acquirements is the result of a progressive accumulation, and of the gradual development of his faculties" (A. Gallatin 1845:181).

More conscious of his critics, the polygenists and degenerationists, Gallatin in his 1845 *Notes* became tighter in his reasoning and built his argument slowly and systematically, employing both historical sources and more conventional ones, such as ancient artifacts, in order to prove his case. To prove his theory of parallel development, he demonstrated that Indian astronomical and agricultural discoveries could only have been made where they were found, that is, in Mexico and Peru. In refuting diffusionist critics, he challenged them to explain why some Old World inventions had been imported but not others, like the wheel and the smelting process.

Gallatin maintained that his denial of diffusion from Europe, as the cause of the higher state of civilization of some of the Indian tribes relative to others, forced any explanations of this higher civilization to rely upon social evolution. However, degeneration still offered a possible explanation of primitivism; the necessity of proving this error still remained. As before, Gallatin fell back upon his theory that geography and climate functioned as limiting factors in man's evolution. That this answer did not completely suffice, Gallatin fully realized. While it did explain why some people had not advanced, it did not explain why, and more importantly how, other peoples had. In the end, Gallatin admitted he was forced to conjecture in suggesting that man's rise from hunter to agriculturalist was made possible by slavery (A. Gallatin 1845:197).

Gallatin's last essay, an introduction to Horatio Hale's *Indians of north-west America*, differed little in structure from previous essays. The problem probed, as well as the answers, were the same. Again Gallatin underscored the significance of geography and climate as limiting factors in man's development. He concluded the essay with a discussion of the ethnological data on the Pueblo Indians of the Southwest which he had received from government exploring expeditions. While he expressed his inability to determine who the Pueblo Indians were relative to other Indians, as he had little linguistic data on which to rely, he found them both interesting and attractive. Their interest for him lay in their having somehow short-circuited the usual developmental route. Without kings, nobles, despots, castes, or priests "of a most execrable worship," the Pueblo Indians were "an exemption of those evils which have often, and in many places, attended the early steps toward civilization of a savage people" (A. Gallatin 1894:xcvi-xcvii). His study of the Pueblo Indian, he wrote, offered "Almost the only refreshing episode in the course of my researches (A. Gallatin 1849:xcvii).

Out of step with his time by the 1840's, Gallatin continued to try to make sense out of man's past with what many considered invalid ethnological assumptions. In 1849 Henry R. Schoolcraft pondered the causes of the degeneracy of the Indians as he set about to write his monumental six volume Indian history. Phrenological investigations had found non-white races innately inferior (Anonymous 1841; Anonymous 1846). Following in the tradition of Samuel G. Morton, both Josiah Clark Nott and George Gliddon not only added support to theories of non-white inferiority but argued the validity of polygenism (Nott and Gliddon 1854).

While many viewed the stages of development in the history of mankind with skepticism or outright derision, not everyone did. In 1847 and 1848, Lewis Henry Morgan conceived of Iroquois history within an evolutionary framework. While it is impossible to establish the direct influence of Gallatin's ethnology upon Morgan's work, there are certain indications that support the plausibility of such a suggestion. Morgan did read an essay on "Government and institutions of the Iroquois" before the New-York Historical Society in April of 1846 (Fenton 1962: xii); as a member, Gallatin was most likely in attendance. Whether the two met then is not known. But it is certain that the venerable ethnologist did make an impression upon the young Morgan, for the latter's "Letters on the Iroquois," which appeared in the *American Whig Review* in the years 1847 and 1848 under the pen name of "Skenandoah," were addressed to Gallatin (Morgan 1847–1848).

REFERENCES

ADAMS, HENRY
1879 [1943]   *The life of Albert Gallatin.* New York: Peter Smith.
ANONYMOUS
1841   The superiority of the Caucasian race. *The American Phrenological Journal and Miscellany* 3:124–126.
1846   Signs of character as indicated by phrenology... illustrated by a like-

ness of Harrahwaukay, the New Zealand chief. *The American Phreno-logical Journal and Miscellany* 8:54–58.

BARTLETT, JOHN R.
   n.d.   Extract from *Albert Gallatin papers*, roll 44. New York: New York University.

BERKHOFER, ROBERT F.
   1965   *Salvation and the savage: an analysis of Protestant missions and American Indian response, 1787–1862*. Lexington: University of Kentucky Press.

BRADFORD, ALEXANDER W.
   1841   *American antiquities and researches into the origins and history of the red race*. New York: Dayton and Saxton.

FENTON, WILLIAM N.
   1962   "Lewis Henry Morgan (1818–1881): pioneer ethnologist," in *League of the Iroquois*. By Lewis Henry Morgan, v–xviii. New York: Corinth Books.

FREEMAN, JOHN F.
   1965   Religion and personality in the anthropology of Henry Schoolcraft. *Journal of the History of the Behavioral Sciences* 1:301–312.

GALLATIN, ALBERT
   1836   *A synopsis of the Indian tribes of North America*. American Antiquarian Society Transactions and Collections 2:1–422.
   1845   *Notes on the semi-civilized nations of Mexico, Yucatan, and Central America*. American Ethnological Society Transactions 1:1–352.
   1848   "Introduction," in *Hale's Indians of north-west America, and vocabularies of North America, with an introduction*. American Ethnological Society Transactions 2:xxiii–clxxxviii.
   1879   [1960]   *The writings of Albert Gallatin*, volume two. Edited by Henry Adams. New York: Antiquarian Press.

GALLATIN, JAMES
   1916   *The diary of James Gallatin, secretary to Albert Gallatin, a great peace maker, 1813–1827*. Edited by Count Gallatin. New York: Charles Scribner's Sons.

HALL, PERCIVAL
   1931   "Albert Gallatin," in *Dictionary of American biography*, volume seven, 103–109. New York: Charles Scribner's Sons.

LEVIN, DAVID
   1959   *History as romantic art*. New York: Harcourt, Brace and World.

MORGAN, LEWIS HENRY
   1847–1848   Letters on the Iroquois. *American Whig Review* 5:177–190, 242–257, 447–490, 507–515.

NOTT, JOSIAH CLARK, GEORGE R. GLIDDON
   1854   *Types of mankind*. Philadelphia: Lippincott, Grambo.

STANTON, WILLIAM
   1960   *The leopard's spots: scientific attitudes toward race in America, 1815–1859*. Chicago: University of Chicago Press.

THOMAS, ISAIAH, *et al.*
   1820   *Origins of the American Antiquarian Society*. American Antiquarian Society Transactions and Collections 1:17–20.

E. George Squier and the Mounds, 1845-1850

E. G. Squier has frequently been cited as the premier American archeologist of his time. His achievements caught the imagination of American
scholars and laymen alike and focused attention on the mounds of the
Mississippi Valley. Nevertheless, Squier owed much to the pioneer archeologists who preceded him and to the learned societies that financially
and morally supported him. Joseph Henry and the Smithsonian Institution in particular influenced Squier by imposing rigorous scientific standards and restricting theories in Squier and Davis' now classic *Ancient monuments of the Mississippi Valley* (1848). This monograph sparked a surge
of archeological enthusiasm in the 1850's, which Secretary Henry subtly
directed into scientific and professional channels. Moreover, Squier's
Smithsonian memoir outlined an intellectual method that eventually, and
probably inevitably, discredited the "romantic school" of American
archeology and its legendary history. The scientific precedents nurtured
by Squier and Henry subverted the Moundbuilder myth. With Henry as
the virtual arbiter of archeological respectability in the United States,
solid evidence replaced conjecture as the dominant archeological method.

Squier was a product of early nineteenth-century interest in antiquities.
He reflected some of the major preoccupations of earlier archeologists and
reacted against others, but the influence was strong in either case. The

This paper is essentially a chapter from my doctoral dissertation, "The development of
American archaeology, 1800–1879," submitted to the Department of History of the
University of Chicago in Autumn, 1973. I would like to acknowledge the critical com-
ments and assistance of Professors Neil Harris and George W. Stocking, Jr. of the
University of Chicago and the generosity of William Stanton of the University of Pitts-
burgh.

social and intellectual context within which Squier's archeology developed is therefore necessary to an understanding of his "moundology." An antiquarian tradition, inherited chiefly from Britain, in many respects molded early American archeology. Like British archeologists, Americans tended to adopt romantic solutions for troublesome questions. Perhaps the best example of this was the conjectural history they developed for an imaginary Moundbuilder race that long before achieved a civilization of awesome magnitude. This myth presumed that invading and savage American Indians destroyed the Moundbuilders and appropriated their lands. The Moundbuilder mythology at once postulated a venerable antiquity of civilization for the United States and condemned the Indian for his brutality. In short order the legendary history became the standard interpretation, and, although American antiquaries might differ over aspects of the paradigm, few disputed its fundamental validity. The acceptance of the tradition insured archeology's popularity, but it limited the perception and contributions of archeologists because their preconceived theoretical constructs confined their vision to unproductive and ultimately untenable channels.

Two groups chiefly constructed the Moundbuilder myth. Western archeologists provided both accurate and spurious information on the mounds. Skilled antiquaries, generally in the East, devised grandiose, pseudo-historical interpretations to fit this data. As archeological methods gradually improved from simple description to accurate surveys, the sophistication and scientific underpinnings of the Moundbuilder arguments also strengthened. By 1845 new proofs were based on racial classification, fanciful comparative ethnology, and, in the case of the Mormons, divine inspiration. The popular and scientific literature, with few important exceptions, both augmented and fortified the foundations of the mythology.

Western archeologists generally preferred describing local surface remains to fabricating world histories. Their style of exploration closely resembled British topographical or "field" archeology. Mound excavation had less attraction than surveying, and diggers preferred treasure to data. Collecting relics became a popular hobby among westerners. By 1845 the Moundbuilder mystique caught the public's fancy and achieved scientific respectability throughout the nation.

Learned institutions became a vital facet of the antiquarian tradition as it developed in the United States. American antiquaries soon emulated the British archeological model by organizing into scientific societies. In 1812 the American Antiquarian Society (AAS) was founded, supposedly to serve the national community. It dominated American archeology for

several decades, stimulated western archeology, and sponsored and published Caleb Atwater's mound researches. Ultimately the society abdi-
cated national responsibility and became one of many eastern "bastions
of localism."

Western intellectual sectionalism in part instigated the regional division
of archeological activity. A series of transient local societies began in
western cities in the 1820's, and replaced the extended eastern organizations as the centers of western science. The western institutions stressed
archeological investigations as one of their major functions. However, too
geographically isolated to attract and maintain the large memberships
needed for continuous activities, they actually accomplished fairly little.
When Squier began his archeological activities in the mid-1840's, public
interest in the mounds was great but scholarly institutions had never
successfully capitalized on it. New kinds of research institutions and innovative archeologists were needed to invigorate the study of American antiquities.

THE DEVELOPMENT OF AN ARCHEOLOGIST

Born in Bethlehem, Albany County, New York, Ephraim George Squier
(1821-1888) grew up on the fringes of the Burned-over District. He had a
zealous and romantic temperament which manifested itself in a direction-
less will to succeed and an aggressive and uncompromising character.
Squier lacked adequate emotional stability, a problem that reduced the
effectiveness of his indomitable will, occasionally infected him with self-
doubts and depression, and ultimately led to insanity. Squier exhibited
striking perseverance during success, but could not easily admit or accept
defeat. He frequently saw a conspiracy in any criticism of himself or his work.
Because of his paranoid behavior, he experienced many personal conflicts
and betrayals, with the result that several close friends became bitter foes.
Like so many of his contemporaries, Squier passionately yearned for fame
and fortune, and he succeeded in achieving a measure of both. He won a
good reputation as a journalist, diplomat, railroad entrepreneur, and
archeologist, but flitted from one occupation to another throughout his
active life, spreading his talents thin.

From his youth Squier had difficulty choosing a career. His family
lacked enough money for his schooling, so he received only a rudimentary
education, perhaps supplemented by lessons from his father, a Methodist
Episcopal minister. During his teens he taught others in the winter and
farmed the rest of the year (*American Whig Review* 1850:347; Duyckinck

and Duyckinck 1875:671). While teaching school Squier studied civil engineering. However, the depression years following 1837 restricted internal improvement projects, putting many civil engineers out of work (Calhoun 1960:141). With engineering no longer profitable, Squier, following his father's advice that he prepare for a teaching career, enrolled in the Troy Conference Academy in West Poultney, Vermont in 1839 (*Squier papers-IHS*, Newman to F. Squier, August 20, 1874; *Squier papers-NYHS*, E. G. Squier to Parents, June 30, 1839). The life of a "dispised and miserable pedagogue — the most illy paid and thankless of all employments" soon palled, and instead Squier embarked on a literary career (*Squier papers-NYHS*, E. G. Squier to Parents, December 30, 1841). He secured an editorial position on Joel Munsell's *New York State Mechanic* at Albany in 1841. At the same time he earned a reputation as a poet. An ardent Whig, Squier also sent legislative reports to the New York *Journal of Commerce*. Working for another man's newspaper failed to satisfy an "ambition that burns like fire in my veins." Squier determined to leave "a NAME to the world" (*Squier papers-NYHS*, E. G. Squier to Parents June 24, 1842). In 1845 Squier changed his job and location. He rejected an attractive offer to edit a Baltimore newspaper, refusing to "live where there are SLAVES!" and moved instead to Chillicothe, Ohio, to edit the weekly *Scioto Gazette* (*Squier papers-NYHS*, E. G. Squier to Parents, January 1, 1845, February 24, 1845).

There Squier found one of his life's passions — the mounds. As a New Yorker he must have seen or at least heard about mounds, but none so impressive as the Scioto Valley earthworks. Squier later wrote that he thoroughly researched the literature on the western earthworks before leaving for Ohio and "the third day after my arrival there found me in the field examining their character" (*Squier papers-LC*, E. G. Squier to Marsh, January 8, 1848; to Henry, March 24, 1847). His earliest letters from Ohio spoke excitedly of the mounds and how he devoted all of his spare time to their study (*Squier papers-NYHS*, E. G. Squier to Parents, July 20, 1845). He soon collected Moundbuilder relics, planned a book on the subject, and sought other Ohioans with similar interests.

Shortly after arriving in Chillicothe he met Dr. Edwin Hamilton Davis (1811–1888), a long-time resident of Chillicothe. Davis, enamored of the mounds since his youth, explored them while a student at Kenyon College, lectured on the subject at commencement, and helped Charles Whittlesey with his topographical surveys in Ohio (*New York Tribune* 1888). After graduating from the Cincinnati Medical College in 1837 or 1838, he married and practiced medicine at Chillicothe. Reserved and somewhat diffident, Davis shared Squier's ambition, but lacked his drive. He must have felt both flattered and pressured by the attention of the younger man. In the summer of 1848, the two reached an informal agreement to explore together the mounds around Chillicothe and to publish an article or book on that subject. Soon both wrote newspaper and magazine articles and corresponded with antiquaries in eastern as well as western learned societies.

From the start Squier and Davis maintained high scientific standards. They recognized that earlier archeologists built "the crudest speculations and the wildest conjectures" on inadequate facts and faulty examination (Squier and Davis 1848:xxxiii). To avoid similar pitfalls the partners vowed to cleanse their minds of all preconceived notions and let their impressions of mounds form upon *tabulae rasae*. Only with original and systematic investigations could accurate data be collected for correct conclusions. Squier and Davis employed techniques which, while not radically innovative, equaled any ever before practiced by American archeologists. Squier used his surveying skills to obtain precise measurements in cases requiring great accuracy. The partners made field notes of every potentially valuable fact, paying particular attention to "the dependencies of the position, structure, and contents of the various works in respect to each other and the general features of the country" (Squier and Davis 1848: xxiv). However, their chief contribution to archeological method rested on their understanding that only examinations of a large sample of mounds warranted meaningful generalizations. In practice, they surveyed and excavated enough mounds to support their conclusions. Lapses in their accuracy can in part be blamed on their old and unreliable surveyor's compass, and, perhaps, even some distortion of their statistics (Fowke 1902:55–58; Thomas 1894:481–482).

Despite their assertions to the contrary, both Squier and Davis were influenced by previous archeological writers and reflected this in their theories. Squier's first published piece on the mounds repeated standard Moundbuilder theory (Squier 1845). However, since he purposefully tried to avoid conjectures, the traditional American prejudice less affected his subsequent work. The chief objective, and the greatest merit, of Squier's early efforts consisted of the logical and systematic categorization of various types of ancient mounds and artifacts. Speculation about origins and purposes was minimal.

Squier frequently remarked that the nation's future lay in the West and even attempted to enter Ohio politics. Yet from the first he sought eastern support for his archeological endeavors. Showing no interest in several western societies that requested his archeological aid, Squier disclosed his discoveries only before eastern organizations (*Squier papers-LC*, Circulars of the Cincinnati Historical Society and the Academy of Natural Sciences of Cincinnati). The fame and fortune he fervently desired could be obtained only from the East. Throughout his life Squier remained an easterner at heart. His New York background and 1844 election to membership in the Connecticut Historical Society undoubtedly influenced his orientation. Dr. Davis made no objection, since he also desired scientific recognition from the East.

Squier's personal ambition twisted his conception of the Moundbuilders in an unorthodox direction. Probably in rebellion against his strict father's religious zeal, Squier adopted an atheistic posture and an antagonism toward religion. Soon after he arrived at Chillicothe he promised his father "to show you some things 'you never dreamed of' in your philosophy" (*Squier papers-NYHS*, E. G. Squier to Parents, March 10, 1846). Squier tried to use the mounds to dispute the chronology and views of man's dispersion espoused by Biblical scholars. He soon allied himself with polygenist writers of the "American School" of Anthropology (Stanton 1960:82–89). Dr. Samuel G. Morton, George R. Gliddon, and Dr. Josiah Nott, who believed American Indians racially distinct by a separate creation, deeply influenced Squier's thinking. They applauded his efforts in support of their theories and encouraged him to extend his studies. Affiliation with these heretical scientists must have appealed to Squier's own rebellious spirit.

Hoping to receive both recognition and financial assistance from eastern societies, Squier rarely mentioned his connections with racial theorists or his desire to prove their contentions. Had he done so his reception might well have been cool. Most of the ethnologists and antiquaries based their interest in man's history upon a foundation of philology and not physical anthropology. Morton's ideas made some inroads in learned societies, but deep-rooted and powerful opposition remained. For example, Albert Gallatin (1761–1849), president of the American Ethnological Society and Squier's patron, vigorously disagreed with Morton on Indian origins (Stanton 1960:97-98). It is unlikely he would have aided Squier had he fully known the latter's views. As it was, the aged philologist took immediate interest in Squier's work upon the archeologist's arrival in New York City in June, 1846, to solicit assistance.

Gallatin's reputation and personality brought many of the nation's foremost antiquaries and ethnologists into the American Ethnological Society's fold and made New York City the center of American anthropology during the 1840's. A great patron of science and a public servant of renown, Gallatin devoted his last years to the study of American Indians and their languages. In 1842 he founded the Ethnological Society in

New York City. His concurrent presidency of the New-York Historical Society (NYHS) from 1843 to 1849 lent it similar prestige and prosperity (Vail 1954:90). The frequency of joint memberships indicated that Gallatin formed the Ethnological Society as an offshoot of the Historical Society in order to study matters outside the realm of New York history. The American Ethnological Society (AES) proposed to study "Man and the Globe he inhabits, as comprised in the term Ethnology in its widest meaning" (AES 1845:ix). With exotic lands rapidly becoming accessible to the western world, the Society believed the time ripe to investigate little-known peoples. Even in America there were unsolved mysteries. Great gaps remained in man's knowledge about the "history and origin of the American races of man," including the ancient civilizations of Middle and South America and "the earth-works of the Ohio and Mississippi valleys and their founders" (AES 1845:x).

Squier quite rightly placed his hopes for support with the Ethnological Society. He soon made many valuable friends among its members and received assurances that it would publish his preliminary work in the next volume of *Transactions* (*Squier papers-NYHS*, E. G. Squier to Parents, June 29, 1846). John Russell Bartlett (1805–1886), along with his close friend, Albert Gallatin, influenced the subsequent direction of Squier's work. As corresponding secretary of both the New York societies, Bartlett communicated with many important scientists throughout the world. Gallatin's frequent illnesses left Bartlett as virtual head of the Ethnological Society and in a strong position to aid Squier. With his partner, Charles Welford, Bartlett operated a bookstore that specialized in foreign and antiquarian literature and served as a meeting place for New York's literati and antiquaries. During the 1840's Bartlett wrote a continuing essay summarizing recent developments in ethnology and archeology (Bartlett 1846:50–54). Soon after Squier's arrival on the archeological scene, Bartlett incorporated his discoveries into the work, giving them both circulation and prestige. In addition, the scholarly Bartlett aided Squier with problems in comparative archeology and referred him to many antiquarian books. As a first-rate bookseller, he obtained many rare volumes for Squier and helped him to amass a large library on American antiquities.

Squier's enthusiastic reception in New York and election as corresponding member of the American Ethnological Society gave him sufficient encouragement to seek further support in New England. The accumulated interest, now exceeding $5,000, on the American Antiquarian Society's fund for archeological exploration lured Squier to Worcester. Bartlett wrote Samuel Foster Haven, the librarian and guiding light of the Society, on Squier's behalf, asking financial assistance from the fund (AAS,

Bartlett to Haven, June 16, 1846). When Haven and the Society's Council met with Squier they promised to consider his plans at their next general meeting and hinted at a generous appropriation. Squier next went to Boston where he met with "over FIFTY of the most distinguished gentlemen of science and learning. . . at the house of Dr. John C. Warren." Edward Everett, Jared Sparks, and William H. Prescott attended this meeting of the American Academy of Arts and Sciences and supported Squier's requests for assistance. The academy made him an honorary member and "offered to publish the results of. . . [his] labors" (Squier papers-NYHS, E. G. Squier to Parents, June 29, 1846).

    Before leaving the East, Squier proposed a "plan of operations" to several learned societies. An early statement of his ideal approach to archeology, it presented an alternative method for archeological activity by societies. Standard procedure allowed only limited support to individuals who investigated antiquities on their own time and money. A society might grant cash awards to help defray expenses and certainly published memoirs, but the relationship remained one of individuals freely offering their services and not the society commissioning archeological explorations. Hence responsibility for the operations rested entirely upon archeologists who derived no authority from their nebulous institutional connections. Squier, who possessed considerable organizational talent, judged this informal policy foolish. He felt that only cooperative archeology could succeed on a worthwhile scale. He himself generally preferred to work under the auspices of learned societies, believing that societies granted personal prestige along with money.

    Squier's envisioned "campaign of investigations" would operate under the joint patronage of several societies. He and Dr. Davis would supervise the entire operation, recruiting subordinates among western antiquaries. These volunteers would receive reimbursement for their personal expenses and, when necessary, additional payment for the "complete and thorough exploration of the antiquities in their vicinity." A letter of instructions would be distributed and the resulting local, systematic surveys sent to Squier within a fixed period, probably a year. The joint efforts undoubtedly would surpass any individual attempt to cover the Mississippi Valley. Finally, Squier and members of the various societies would analyze the data and compile the complete story of the mounds of the United States. This plan, Squier added, "is identical with that accepted by the General Government, in collecting information for specific objects" (Squier papers-NYHS, E. G. Squier to Warren, July 6, 1846; Haven papers, E. G. Squier to Haven, July 6, 1846). Its successful implementation rested entirely with the eastern societies since only they could afford the large expenditures necessary for success. Squier hoped the American Antiquarian Society would underwrite the costs but thought even their large fund insufficient and therefore requested other assistance.

The societies' leaders agreed to broach the matter to their memberships. Ultimately all either postponed decision or rejected the plan outright. In August, 1846, the American Antiquarian Society deferred judgment for a year, when Squier's expected memoir could be assessed (*Squier papers-LC*, Haven to E. G. Squier, August 28, 1846; *Bartlett papers*, E. G. Squier to Bartlett, September 21, 1846). The American Academy of Arts and Sciences found their funds "exceedingly low" and offered no help (*Squier papers-LC*, Warren to E. G. Squier, August 28, 1846; *Bartlett papers*, E. G. Squier to Bartlett, September 21, 1846). It remains unclear whether the American Ethnological Society accepted Squier's proposal. Gallatin and Bartlett probably agreed to it only on the condition that other organizations participate.

Even Dr. Davis demurred at Squier's plan. He disliked delegating the archeology, believing that "you might as well expect information from the moon by addressing the Man there, as to get anything of value from most correspondents." Furthermore, Davis felt that five years "will be required to. . . do justice to the subject, ourselves, and the country" (*Squier papers-LC*, Davis to E. G. Squier, July 7, 1846). The learned societies probably shared Davis' poor opinion of the value of correspondents. Too much depended on Squier's choosing competent assistants. Unless the correspondents performed uniformly well the final results would suffer immensely. The problem of regulating the quality of individual contributions on a subject prone to imaginative treatment must have discouraged the societies and in part led to their refusals. Correspondents made fine society members, especially if they paid dues and donated artifacts. However the Jacksonian idea that anyone could contribute to science had little appeal when it drained the societies' treasuries. The unenthusiastic reception of the scheme eventually led Squier to abandon it. He steadfastly resolved to continue his explorations as long as possible and alone if necessary (Historical Society of Pennsylvania (HSP), E. G. Squier to Silliman, December 16, 1846; *Bartlett papers*, E. G. Squier to Bartlett, September 21, 1846).

Squier returned to Chillicothe in August, having received enthusiastic praise and a promise of publication, but no money. Bartlett therefore advised that he quickly write his article for the Ethnological Society's *Transactions*. That would be "the best feeler we can throw out. . .With this we can come forward and ask for aid in the larger work." While "a few thousand dollars in advance. . . is quite desirable," he did not see how

Squier could "call upon people who know nothing of the work or what it will contain" (*Squier papers-LC*, Bartlett to E. G. Squier, September 10, 1846). Acting on this advice, Squier and Davis spent the fall completing their surveys and excavations in the Scioto Valley. Each wrote several archeological articles for *Silliman's Journal* and other periodicals in order to keep their subject "warm" before the public (*Bartlett papers*, E. G. Squier to Bartlett, August 24, 1846).

A substantial portion of their archeological data came from correspondents or conversation, but they personally surveyed the majority of the earthworks. Among their best informants were Samuel Hildreth whom Squier "pumped. . . dry," Charles Whittlesey, and James McBride. The latter two volunteered their notes, surveys, and drawings for the publication. Their reliability allowed Squier and Davis to forego surveying the described earthworks. Other important correspondents included Gerard Troost, Benjamin L. C. Wailes, Robert Morris, U. P. James, Dr. M. W. Dickeson, and J. G. M. Ramsay. In its final form the book included many surveys by these contributors. Squier and Davis gathered their information about southern earthworks and Wisconsin and Iowa effigy mounds almost entirely from correspondents, and therefore could not guarantee accuracy. Because of generous acknowledgments, the borrowed surveys are easily identifiable. The personal efforts of Squier and Davis therefore can also be isolated. In general, the partners confined their activities to southern Ohio and surrounding regions. Thus, in the end, Squier succeeded in implementing his rejected plan on a small and informal scale.

While they used the surveys of others, Squier and Davis retained complete responsibility for the contents of their book. Their unequal roles in the partnership, however, caused strains in their relationship and eventually led to a breakdown in communications. Dr. Davis' medical duties often prevented his leaving Chillicothe, so the burden of the surveying, digging, drawing, and writing fell to Squier (*Bartlett papers*, Davis to Bartlett, October 27, 1846). The two combined their collections of relics upon entering partnership. Davis assumed the responsibility for the whole, cleaning, repairing, and labeling the artifacts that he arranged in his house. Better educated than Squier, he contributed his knowledge of natural history, but Squier, with his seemingly endless energy, clearly led the team.

Squier continued his attempts to raise money throughout the fall and winter. Disappointed, he investigated alternative employments in case archeology failed him. He learned in September, 1846, that Dr. M. W. Dickeson was intruding on his scientific territory and eroding his strength in the eastern societies. Dickeson presented a paper at a meeting of the

Association of American Geologists and Naturalists and visited Dr. Morton and others with news of great discoveries in southern mounds. For a few months Dickeson's eminence eclipsed Squier's in journals and newspapers. Both Bartlett and Morton praised him, undoubtedly wounding Squier's vanity (*Squier papers-LC*, Bartlett to E. G. Squier, September 10, 1846; Morton to E. G. Squier, December 8, 1846).

Perhaps in response to this threat Squier ran for the clerkship of the Lower House of the Ohio Legislature, a post that "gives a man some little ECLAT, which is sometimes worth more than money" (*Squier papers-NYHS*, E. G. Squier to Parents, November 2, 1846). He won that election, quit his post on the *Scioto Gazette*, and moved to Columbus for the winter. His spirits raised by success, Squier renewed his hope of making a complete survey of the mounds. He now felt certain of associational support and definitely decided to remain a "Moundologist." At last he found a suitable profession in a field which "is a wide and rich one and holds out a bright prospect of reputation and REMUNERATION to the person who engages in it, in the right spirit and with a proper determination" (*Squier papers-NYHS*, E. G. Squier to Parents, December 30, 1846). By January, 1847, Squier and Davis excavated nearly 130 tumuli and surveyed about one hundred others (*Squier papers-LC*, E. G. Squier to Morton, 1847).

By early 1847 Squier had finally settled on a career in archeology. He decided that a scholarly life could satisfy the fiery ambition that drove him to seek personal success, a goal he shared with many young men of Jacksonian America (Ward 1955:166–180). To a degree this same will to succeed led him to fault earlier archeologists in order to enhance his own achievements. Actually Squier operated similarly to his predecessors. He linked his aspirations to the prestige of eastern learned societies and tried to reshape rather than revolutionize their methods of archeological exploration. His early archeological theories buttressed the legendary history. His most important contribution was to subordinate hypothesis to data-collecting, although the subordination was never as clear as Squier suggested. If the history of American archeology reached a turning point with the work of Squier and Davis, it was the influence of Joseph Henry, the Secretary of the Smithsonian Institution, as much as the activities of E. George Squier, that was responsible.

SQUIER AND THE SMITHSONIAN INSTITUTION

Perhaps Squier and Henry's greatest archeological achievement rested in the initiation of a gradual and subtle process that finally replaced romantic antiquarianism with scientific archeology. Each man wanted to re-examine American antiquities from an unbiased position. This entailed a large-scale mound survey to collect raw data unsullied by preconceived theories. The success of Squier's memoir gave its publisher, the Smithsonian Institution (SI), pre-eminence among antiquarian organizations and motivated many archeologists to associate with it. This factor and Henry's insistence on original and empirical mound research rang the death knell for the romantic tradition, which relied heavily on comparison and conjecture.

Neither Squier nor Henry, of course, anticipated the impact their alliance eventually had on archeology. When Squier's friend, Congressman George Perkins Marsh (1801–1882) of Burlington, Vermont, first discussed Squier's proposed monograph with Henry, neither man knew the other. The first Secretary of the Smithsonian Institution, Joseph Henry, soon offered to publish an expanded version of Squier's article on the mounds as part of the initial volume of "Smithsonian Contributions to Knowledge" (Squier papers-LC, Marsh to E. G. Squier, March 6, 1847). The Board of Regents of the Smithsonian Institution authorized the series in January, 1847 with an annual sum of $1,000 to cover expenses. Henry decided to use this money to publish learned monographs with little popular appeal and a limited market (Lowenthal 1958:86). Squier's memoir, which promised to be a scholarly and expensive book on a widely-discussed topic, therefore seemed appropriate.

Early in April, Henry officially offered to print Squier's monograph with ample illustrations in a quarto-sized volume. He did not offer a cash award, but for an honorarium Squier would receive "a sufficient number of extra copies," free use of the engravings, and possibly a second edition for private sale. With acceptance by the regents understood, Henry anticipated no difficulties. He stressed above all else the scholarly recognition Squier would gain from the arrangement. Publication with a "respectable Institution" would make Squier's results "known to all engaged in the same pursuit throughout the civilized world and thus establish on some grounds the foundation of a lasting reputation." Henry's plan closely resembled the procedures "usually adopted by men of science abroad," to guard legitimate science against new, but undeserving, scientists or charlatans. Scientists might view an independent publication by Squier as "an appeal to the public generally for that consideration which it is the privilege of only the learned few to grant." Such a course inevitably prejudiced against the book "those who are best qualified to appreciate its merits and on whose judgments its character must ultimately depend" (Squier papers-LC, Henry to E. G. Squier, April 3, 1847). Whether convinced by Henry's argument or just satisfied to get a paying publisher, Squier and Davis agreed to the proposal. In May, 1847, both traveled East to consult with Henry and to finish the article for the Ethnological Society (*Squier papers-NYHS*, E. G. Squier to Parents, May 15, 1847).

Joseph Henry's letter to Squier illustrated his view of science and society. Only experts should judge, but any talented amateur could contribute to the sum total of human knowledge. The Smithsonian Institution would function as a scientific agent, first appraising the scientific value of a contribution and then delivering it to the scholarly world. The contributor gained scientific respectability and the Institution earned prestige as the commissioner. Henry's vision of the Institution's role in science changed gradually over time. Eventually he had the Smithsonian initiate scientific investigations instead of only processing them.

Acutely aware that any precedents he set during the Smithsonian Institution's first years would probably become common practice, Secretary Henry carefully weighed the future consequences of every action (*Squier papers-LC*, Henry to E. G. Squier, June 23, 1847). Therefore he decided to publish the correspondence relating to the Squier and Davis memoir so as to show the non-political nature of the choice. Henry enlisted a committee of the American Ethnological Society to judge the manuscript. Such a committee promised to be a rubber-stamp since the leadership of the Society, personal friends of Squier, originally recommended the archeologist. Had Henry desired the required "careful examination by a commission of competent judges," he would probably have referred the manuscript to the American Antiquarian Society, an organization to which Squier had no formal ties (SI 1848:185). As expected, the committee of the American Ethnological Society submitted a highly favorable report with Gallatin's full approval (*Gallatin papers*, Gallatin to Henry, June 16, 1847).

Henry insisted on the emendation of several technical, but misleading, faults in the committee's report before publication of the correspondence. For one thing, the committee called the Smithsonian a "National Establishment." Henry considered it "the Establishment of an individual [James Smithson] and the more widely it is separated from the Government the brighter will be its prospects." Furthermore, the report failed to mention that the memoir rested on original research. It wrongly stressed the American origin of the work, implying that only American authors could publish in the "Smithsonian Contributions to Knowledge" (*Squier papers-LC*, Henry to Bartlett, June 23, 1847; to E. G. Squier, June 23, 1847).

Henry set a clear precedent by publishing the correspondence both in his first "Report of the Secretary" and at the front of Squier's volume. It demonstrated that he sought a society's opinion about an anonymous manuscript and dispelled the impression that the Ethnological Society originally submitted the memoir. Henry hoped this course would prevent other societies from deluging the Institution with unsolicited and unacceptable manuscripts. To this end Squier and Henry subtly altered the committee's "Report" and exchanged back-dated letters, manufacturing the correspondence they wished they had written (*Squier papers-LC*, E. G. Squier to Henry, June 26, 1847; *Bartlett papers*, Turner to Bartlett, July 7, 1847).

While conferring with Henry, Squier put to press his article for the American Ethnological Society's *Transactions*, Gallatin paying all costs. At the same time he again requested a research grant from the American Antiquarian Society. Jared Sparks, corresponding secretary of the Society and Harvard professor of history, strongly seconded Squier's application for support. He believed Squier would fulfill the Society's original objectives by throwing "all the light, which can ever be attained, on the early races of this continent" (*Haven papers*, Sparks to Haven, May 18, 1847). In response to pressure by Sparks and other members, the Society on May 28, 1847, appropriated two hundred dollars for Samuel F. Haven to visit Squier and Davis in Ohio and evaluate their work (AAS 1912:520). Haven spent three days with Dr. Davis (Squier being in New York City) in late June and returned East with a favorable impression of "the science, industry, and judgment" of the partners (*Squier papers-LC*, Davis to E. G. Squier, June 27, 1847). To Squier's disgust, the Worcester Society still offered no money.

Another blow to Squier soon followed which disrupted his partnership. The American Ethnological Society's release of an unrevised copy of their "Report to the Smithsonian Institution" in early autumn, 1847, initiated a long and bitter feud between Davis and Squier. The report incorrectly named Squier as sole author of the forthcoming book and listed Davis as his assistant (*Literary World* 1847:158). Angered by this slight, Davis blamed Squier and wrote Henry and others that he and Squier, as equal partners deserved equal credit. While Squier did all the actual writing, he, Davis, provided the requisite scientific knowledge and "archaeological acumen" (*Squier papers-LC*, Davis to E. G. Squier, September 22, 1847). Squier denied any responsibility for preparation of the report and refused any apology. He maintained that he always considered Davis as an equal partner and friend (*Squier papers-LC*, E. G. Squier to Davis, September 30, 1847). Bartlett attempted to mollify Davis, but failed. The doctor traveled to Washington and complained in person to Secretary Henry who questioned Squier's conduct. This elicited a belligerent response.

Squier not only proclaimed complete innocence in the matter, but contended that only his generosity and friendship continued the partnership in which he alone produced anything. Because of Davis' betrayal, Squier demanded that Henry publish the memoir solely under his name or not at all (*Squier paper-LC*, E. G. Squier to Henry, December 31, 1847; to Marsh, January 8, 1848). After Henry, Marsh, and Bartlett advised him to share the ample honors with Davis, Squier reluctantly acquiesced and restored an uncertain peace (*Squier papers-LC*, Marsh to E. G. Squier, January 7, 1848; *Barlett papers*, E. G. Squier to Bartlett, February 1, 1848). With the problem of authorship settled, Squier finished and submitted his expanded memoir to Henry.

In editing Squier's manuscript, Secretary Henry strictly adhered to the policy that every monograph be a basically original and "positive contribution to existing knowledge" (*Squier papers-LC*, Henry to E. G. Squier and Davis, February 16, 1848). He allowed very few theoretical views and eliminated most contentions based on other published sources. Therefore he rejected Squier's theory of the interrelationships between the monuments, religions, and mythologies of the North American Indians and the peoples of Central America and Southern Asia. Henry suggested that Squier publish his analogies in a separate work (*Squier papers-LC*, Henry to E. G. Squier and Davis, February 16, 1848; Squier and Davis 1848:304). These deletions greatly annoyed Squier who considered himself "quite as competent to judge of what is pertinent and proper as the sect. of the Smithsonian Inst." (*Squier papers-LC*, E. G. Squier to Henry, February 21, 1848). Henry, having final say about what could or could not appear in a Smithsonian memoir, prevailed. Considering that most reviews praised the absence of theories, Squier did well to accede to Henry's demands.

Henry's editorial authority, as much as any single factor, affected the Institution's role in the development of a new type of archeology. The success of Squier's publication encouraged other American archeologists to publish with the Smithsonian Institution. To do so they bowed to Henry's insistence on original research and elimination of theory. Over the course of three decades a scientific archeological model pervaded the publication policies of most American learned societies. Original research soon replaced the theorizing in vogue, and *Ancient monuments of the Mississippi Valley* became an archeological paragon to be emulated.

Squier had no such excellent examples to follow. The archeological literature gave an inadequate picture of the mounds and the public generally accepted the fallacies perpetuated by dozens of popular writers (Haven 1856:118). Most meritorious archeological writings had small distributions, leaving Squier a wide, untapped readership. Actually, the content of his book justified the recommendations the American Ethnological Society heaped on it. A preface individually named the dozens of local archeologists who aided Squier and the eastern antiquaries who helped write the work. Chapters on each type of earthwork followed. Squier categorized the ancient monuments by their supposed function, thus labeling them as sacred and defensive enclosures and as altar, temple, and sepulchral mounds. He provided examples of detailed surveys for each type, often with complete descriptions and cross-sectional stratigraphic diagrams of specific earthworks. From this data he incorrectly determined that the mounds were perfect circles and that their builders were skilled in mathematics. He believed the placement of fortified enclosures throughout the country indicated that the Moundbuilders conducted a slow, southerly retreat in the face of an invading people, presumably the Indians. After a lengthy treatment of the mounds, he described examples of art found in the mounds, including sculptures and pottery, stone, and metal implements and ornaments. These he judged superior to the productions of modern Indians, but not equal to artistic achievements of civilized peoples. Squier dismissed most accounts of iron implements and inscribed stones as either intrusive, fraudulent, or of Indian manufacture.

Squier's last short chapter contained virtually all of the conjectures in his 306-page volume. In it he hinted at his real views on the history of man in America. His statements implied a strong belief in the great age of the earthworks. Referring to tree-ring dating and the existence of mounds on all but the lowest terraces of the Ohio valley, he alluded to the immense antiquity of the mounds. Equally important, a Moundbuilder cranium disinterred by Squier proved, in Morton's words, to be "a truly aboriginal skull. . . a perfect type of the race. . . which is indigenous to the American continent" (*Squier papers-LC*, Morton to E. G. Squier, April 10, 1847; E. G. Squier to Morton, April 4, 1847). Cranial examination by Dr. Morton confirmed the identity of physical type between the American Indian and the Moundbuilder. Linkage with the Indians militated against claims of a high Moundbuilder civilization in America. Although the Moundbuilders were more advanced than their later relatives, they at best attained a semi-civilized status. Squier also believed that the Moundbuilders were a populous, homogeneous, agricultural, and stationary people, with a vast trading network extending from Lake Superior to Mexico (Squier and Davis 1848:306). Great antiquity, continuity of racial type, and lack of geographical movement all showed that the Moundbuilders and Indians did not migrate to America. Therefore they must have originated in the New World by a separate creation (Stanton 1960:85). Of course, it was up to the reader to interpret these hints. That many did not perceive Squier's polygenism is evidenced by reviewers who were entranced by the idea of a lengthy antiquity for America and who raved about Squier's scientific bearing and accuracy.

Squier's treatment of the mounds generally ignored the traditional Moundbuilder myth. He had no real interest in proving or disproving either Moundbuilder civilization or savagism. Neither did he draw many analogies between modern Indians and their forebears. While he devoted his whole first book to describing mounds and relics, Squier personally preferred ethnological comparisons. Only because of Secretary Henry's refusal to publish his theories did Squier's volume remain objective. One suspects that given a free hand, Squier would have liberally sprinkled cross-cultural comparisons throughout the text. In this respect he resembled most early archeologists. His romanticism, obscured by a self-styled scientific aura, led him to use archeology to illustrate large ethnological problems. For instance, the occurrence of the serpent symbol in artifacts from the mounds and in effigy mounds themselves led Squier to seek parallel developments throughout world history. His interest was less in the earthworks than in clues they might provide for a history of American man.

Henry and Squier finally put *Ancient monuments of the Mississippi Valley* to press in early March, 1848. The Smithsonian edition of 1,000 copies came out in July. Bound in red moroco and filled with dozens of beautifully engraved plates, it undoubtedly impressed the public with the expertise of the writers and the splendor of the Smithsonian Institution. The regents previously modified the 1847 agreement made with Squier and Davis. Since the clause which gave the authors an unspecified number of copies established a difficult precedent, the regents decided instead to pay them a sum of money (*Squier papers-LC*, E. G. Squier to Henry, January 3, 1848). This offer included the book's copyright and free use of plates, engravings, and type for a private edition to be sold at least two months after the Institution's distribution. Ultimately, the regents refused any cash payment, again because of precedent, and voted the authors 200 copies of the work (SI 1849:7, 11–12).

Squier and Davis, still feuding, decided to print an edition of their own. Most publishers refused to handle the book, fearing the Smithsonian edition would cut too deeply into the potential market (*Squier papers-NYHS*, E. G. Squier to Parents, March 10, 1848). Wryly commenting that only "RICH MEN can possibly afford to be patronized," Squier privately printed a second edition of 800 copies (*Bartlett papers*, E. G. Squier to Bartlett, February 1, 1848). Bartlett and Welford published Squier's edition for eastern sale, as did Davis' friends, J. A. and U. P. James in Cincinnati for the West. The volumes sold by subscription at ten dollars a copy. Squier issued a propectus to attract subscribers and raised half of the $ 700 he needed for the edition. Albert Gallatin, to whom he dedicated the book, loaned him the rest (*Squier papers-NYHS*, E. G. Squier to Parents, March 10, 1848, March 18, 1848, May 3, 1848). Squier's copies sold quickly and earned him a tidy sum.

Even before the printing of his first book, Squier began work on a second. He wanted to extend his archeological research over the rest of the country but to do so he needed financial assistance. He spent much of late 1847 and early 1848 writing articles and giving lectures to establish his reputation. In October, 1848, he presented a paper to the Association of American Geologists and Naturalists at Boston. When that body reorganized as the American Association for the Advancement of Science in 1848, he became a charter member. In June, 1848, he received an honorary Master of Arts (A.M.) degree from the College of New Jersey (now Princeton University). Henry's influence lay behind this honor. In writing Squier of the award, Henry instructed him to use the initials after his name to complement Davis' "M.D." He candidly added that "these titles will have a good effect on the reception of the work abroad and will detract nothing from its respectability at home" (*Squier papers-LC*, Henry to E. G. Squier, June 28, 1848).

Despite his new degree and the honorarium, Squier became disgusted with learned societies in general and the Smithsonian in particular, for none provided him funds and freedom to "resume the field again" (*Hammond papers*, E. G. Squier to Hammond, April 17, 1848). He considered applying to Congress for money "under some disguise or other", sounded out South Carolina Governor James H. Hammond about this possibility, and received an encouraging response (*Squier papers-LC*, Hammond to E. G. Squier, April 20, 1848). However, for another year Squier made no direct pleas for governmental patronage. Instead he repeated his earlier requests for associational support. Through Jared Sparks, Squier once again appealed to the American Antiquarian Society, now resting his case on solid achievement (*Haven papers*, Sparks to Haven, July 11, 1848). The "conservative gentlemen" of that society still declined to aid him (*Squier papers-LC*, Henry to E. G. Squier, July 18, 1848; Sparks to E. G. Squier, July 30, 1848). The New York Historical Society and the Smithsonian Institution proved more fruitful grounds. Both organizations paid him to explore western New York mounds. Henry, anxious to complete a national mound survey, gave Squier one hundred dollars on the condition that the Historical Society grant an equal amount and that he publish his results in the "Smithsonian Contributions to Knowledge" (*Squier papers-LC*, Henry to E. G. Squier, September 30, 1848; *NYHS* 1848:163). Having no available funds, the Historical Society raised the money by a special collection. Many influential members also furnished Squier with letters of introduction to friends in western New York (*Squier papers-LC*, Moore to E.G. Squier, October 20, 1848; NYHS 1848:171–177).

Squier made a whirlwind trip, leaving New York City in late October and returning in early December, 1848, forced by cold and snow to cease his activities. In that time he surveyed about sixty mounds, excavated a few, and collected many relics (*Squier papers-NYHS*, E. G. Squier to Parents, December 8, 1848; Squier 1849a:11). Upon his return to New York City he wrote his second monograph and lectured on New York antiquities before the Historical Society (*Squier* 1849b). Generally favorable reviews of his earlier book frequently appeared in early 1849. Taking advantage of his fast-growing scientific reputation, Squier applied for a diplomatic post to Guatemala. A long list of distinguished scholars including Albert Gallatin, Edward Everett, Jared Sparks, William H. Prescott, Benjamin Silliman, Washington Irving, Dr. Samuel G. Morton, Francis Lieber, Dr. Josiah Nott, Luther Bradish, and Brantz Mayer urged Squier's appointment (*Morgan papers*, E. G. Squier to Morgan, March 20, 1849). Squier presented his reasons for seeking the post in terms of scientific expediency. He wished to investigate the connections between the North American and Latin American monuments and to search for living descendants of their builders. Gallatin and other members of the American Ethnological Society intended to sponsor his expedition, but political disturbances in Central America rendered travel too dangerous. A vacated Chargé d'Affaires post for the region promised the "aid and PROTECTION, without which. . . it is not likely much could be accomplished" (*Fish papers*, E. G. Squier to Fish, March 10, 1849). John Lloyd Stephens' successful combination of archeology and diplomacy less than a decade earlier gave clear precedent for such a scientific appointment.

While Squier based his application upon "broad scientific grounds," and insisted that the "honors and emoluments of the post" held no interest for him, he also alluded to his past support of the incumbent Whig Party (*Fish papers*, E. G. Squier to Fish, March 10, 1849). His allies stressed still other reasons for the appointment. Office holders and diplomats praised Squier's political contributions. An official committee of the New York Historical Society stressed the foreign example. It asserted that "it is concurrent practice of the enlightened Governments of Europe to so arrange their foreign appointments as to afford facilities for scientific investigation in regions of interest not otherwise accessible." Such policies resulted in "large additions to the sum of human knowledge and consequent augmentation of National Glory" (*Squier papers-IHS*, Members of the NYHS to Clayton, no date). Squier's petition succeeded.

Squier took the scientific nature of his mission very seriously. He urged other scientists to join his exploration of Central America, but found no volunteers (Academy of Natural Sciences of Philadelphia (ANSP), E. G. Squier to Cassin, April 7, 1849). However, he received many letters of introduction to influential Central Americans, notably from his friend, John Lloyd Stephens. Charles Eliot Norton and Jared Sparks again ineffectually pressed the American Antiquarian Society to aid Squier's archeological research (*Squier papers-LC*, Norton to E. G. Squier, April 29, 1849). Squier's post proved no sinecure, and, due to dangerous diplomatic situations, he found little time for archeology while abroad. However, he insured that the discoveries he did make received ample publicity (Stansifer 1959). His frequent letters to John Russell Bartlett contained many archeological tidbits. As corresponding secretary of the American Ethnological Society, Bartlett often read these letters at meetings and released them to the press, using Duyckinck and Duyckinck's *Literary World* as chief medium (*Squier papers-LC*, Duyckinck to E. G. Squier, October 25, 1849; Bartlett to E. G. Squier, December 10, 1849). Squier shipped many carved columns and idols to the United States, including at least six monuments destined for the Smithsonian Institution (SI 1851:78–80).

Exhausted and wishing to replace his artist and procure scientific instruments, Squier returned to New York after a year's absence (*Clayton papers*, E. G. Squier to Clayton, March 10, 1850). He planned a speedy return to Central America to devote further time to archeological and geographical surveys. However, President Taylor died in the meantime and Daniel Webster, the new Secretary of State, for political reasons, dropped Squier as Chargé d'Affaires (*Squier papers. NYHS*, Webster to E. G. Squier, September 13, 1850).

After his sudden dismissal from diplomatic service, Squier returned his full attention to archeology. While he was abroad the Smithsonian Institution officially accepted his monograph on New York antiquities as part of the second volume of "Contributions to Knowledge." Once again Secretary Henry chose two of Squier's associates in the American Ethnological Society, Brantz Mayer and W. W. Turner, for expert approval. They, of course, responded favorably. In his *Aboriginal monuments of the state of New York* Squier decided that fairly modern Indians built the New York earthworks, which had no connection with the older mounds of the Mississippi Valley (Squier 1849a:10–11). The main portion of the memoir described Squier's findings in New York. A lengthy appendix followed, presenting new information relevant to the earlier book and many detailed comparisons with Old World archeology. Squier demonstrated knowledge of recent European archeological discoveries and Thomsen and Worsaae's comparative dating of Danish barrows according to their stone, bronze, and iron contents (Squier 1849a:118). He also referred to Richard Colt-Hoare's work on ancient Wiltshire, England.

Henry allowed Squier latitude for theorizing, comparative analysis, and documentation from published sources, but confined this material to an appendix. Perhaps Henry allowed this freedom because of Squier's success with the earlier volume. Also, being in Central America, Squier could not defend his work. Henry may have intended his generous action as atonement for not recommending Squier for the Central American post (*Henry papers*, Davis to Henry, May 8, 1849; *Squier papers-LC*, Henry to E. G. Squier, April 25, 1851; Coulson 1950:159, 165, 184).

Squier, who lacked Henry's scientific temperament, frequently criticized the other as overcautious. In fairness he had no real cause for complaint since he ultimately benefitted from his connection with the Smithsonian Institution (*Squier papers-NYHS*, E. G. Squier to J. Squier, September 17, 1848; *Bartlett papers*, E. G. Squier to Bartlett, November 12, 1848). Squier's early archeological fame rested far more upon his association with the Smithsonian Institution than on his relation with any other learned society. Even without Henry's recommendation, the scientific aura attributed to the Smithsonian certainly influenced Secretary of State Clayton's choice of Squier as Chargé d'Affaires. Joseph Henry proved correct when he advised Squier to "establish a reputation" by publishing with the Institution. Learned societies throughout the world received Squier's publication with great praise.

Squier's archeological reputation opened many doors in the United States as well. With Gallatin dead and Bartlett serving on the Mexican Boundary Survey from 1850 to 1853 and then moving to Providence, Squier became the principal ethnological authority in the declining American Ethnological Society. In 1848–1849 he wrote six ethnological and archeological articles for the *American Review* of New York. His *Serpent symbol and the worship of the reciprocal principles of nature in America* (1851) became the first and only volume of Putnam's American Archaeological Researches series. Also in 1851 he privately issued a revised edition of his volume on New York mounds with a long appendix summarizing his first memoir. In succeeding years he published several books on Central America. These included some of the earliest detailed descriptions of the environment and inhabitants of that area and sold very well in the United States and Europe.

Squier long desired a position as curator or professor in an archeological museum or institution. When he urged Joseph Henry to establish a "National Archaeological Museum" at the Smithsonian Institution, Squier undoubtedly meant the directorship for himself. In his best administrative manner Squier boldly outlined his plan for the museum. It would be a central depository for the antiquities of all of the Americas, but particularly of the United States. He believed that "most persons possessing collections would not hesitate to surrender them to augment the central stock." Squier felt that only by gathering small collections together could meaningful archeological comparisons be made. The Institution if it guaranteed reimbursement could persuade American agents in foreign countries, "army and naval officers in frontier or foreign service, and our traders generally residing abroad," to procure and transmit artifacts. Squier considered it a national shame that the Louvre in Paris exhibited nearly a thousand relics of American antiquity while "we have no public collection of this kind worthy to be mentioned." To help rectify this unfortunate situation he promised "to contribute whatever monuments of the past, or relics of aboriginal art which I possess, or may hereafter collect." Squier stipulated only that "they shall have a specific place assigned them. . . and that my classification when finally made, shall not be disturbed" (SI 1851:78–80). This clause insured that his collection would be displayed and not locked away in some storage room. Henry agreed about the importance of an archeological museum and printed Squier's letter in the *Annual report* to emphasize the need. However, the secretary believed any Smithsonian Institution museum should be dedicated to specific objects and not become an "*omnium gatherum* of the odds and ends of creation" (*Squier papers-LC*, Henry to E. G. Squier, December 5, 1850). Nearly three decades passed before the Smithsonian started a strictly archeological museum. In the meantime archeological holdings became incorporated in the Natural History Museum directed by Spencer F. Baird.

After Squier achieved a reputation as a first-class archeologist from his two Smithsonian memoirs, he discontinued his active association with the Institution and turned to ethnology. In his subsequent scientific career, Squier concentrated on Central American and Peruvian studies. During the 1850's he spent the greatest part of his energies promoting the Honduras Inter-Oceanic Railway, which ultimately failed. As editor of Frank Leslie's publications during the 1860's he achieved journalistic stature. However, his mind and health broke when his wife divorced him in 1873 to marry Leslie (Stern 1953). Squier remained secluded in mental institutions and under his half-brother's care until his death.

The details of E. George Squier's early life tell more than just the story of America's first important archeologist. Squier, by his ambition and talent, illustrated the variety of experiences any mid-nineteenth-century archeologist might have faced. He embodied elements of both the scientific and romantic strains of archeology and tried to secure the most from each. In some respects Squier typified the Jacksonian "man on the make" by his intense desire for wealth and fame. That he tried to use archeology as a stepping-stone to greatness is undoubted, but he also felt an obligation to give his best to the science. The diversity of his life highlighted the human aspects of archeology. No discussion of learned institutions, museums, methods, or theories can describe so well the place of the archeologist in American society.

In addition to portraying the frustrations and successes of an archeological career, Squier's life shows the importance scholarly institutions held for "moundologists." There can be no doubt that Squier's contributions to American archeology would have greatly diminished had no such institutions existed or had they rejected his overtures. Of course, the exchange between Squier and scientific organizations ran in both directions. Squier helped shape and even initiated several societies. Despite the fact that Secretary Henry's Smithsonian Institution molded Squier's major archeological achievement by insisting on a descriptive rather than an interpretive presentation, the atmosphere of the American Ethnological Society better reflected Squier's thinking.

The Ethnological Society served as a forum for many of the nation's most active ethnological theorists. Its discussions covered a wide range of subjects and geographical areas. One suspects that Squier's association with men interested in making broad anthropological generalizations influenced him to try to put his narrow speciality of mound archeology into a global perspective. The free-wheeling interchange of conjectures and facts appealed to Squier's romantic nature more than the strictly scientific method imposed by Henry. He became deeply involved in ethnological discussions and occasionally engaged in bitter debates. Sometimes this dissension resulted in an exchange of personal recriminations. The vanity and volatile tempers of Henry R. Schoolcraft and Squier frequently clashed. Each believed himself the leading American ethnologist and resented the other's pretensions (Freeman 1959:388; *Schoolcraft papers*, E. G. Squier to Schoolcraft, July 22, 1854).

Such interchanges contrasted starkly with the serious and conservative milieu of the Smithsonian Institution. In opposition to the Washington research institution, the American Ethnological Society was preoccupied with interpretation without the requisite collection of data. Beset with the problem of pleasing and entertaining its membership, the society could not easily rise above the vagaries of individualistic members. The Smithsonian Institution, however, so long as it pleased Congress, operated along a strictly supervised plan calculated to maximize its efficiency and output.

The relationship between Squier and the Smithsonian Institution as personified by Joseph Henry, while not always happy and placid, benefitted all parties involved. Squier gained an impressive reputation and laid the groundwork for an anthropological career, and the Smithsonian received two important monographs. Archeology also made great gains, not only because of Squier's contributions, but because public attention increased. People who showed no previous interest in antiquities suddenly were fascinated by them. Joseph Henry, far from expert about the mounds when he first learned of Squier's researches, quickly became one of the nation's foremost advocates of archeological investigations. The Smithsonian Institution's long series of archeological endeavors merely started with Squier's explorations. Thereafter, the Institution grew far more important as its role shifted from passive publisher to active initiator of archeological research.

REFERENCES

AMERICAN ANTIQUARIAN SOCIETY (AAS)
  1912   *Proceedings of the American Antiquarian Society, 1812–1849.* Worcester: American Antiquarian Society.
  n.d.   *Letters to the Society.* American Antiquarian Society.
AMERICAN ETHNOLOGICAL SOCIETY (AES)
  1845   Preface. *Transactions* 1:ix–x.
AMERICAN WHIG REVIEW
  1850   Our foreign relations: Mr. E. G. Squier, Chargé d'Affaires, Central America. *American Review* n.s. 6:345–352.
ACADEMY OF NATURAL SCIENCES OF PHILADELPHIA (ANSP)
  n.d.   *Letters to the Academy.* Academy of Natural Sciences of Philadelphia.
BARTLETT, JOHN RUSSELL
  1846   "Observations on the progress of geography and ethnology, with the historical facts deduced therefrom," in *Proceedings*, 149–219. New-York Historical Society.
Bartlett papers
  n.d.   *John Russell Bartlett papers.* John Carter Brown Library, Brown University.
CALHOUN, DANIEL H.
  1960   *The American civil engineer.* Cambridge: M.I.T. Press.
Clayton papers
  n.d.   *John M. Clayton papers.* Library of Congress.
COULSON, THOMAS
  1950   *Joseph Henry: his life and work.* Princeton: Princeton University Press.

DUYCKINCK, E. A., DUYCKINCK, G. L
  1875 *The cyclopedia of American literature*, volume two. Philadelphia: T. Ellwood Zell.
Fish papers
  n.d. *Hamilton Fish papers.* Library of Congress.
FOWKE, GERARD
  1902 *Archaeological history of Ohio.* Columbus: Ohio State Archaeological and Historical Society.
FREEMAN, JOHN FINLEY
  1959 "Henry Rowe Schoolcraft." Unpublished doctoral dissertation, Harvard University.
Gallatin papers
  n.d. *Albert Gallatin papers.* New-York Historical Society.
Hammond papers
  n.d. *James H. Hammond papers.* Library of Congress.
HAVEN, SAMUEL F.
  1856 *Archaeology of the United States.* Smithsonian Contributions to Knowledge 8. Washington, D.C.
Haven papers
  n.d. *Samuel Foster Haven papers.* American Antiquarian Society.
Henry collection
  n.d. *Joseph Henry collection.* Smithsonian Institution Archives.
HISTORICAL SOCIETY OF PENNSYLVANIA (HSP)
  n.d. *Autograph collection.* Historical Society of Pennsylvania.
Literary World
  1847 American archaeology. *Literary World* 2:157–158.
LOWENTHAL, DAVID
  1958 *George Perkins Marsh, versatile Vermonter.* New York: Columbia University Press.
Morgan papers
  n.d. *Lewis Henry Morgan papers.* University of Rochester Library.
NEW-YORK HISTORICAL SOCIETY (NYHS)
  1848 *Proceedings.*
New York Tribune
  1888 "Death of Dr. Edwin H. Davis," *New York Tribune* (May 16).
Schoolcraft papers
  n.d. *Henry R. Schoolcraft papers.* Library of Congress.
SMITHSONIAN INSTITUTION (SI)
  1848 *Annual report.*
  1849 *Annual report.*
  1851 *Annual report.*
SQUIER, E. G.
  1845 American antiquities. *Scioto Gazette* (October 23).
  1849a *Aboriginal monuments of the state of New York.* Smithsonian Contributions to Knowledge 2. Washington D.C.
  1849b "Report upon the aboriginal monuments of western New York," in *Proceedings*, 41–61. New-York Historical Society.
  1851 *Serpent symbol and the worship of the reciprocal principles of nature in America.* American Archaeological Researches 1. New York: Putnam.

Squier papers-IHS
n.d.   *E. G. Squier papers.* Indiana Historical Society.
Squier papers-LC
n.d.   *E. G. Squier papers.* Library of Congress.
Squier papers-NYHS
n.d.   *E. G. Squier papers.* New York Historical Society.
SQUIER, E. G., E. H. DAVIS
1848   *Ancient monuments of the Mississippi Valley.* Smithsonian Contributions to Knowledge 1. Washington, D.C.
STANSIFER, CHARLES L.
1959   "The Central American career of E. George Squier." Unpublished doctoral dissertation, Tulane University.
STANTON, WILLIAM
1960   *The leopard's spots.* Chicago: University of Chicago Press.
STERN, MADELEINE B.
1953   *Purple passage: the life of Mrs. Frank Leslie.* Norman, Oklahoma: University of Oklahoma Press.
THOMAS, CYRUS
1894   "Report of the mound explorations of the Bureau of Ethnology," in *Twelfth annual report of the Bureau of American Ethnology.*
VAIL, R. W. G.
1954   *Knickerbocker birthday.* New York: New-York Historical Society.
WARD, JOHN WILLIAM
1955   *Andrew Jackson: symbol for an age.* New York: Oxford University Press.

Bachofen and the Concept of Matrilineality

STEPHEN F. HOLTZMAN

Johann Jakob Bachofen (1815–1887), German Swiss jurist and student of classical antiquity, is remembered by anthropologists and ethnologists as the first scholar to emphasize the importance of matrilineality (e.g. Lowie 1937:43). However, his particular formulation of stages of mother right preceding father right has not received much attention in terms of his methodology. Also, it is often forgotten that, in fact, Bachofen brought attention to the IDEA of matrilineal succession in the context of an impressionistic approach to a science of history in the German romantic tradition.

Bachofen was born in Basel on December 22, 1815, to a prominent and wealthy family. He studied at the Universities of Basel, Berlin, and Göttingen; his interests were in classics and law. At Berlin under the influence of Savigny, Bachofen became interested in Roman law and submitted a doctoral dissertation to the University of Basel in 1840. For the next two years he continued his studies at Paris, Oxford, and Cambridge. On returning to Basel, Bachofen, then 27, was appointed to the chair of Roman law at the University, from which he resigned in 1844 for personal and political reasons under pressure from the left. From 1842 to 1866 he was a judge in Basel. Bachofen published significant works on Roman law in 1847 and 1848. However, by then his interests had widened to embrace all of the ancient world.

Friedrich Carl von Savigny (1779–1861) is credited with founding the "older, or romantic, branch of the German historical school of jurisprudence" (Kantorowicz 1934:547). Savigny came from a noble and wealthy family. He was against the codification of law in the German states on a rationalistic basis; specifically, he was against using the French

(Napoleonic) and Austrian codes as models. Rather, he believed law proceeds in its essence out of custom; law is an emanation from what was later to be called the *Volksgeist*. Thus, he advocated empirical and systematic treatment of traditions, a science of the history of law. Positive law is the result of the organic, collective development of the personality of a people; it cannot be altered successfully by arbitrary legislation inspired by foreign sources. Savigny reacted negatively to the idea of a universal, natural law as embodied in the principles of the *Aufklärung* and the French Revolution. Comparative jurisprudence was to be reformed through historical research on the customs of peoples. Savigny's particular ideas were criticized by younger German legal historians. However, his historical and nationalistic bent very much influenced *"Die Brüder Grimm,"* who set themselves to recover the mythos of peoples by means of scientific historicism (Stadelmann 1932: 173). And Savigny's conservative and historical inclinations appear to have influenced the young Bachofen, who proceeded to analyze myths and legends from antiquity to discern the prehistoric development of the establishment of the modern world.

On his first trip to Italy, in 1842–43, Bachofen was impressed esthetically by symbols marked on ancient tombs. "The supreme aim of archeology consists... in communicating the sublimely beautiful ideas of the past to an age that is very much in need of regeneration" (Bachofen 1967:23). He demonstrated his method in *Versuch über die Gräbersymbolik der Alten* (1859).

For Bachofen myths were exegeses of the symbol. In the symbol various aspects of a people are "joined in the unity of one supreme idea" (Bachofen 1967:120). A system of mythology "unfolds in a series of outwardly connected actions what the symbol embodies in a unity" (Bachofen 1967:48). According to Bachofen (1967:49ff.), "The symbol awakens intimations; speech can only explain. The symbol plucks all the strings of the human spirit at once; speech is compelled to take up a single thought in time. The symbol strikes its roots in the most secret depths of the soul; language skims over the surface of the understanding like a soft breeze. The symbol aims inward; language outward." Therefore, by subjectively experiencing symbols and objectively analyzing myths, one can derive insight into the mythos or *geist* of an ancient people. To be sure, according to Bachofen, "To penetrate to the structure of a mind different from our own is a hardy work" (in Resek 1960:136). One "must everywhere stress the particular and only gradually progress to comprehensive ideas" (Bachofen 1967:119).

Das Mutterrecht (1861) is the first attempt at a scientific history of the family. Bachofen knew that before the advent of the historical Greeks and Romans, millennia had passed during which other peoples, such as the Etruscans, lived in Italy and Greece. He hoped to grasp the genius of those peoples whereby they differed quintessentially from the known patriarchal peoples of Greece and Rome. In so doing Bachofen appears to have emphasized the notion of matriarchy.

Bachofen's approach was holistic. The spirit of a people was understood in terms of the juxtaposition of ideas, attitudes, and practices as part of a structure underpinned by a single, sexual principle. There were three stages in the development of the family: two stages of mother right followed by the stage of father right. Bachofen postulated an original stage of no marriage rules, men having access to women at will. Thus, descent had to have been through the mother as paternity was unknown. This stage was pre-agricultural and ideas were earth-bound. Indignant at degrading treatment at the hands of men, women revolted and set up marriage rules and tended to take control of society. This second, prehistorical stage of mother right was agricultural, and ideas were more elevated. It is this second stage that Bachofen believed he analyzed and intuited from the myths and symbols of ancient Greece and Rome. Dominance by women eventually became intolerable to men, who in their turn revolted and set up patriarchy. This third, historical stage, in which descent was reckoned through the father, was characterized by the rise of civilization and the creation of law. Though this whole scheme was developed, for the most part, on the basis of analysis of ancient classical cultures, Bachofen evidently considered it to be universal. "The scientific approach to history recognizes the stratifications of the spiritual modes that have gradually made their appearance, assigns to each stratum the phenomena that pertain to it, and traces the genesis of ideas" (Bachofen 1967:246). That mother right preceded father right is, then, a basic law of the epigenesis of the soul.

Bachofen has been called "a typical evolutionist of the old school" (Lowie 1937:41). But, as Stocking (1968:1188) has pointed out, his stages "were encompassed within a general sexual dialectic...." According to Bachofen (1967:109ff.), "Maternity pertains to the physical side of man, the only thing he shares with the animals; the paternal-spiritual principle belongs to him alone. Here he breaks through the bonds of tellurism and lifts his eyes to the higher regions of the cosmos." Bachofen's evolutionism amounts to the progressive development from the chthonian to the spiritual, the successive manifestations of the life force of the soul as represented in the dialectical opposition of the male and female principles. It is "a great truth borne out by all history that human culture advances only through the clash of opposites" (Bachofen 1967:227).

It has been charged that Bachofen "thoroughly confused the phenomenon of matrilineal descent with a matriarchate..." (Lowie 1937:43). It
would be more correct to say that he simply did not distinguish between
the two concepts. It was Bachofen's purpose to demonstrate the preced-
ence of the female vis à vis the male principle in order to explain the rise of
civilization and law in ancient Rome. It should be noted that "mother
right" is not synonymous with either "matrilineality" or "matriarchy."
Mother right refers to right THROUGH the mother, but it also refers to the
notion of rights OF the mother. Bachofen emphasized what was later to be
called matrilineality, retaining connotations of matriarchy. As his emphasis was on the genius of the people, specifics were not ultimately important. For all of his meticulous scholarship, Bachofen was not concerned
with that "rationalistic self-conceit that sets itself above history. Abundance of information is not everything, it is not even the essential"
(Bachofen 1967:16). A romantic, he was ultimately concerned with es-
sences, with principles.

In 1870 Bachofen published *Die Sage von Tanaquil*. In it he used his
method of intuition of symbols by myth analysis and by comparison to
demonstrate an historical, genetic connection between the supposedly
matrilineal peoples of prehistoric Greece and Italy and matrilineal peoples
of western Asia. He argued that the late prehistoric Italians and Greeks
were immigrant agriculturalists. In this work ethnological concerns are
clearly evident.

Bachofen often has been considered an early anthropologist or ethnologist. Actually he was a student of Roman law in the German romantic
tradition of historical scholarship. His interests led him to formulate a
plan by which he believed he could recover intellectually through empathy
the spirit of preclassical society. In *Das Mutterrecht* he used little ethnographic data from societies outside the Mediterranean area. By 1870,
however, having become aware of developments in the then newly institutionalized science of anthropology, he had decided to revise *Das Mutterrecht*. "My task is now to assemble the evidence of the maternal system
from all peoples of the earth.... We have been brought up in just too
limited a classical way..." (Bachofen 1967:lii). Bachofen died in Basel on
November 27, 1887, before his project was carried out.

A student of historical jurisprudence, Bachofen conveyed the importance
of the concept of matrilineal succession to anthropology and ethnology in
an attempt at conscious intuition, from antiquities and from analysis of
myths, of the social organization of prehistoric peoples. This procedure
necessarily involved Bachofen in impressionistic science of mankind.

REFERENCES

BACHOFEN, JOHANN JAKOB
1859 *Versuch über die Gräbersymbolik der Alten.* Volume four of *Gesammelte Werke* (1954). Edited by Karl Meuli. Basel: Schwabe.
1861 *Das Mutterrecht.* Volumes two and three of *Gesammelte Werke* (1948). Edited by Karl Meuli. Basel: Schwabe.
1870 *Die Sage von Tanaquil.* Volume six of *Gesammelte Werke* (1951). Edited by Karl Meuli. Basel:Schwabe.
1967 *Myth, religion and mother right: selected writings.* Translated by Ralph Mannheim from *Johann Jakob Bachofen: Mutterrecht und Urreligion* (1926), edited by Rudolf Marx; Preface by George Boas; Introduction by Joseph Campbell. Bollingen Series 84. Princeton: Princeton University Press.

KANTOROWICZ, HERMAN
1934 "Savigny, Friedrich Carl von," in *Encyclopedia of the social sciences*, volume thirteen, 546–548.

LOWIE, ROBERT H.
1937 *History of ethnological theory.* New York: Holt, Rinehart, Winston.

RESEK, CARL
1960 *Lewis Henry Morgan, American scholar.* Chicago: University of Chicago Press.

STADELMANN, RUDOLF
1932 "Grimm, Jacob Ludwig Karl and Wilhelm Karl," in *Encyclopedia of the social sciences*, volume seven, 173–174.

STOCKING, GEORGE W., JR.
1968 Review of *Myth, religion and mother right: selected writings. American Anthropologist* 70:1188–1190.

Modern Theoretical Views of a Croatian Ethnologist of the Late Nineteenth Century (Antun Radić, 1868-1919)

VITOMIR BELAJ

The following contribution attempts briefly to explain the theoretical views of the first Croatian ethnologist to conceive of ethnology as a single science and to establish it on a theoretical basis in the Croatian region. The essay is about Antun Radić (1868–1919), who is otherwise much better known as an ideologue of the Croatian peasant movement and the true founder of the Croatian Republican Peasant Party in 1904.

Antun Radić was born in Trebarjevo, a village in the vicinity of Zagreb, at a time when over 95 percent of all Croatians were still peasants. Feudal service and duties had been abolished just a few decades earlier, and at this time the peasant society was under a constantly growing pressure from a new and strange urban way of life to change. The conflict between these two spheres, the peasant and the urban, had bad consequences especially for the peasants, for it threatened to destroy their old, familiar, balanced way of life. Throughout his entire life Radić worked toward a single goal. He wanted to alleviate the economic, social, and cultural suffering which had followed the conflict. He wanted to save the peasants' world.

Radić studied Slavic philology in Zagreb and Vienna (with Jagić) and received his diploma in 1892. Independently, however, he devoted himself to the study of ethnology. As editor of the *Zbornik za narodni život i običaje Južnih Slavena* [Journal of the Folklife and Folklore of the Southern Slavs] of the South Slav Academy of Science and Art in Zagreb from 1897 until 1901, he became the first and for a long time the only

Translated from original German by Timothy Thoresen, with the assistance of Gerhard Zednik.

professional Croatian ethnologist. His scientific activity, however, was limited to the short period of time from 1896 to 1899. After that he became involved in political affairs, and together with his brother Stejpan, he founded the Croatian peasant movement and its party. Shortly before the First World War, in 1913 and 1914, he appeared again with his cultural-historical studies.

Nevertheless, in the relatively short time span of only four years, Radić developed a comprehensive understanding of culture and its history, and established the basic theory underlying Croatian ethnology. At the same time, his conception of ethnology as a science with folklore as its subject matter remains for us an undeveloped body, for he never wrote it down systematically. The motive force of his entire work as ethnologist — and politician as well — derived from the fact mentioned above, that among Croatians as elsewhere in Europe, two groups of directly antagonistic people lived beside each other: a broad peasant class with its own way of life, and a much narrower dominant class made up mostly of urbanites. The strong opposition between these two classes, these two parts of the nation, seriously endangered national development. Yet according to Radić, the opposition was not based in economic, social, or political conditions; any social difference between the nation and the peasantry (that is, the lower classes) cannot stand scrunity ([1897]: 1, 265).[1] Rather, the opposition was culturally conditioned, an idea inspired by Jules Michelet's *Le peuple*. The opposition was therefore between two cultures of diverse character and diverse origin: the essential Croatian folk culture (the culture of the Croatian peasant), and Greco-Roman culture (or civilization, which in Croatia was the culture of the urban or upper classes).

For Radić, this contrast legitimated folk culture as a special subject for study and research. Folk culture ought therefore to be the subject of its own science, ethnology, because culture history, literary history, and so on are primarily concerned with the culture of the other segment of the population, that is, with "civilization." In Radić's conception, where the continuity of European civilization begins, there ethnological studies cease and general studies begin ([1898]: 1, 290). The distinction was important, for folk culture has its own value, and its achievement ought not to be measured with a standard of value from a past civilization. If the

---

[1]   Editor's note: In order to achieve a fairly idiomatic English, all direct quotations in the original text have been rendered here as paraphrase. References in the text indicate year of publication of the original passage, followed by volume and page as the passage is found in the collected works of Antun Radić, *Sabrana djela Dra Antuna Radića* (Zagreb: Seljačka sloga; 1936).

folk has its own culture, Radić wrote, what it is and how it continues to exist ought to be studied; one ought as well to allot it a place beside other cultures, not under them ([1897]:1, 15).

Radić defined culture itself in the following manner: What is culture? All that which man has at some time and at some place done and created to make his life easier and more beautiful one calls cultural behavior and cultural products. All together, that which several people have done toward this end, or what a people has done toward this end, namely, to make life better and more beautiful – that ought to be called culture ([1909]:8, 65; this is a revised definition of one given in 1896, for which see 1, 189).

Radić realized that in reality, individual culture elements are more than loosely interrelated with each other. Rather, they are bound together in an intricate web, a web whose obvious filaments both bind individual culture elements with each other and also bind culture as a whole to its creator and bearer, man. For this reason, Radić demanded two important requirements: (a) every writer ought to collect his data in only one region or even only one village ([1897]:1, 68) and (b) preferably a writer should collect his data in the dialect spoken in that particular region ([1897]:1, 70). Written speech, Radić believed, is a conventional language; it is appropriate for our scholarly, learned, disciplined thought, and is learned for a context of scientifically derived notions. Everything outside this context either (a) cannot be expressed in conventional written language as it ought or (b) when drawn into this context it becomes a different and distorted expression ([1898]:1, 94). This is significant, for the folklorist describes not only houses and similar things but also the inner life, the thought. All this exists outside our formal education and for which there are neither concepts nor words. Further, houses and similar things should not only be described as they are seen but also as they are felt ([1898]:1, 95). One ought to consider, for example, that in contrast to the civilized cosmopolitan (*Ubi bene, ibi patria!*), the peasant feels intimately bound to his home. These feelings are an important component of the peasant's culture, and whoever intends to describe the culture must recognize, experience, and finally be able to express these feelings. An exact description of this kind is not easy but neither is it such a hard thing, Radić wrote. Whoever knows well the region, the population, and the dialect (without which there can be no ethnographers!) will find that the work seems easy ([1897]:1, 70–71).

These demands on field studies became even more pointed: intelligent, literate peasants themselves could best of all write about the folk life ([1897]:1, 69). Such description would on that account be valuable precisely because it would be both objective and subjective ([1898]:1, 97). In order to make such work easier for ethnographers, especially the peasants, but also in order to obtain sufficiently complete, classifiable, and comparative material, Radić wrote his *Osnova za sabiranje i prou-čavanje gradje o narodnom životu* [Outline for the collection and investigation of folk life materials] ([1897]:1, 3–85) which did bring in much valuable material, some in fact written by peasants.

Radić, however, was not content with just this much. He was not merely interested in the question "what" and "how" – What is culture? How does it appear? How is it structured? How does it function? The next step had to be the investigation of the HISTORY of culture. The single correct point of view from which our folk life ought to be considered, he wrote, is and can only be cultural, which in this case means cultural-historically ([1913]: 16, 148). Through a study of the history of culture, Radić expected to to discover the general laws according to which the folk live and think, and also the origin of these laws ([1897]:1, 13). Thus one could learn whether and to what degree the folk IN THEIR ESSENCE have a capacity for life and development ([1897]:1, 16). Here the beginning of Radić's political activity was already evident. His goal, which he even called the "aim and objective of ethnology," was a reconciliation of the two major divisions of the people by means of an advancement of scientific knowledge. That is, he hoped to achieve a distinct culture in which finally the entire nation would be able to work harmoniously together ([1897]:1, 16).

The course of the history – or as one might prefer, the evolution ([1896]: 1, 191) – of culture for Radić, however, was on no account unilinear. Yet the laws which culture followed in its development were in accordance with the laws we know in the natural sciences. Cultural forms originate, develop, flourish, and decay. Here under certain life conditions they are thus; there, in other circumstances, they are different; and perhaps some forms do not appear at all ([1899]:16, 33). They (just as the words about which Radić wrote) changed their forms not only according to similar laws whose origin lay in the organs, but such changes could also have their origin in history, that is, in the thought, aspirations, and culture of each particular time in which we locate the appearance of change ([1898]:1, 183). Radić was skeptical of classical evolution in ethnology. If one looks over the schemes and sometimes the manner of expression of a scholar, he maintained, then even the most sober explanations seem somehow like a new social mythology ([1896]:1, 232). In contrast, Radić recognized the importance of the spatial distribution of individual culture elements. Thus he gave approval to M. Dragomanov's formulation that variations ought to be arranged according to the geographic locations in which they had been recorded ([1896]:1, 211), and he himself acted accordingly (see [1899]:1, 127–139). Also, Radić recognized the phenomenon known as culture sediment. Culture and its forms arise and develop in the highest societal layers and then generally diffuse. Just as he conceived of the idea of culture, so also its particular features ([1899]: 16, 33).

Radić did not plan a single method of ethnology. At the time he really did not need one at all. First he would have to bring together sufficient material. For that reason he restricted himself to his *Osnova* and to the principles of field research. Worth mentioning, however, are single appropriate observations. The first work in research, Radić wrote, will be classification ([1897]:1, 85). The method is the same as in other noological sciences, as for example in the history of literature ([1897]1, 83; one can see that Radić began his studies in philology!). In the search for the origin of the phenomenon of the folk soul, ONE OUGHT ALWAYS, Radić believed, to proceed comparatively and only sometimes psychologically or, in a certain sense, *a priori* ([1897]:1, 85). Radić made us aware of the danger in too quickly reducing cultural problems to psychic factors. Were that possible, he maintained, ethnology would become superfluous. Therefore one should proceed slowly and in the proper sequence. Psychology will be unable to approach an understanding of psychic factors until ethnology has gathered its data ([1898]:1, 92–93).

Radić's theoretical principles and especially his *Osnova* strongly influenced Croatian ethnology. However, since he wrote in a language that at the time was scarcely known or noticed in Europe (the position of Croatian is not much better today!), his ideas generally met no response from the international community of ethnologists. Nevertheless it is interesting and today even instructive to include Radić in the history of the theory of our science. One can then see how a nineteenth-century thinker, who unfortunately because of language barriers remains unknown, could yet develop ideas that appeared in the official science relatively later. Here I refer to the theory of two cultures (an idea, for example, that Lenin also developed from a sociological perspective in 1913); or to the demands on field research which Malinowski later, although not so consistently, required; or to Radić's conception of culture as a structure (a word which Radić himself did not use), which Claude Lévi-Strauss a half century later first transplanted to ethnology from linguistics where it had made its first appearance around 1916 in the work of F. de Saussure. But, to me, just as important as these principles are Radić's contemporaneous researches carried out according to historical (not in an evolutionary sense) principles; his reference to an especial historical causality in culture which is different from causality in the natural sciences; and the recognition of the spatial factors in cultural history as criteria of quantity and quality (a contention which, however, Radić was not able to formulate very clearly) – in short, all the basic principles of what later became cultural-historical ethnology.

Such a historical survey as this admonishes us modern "progressive" scientists not to be too self-satisfied with our insights and not too exclusive in our teaching. Many of our new discoveries have already long been discovered, many of our new insights were also well known to our ancestors, and some of the important recognized or at least anticipated connections were lost for us. It is a waste of time and energy – which we tend to squander today – to go a way that has already been gone. To prevent such waste is the task of a well-written history of scientific theory. Hopefully this sketchy summary of Radić is a small contribution toward that history.

The History of Physical Anthropology in Hungary

JÁNOS NEMESKÉRI

The year 1973 is a centenary for us Hungarians, for in 1873, Samuel Scheiber presented a proposal for organizing a museum and for establishing a chair in physical anthropology at Budapest University. I feel a special honor – now after one hundred years – to have the opportunity to write about the history of Hungarian physical anthropology and to sketch the outstanding events in its development.

Demand for a scientific understanding of Man was brought into focus by the general interest in the natural sciences during the nineteenth century. From an earlier philosophical approach, emphasis began to move toward the development of a scientific physical anthropology. In Hungary, the effort to fulfill the demand for a natural science approach to the study of Man – what today would be called a "biological" approach – was linked to the names of five scientists who worked in the last decades of the nineteenth century: Samuel Scheiber, József Lenhossék, József Körösi, Aurél Török, and János Jankó. These five researchers aimed at a common target – the creation of a Hungarian program of anthropological education and systematic research work – from different directions.

The first of these was Samuel Scheiber, a neurologist who began a pioneering work in the field of body growth and, as early as 1876, presented data on 77,579 recruits. At the same time his intense activity showed his interest in establishing an anthropology section in the Hungarian National Museum.

József Lenhossék, an excellent anatomist, published in 1875 a book entitled *Cranioscopia* in which he laid a foundation of scientific criteria for craniology that supported anthropological aspects beyond anatomy.

József Körösi, famous in Europe as a statistician, demographer, and anthropologist, approached the problem of understanding Man through a convergence of his three fields of science. Within a short period of time he organized researches on a national level in order to study various qualitative and quantitative anthropological characteristics. In his correspondence with Galton he raised genetic problems related to his work in demography.

The early development of Hungarian anthropology was promoted and influenced greatly by the International Congress on Anthropology and Prehistory held in Budapest in 1876. Experts who came to anthropology from other fields presented the results of their studies in nearly every field of the physical anthropology of that day. As one of the most important consequences of this Congress, the importance and necessity of establishing an anthropology chair at Budapest University became generally known and supported public opinion. Thus in 1881, as the fourth of its kind in the world, a chair in anthropology was established through the arrangements of the then minister of cultural affairs, Ágost Trefort. The first professor to hold the chair was Aurél Török, by then already famous as an anatomist.

Aurél Török outlined the program of the newly established institute as follows: Anthropology is a branch of the natural sciences which is very important, because in dealing with Mankind itself, one of the main subjects of all sciences, in endeavoring to determine the natural character of races, populations and nations, in tracing the origin and development of Man as well as the steps and causes of his evolution, and further in trying to detect the cultural level of prehistoric times, in all these it is searching for the basic causes of our physical, mental, moral, social and historical existence. Thus it is not only the auxiliary science of philosophy, biology, and the social and historical sciences, but it serves as the basis for all of them. This program, if translated into modern words, would cover the total scope of physical anthropology, namely the problems of human evolution and variation and the importance of cooperation with the social sciences. The realization of this broad program required a great knowledge, sense of responsibility, and talent for organization on the part of the professor of the new university institute, Aurél Török.

In the interest of his program, Török went on a study-tour of France, and under the guidance of Broca, Topinard, and Manourvrier, learned the scientific goals governing the anthropology of that time. Arriving home, he became an excellent teacher and organized a collection, but he was not equal to all the tasks that he set for himself in the fields of historical and ethnical anthropology. That is a special national task.

Török's ambitions did not get the required support, and as a consequence of his disappointment, he turned toward general anthropological problems. He constructed excellent instruments (craniophor, orbitastat, sphenoidalganiometer, facial ganiometer, etc.), later dealt with the revision of his craniology, and was published abroad. His work entitled *Über den Yezoer Aino-Schädel* represented a scholar withdrawn into himself, separated from his original program. During his university career of nearly thirty years, he gained an international reputation for his institute, but the beginning – I willfully use this expression – of the realization of his program is linked with the names of two other experts, both of whose careers were cut off unexpectedly.

Károly Pápai (1861–1893), a highly trained anthropologist, together with Bernát Munkácsi performed anthropological investigations among the Mari and Komi (Finno-Ugrian) populations at the river Ob (Siberia). He wrote a monograph on the results of his investigations of nearly 340 individuals and presented it at the Hungarian Academy of Sciences, but its publication was hindered by his early death. Recently Pál Lipták evaluated the significant work of Károly Pápai with high appreciation and excellent recognition.

The ethnographer-anthropologist János Jankó (1867–1902) was a founder of Hungarian anthropology in its modern form. In accordance with the program laid down by Aurél Török, he organized the Anthropological Laboratory and a collection in the Ethnographic Department of the Hungarian National Museum. During his short career – he died at the age of thirty five – he organized an expedition to North Africa and carried out an anthropological investigation of Berbers. His research work in Western Siberia was significant from the point of view of Hungarian prehistory. As a result of this work, he was able to add fifty valid Osztjak crania to the collection he had initiated. Further, he was the first to do ethnic anthropological investigations in the western part of Hungary, at Lake Balaton and in Transylvania (Torda, Aranyosszek, Torocko). His researches, besides being systematic investigations, drew a picture of the structure of these populations by analyzing ethnographic and genetic characteristics.

The first period of Hungarian anthropology ended with the deaths of János Jankó and Aurél Török. This period can be characterized by the establishment of comprehensive concepts with biological and social science plans as well as adequate university institutions and museum centers. After this period the development of Hungarian anthropology came to a standstill. The Budapest University chair discontinued its work for a long time. The second period of development began with the work of a great personality, Lajos Bartucz, who saved the foundations built by Török and Jankó and, between the two World Wars, almost alone realized their concepts concerning Hungarian anthropology.

Lajos Bartucz was the successor to János Jankó at the Ethnographic Museum. There he organized the Anthropological Collection as the basis for historical anthropological research. He established close cooperation with archeologists and in two decades developed a collection of crania and skeletons containing nearly 3,000 units. The collection served as excellent source material for studying the populations which had lived in the territory of our country from the Neolithic to the fourteenth century. Parallel with the collecting work and its organization, Bartucz published many studies; his works in Hungarian prehistory and on the populations of the great migrations followed.

In his efforts, Bartucz did not neglect to study the present population. Continuing the work of János Jankó, he carried out numerous investigations of the various ethnic groups of the country. He published an excellent analysis and comparative study of the Paleanthropus find excavated in the Subalyuk Cave in Northern Hungary. Later he taught at Budapest University and afterward in Szeged, at the newly established chair in anthropology. His name and activities were linked to the development of a really systematic research in the field of historical anthropology. His predecessors had been craniologists in the classical sense of the word, whereas he studied predominantly the populations which had lived during the historical period within the territory of our country, analyzing them and presenting reliable data and syntheses on their origins. His interests covered all the field of physical anthropology (investigations of children, body growth and development, paleopathology, etc.), and, most importantly, he severely adhered to the objectivity of the natural sciences, removing himself in his scientific activity from the unscientific and inhuman race-biology prevailing between the two world wars.

Periods of development in the sciences cannot be defined strictly by dates, but it is true that the development itself is influenced by historical and social changes which can serve as useful landmarks. The creation of the new socialist social system was such a landmark in our country, and as it was a factor in developing other sciences, so too did it affect physical anthropology. Earlier, and for historical reasons, physical anthropology had been an auxiliary science of archeology and ethnology. The third period in its development began when it took its place among the biological sciences, though previously its character as a natural science had never been disputed. The change was manifested in three organizational events. In 1945, an independent Department of Anthropology was established within the Natural History Museum, organized by the author of this paper. In 1952, an Anthropological Committee was formed within the Section of Biological Sciences of the Hungarian Academy of Sciences. Finally, also in 1952, the Hungarian Biological Association was organized and became, with the Section of Anthropology, the joint sponsor of a quarterly publication entitled *Anthropological Közlemények* [Anthropological Publications]. This organizational frame ensured the possibility of Hungarian anthropology developing and carrying on systematic research on the basis of new trends, with widened contents, preserving aspects of classical anthropology but meeting the requirements of modern human biology.

Among the presently existing four anthropological institutions, the Anthropological Collection of the Museum of Natural Sciences (Budapest – director: Dr. Tibor Tóth) and the Anthropological Institute of Jozsef Attila University (Szeged – director: Prof. Dr. Pál Lipták) are the centers for paleoanthropological research. Both of these institutions have anthropological collections significant on a world level, with important and valid finds from archeological excavations. The Anthropological Institute of Eötvös Lóránd University (Budapest – Dr. Ottó Eiben, Assistant Professor) is the center of constitutional and human biological research. The Anthropological Institute of the Kossuth Lajos University (Debrecen – Dr. János Nemeskéri, Senior Research Associate) deals mainly with human genetic and biodemographic investigations. Such research was initiated by Mihály Malán, the first professor of the chair.

Besides work in these institutions, active historical anthropological and biodemographic researches are carried out in the Archeological Institute of the Hungarian Academy of Sciences (Budapest – Dr. Imre Lengyel, Dr. István Kiszely) and in the Demographic Research Institute of the Central Statistical Office (Budapest – Dr. János Nemeskéri). The Demographic Research Institute, directed by Dr. Egon Szabady, organized and conducted biodemographic investigations through nationwide sample surveys on various phenomena, e.g. early births, multiple births, endogamous populations, etc.

In the development of anthropology in Hungary after World War II, three periods can be arbitrarily delineated. From 1945 to 1955, the most important task, the foundation of adequate organization frames, was completed. The second period, the following decade, brought results from the first researches and widened the field of studies. Historical anthropological topics, ethnic anthropological investigations, as well as general anthropological and biological studies took shape. A symposium and a conference were held in which scientific results were presented for both international and home audiences. International relations and cooperation began. Significant development of human paleontologic research, biological reconstruction, and paleodemographic investigations already influenced anthropological studies in Hungary at that time.

The third period, the years after 1966, is characterized by a widening research program and its systematic arrangement and coordination. The most significant event in Hungarian anthropology during these years was connected with the study of human evolution: Homo (erectus seu sapiens) paleohungaricus was excavated at the Vértesszölös site, and its excellent anthropological analysis by Andor Thoma gained an international reputation for anthropology in Hungary. A new field of research, the chemical analysis method of investigating prehistoric bone finds, was elaborated by the pioneering of our researchers, principally Imre Lengyel. Population-genetic demographic investigations and research by family reconstruction, sponsored by the International Biological Program, have been carried out in cooperation with the Anthropological Institute of Mainz University.

This picture of the historical development of anthropology in Hungary naturally is not complete. The intention has been only to sketch the main developments.

The Magyarization of Hungarian Ethnography (1889-1919)

MICHAEL SOZAN

The scientific achievements of small nations are all but ignored by Western thinkers. Whereas biographical notes on accomplished scientists such as Malinowski, Róheim, and others working in the West rarely neglect to mention their national backgrounds, little attention is focused upon the scientific traditions of their nations of origin. This gap in our knowledge is comprehensible only insofar as the scientist caught up in the westward "brain drain" is expected to be assimilated into his new disciplinary environment and to weaken his allegiances to his former colleagues and tradition.

My intention here is to delineate the rise of Hungarian ethnography, a science of considerable importance within Hungary, and one which is to a great extent typical of east-central European ethnography/ethnology in its evolution, purpose, and scientific method. I do not intend to compare Hungarian ethnography with Anglo-American cultural/social anthropology. The pitfalls of such comparison are much too dangerous and obvious (compare, for example, Ishida 1965). Instead, important contributing factors to, and the organizational development of, Hungarian ethnography will be examined. The picture presented below is not complete; it merely represents what I feel are the most significant mechanisms responsible for the emergence of modern-day Hungarian folk science and how this discipline became "Magyarized" within the larger, political processes felt by the people of the Carpathian Basin at the turn of the nineteenth century.

Editor's note: During the last stages in the preparation of this volume of essays, Professor Sozan was engaged in field research in Austria and was unable to approve the final editorial revisions made in his essay. The editor of the volume therefore assumes responsibility for this version of Professor Sozan's essay.

1. SOCIO-POLITICAL BACKGROUND

In Hungary, the period between 1850 and 1896 was one of tranquility, economic growth, and scientific progress, often described as the "good old peaceful times." The nation "was in a position which in many ways was more favourable than it had enjoyed since [the sixteenth century]; in some respects, the nation had never before in its history been so truly master of its own destinies" (Macartney, quoted in Sugar and Lederer 1969:276). Austria's colonial advances were checked by the Compromise of 1867, which facilitated domestic economic growth as well as political independence. In 1896, land reforms of the 1850's were updated, facilitating a substantial increase in the number of landed peasants (Szabó 1940:75). In two respects, however, this period was stagnant, if not retrogressive. These were in the area of social reform, and the gradually worsening problem of the nationalities. Under the Tisza and the Bánffy regimes, industrial and agricultural labor strikes – the goals of which were to achieve better working conditions and higher wages – were monthly occurrences. The problems of the growing working class reflected the government's inability to alleviate the pains of transition from a feudal to a capitalistic system. The social problems of the Hungarian working class, however, were only a fraction of what the nationalities had to endure in this multi-ethnic society. Their plight intensified until the end of the Dual Monarchy, when finally they succeeded in breaking away from the Empire.

The political system of the Monarchy was incapable of solving the most urgent problems of the survival of centuries-old vested interests among the ruling classes. For the most part, the best solution seemed to be the creation of unity through a renewed movement of nationalism. "The late nineteenth century regimes aimed to unify the Magyar middle and upper classes by the kindling of nationalism" (Molnár 1967:II, 145). An important psychological reinforcement of nationalism was the celebration of Hungary's 1,000-year-old statehood. Preparations for the millennial began some years before 1896. These included enormous city and road building projects as well as statistical and ethnic surveys, although other aspects of the revivalism contained expressions of Magyar racial and governing superiority at the expense of the nationalities.

As the years gradually advanced toward the climax of the celebrations, the nation was carried to the point of an unprecedented frenzy. What was to be the role of ethnography in this age of Magyarization and revival? There is a great deal of evidence that ethnographers were caught up in the movement and utilized it to their advantage. By 1896, the

Ethnographic Society of Hungary was considered to be an important repository of folk culture research and an organization vested with the task of tracing Magyar origins. This gathering of "concerned" linguists, folklorists, ethnohistorians, and students of material culture gained its first impetus from the millennial.

Naturally, the preparations for the celebrations defined certain priorities within the historical and social sciences, favoring a certain type of research while neglecting others. The overall effect of the millennial may be grouped in three categories. First, there was a growing need for ethnogenetic studies. Therefore, history, archeology, folklore, and to some extent, material ethnography gained notable advances. Second, the longevity of Hungary's ancient culture as expressed in folk life became of primary importance, stimulating salvage ethnography. Third, and related to the above, a need for the demonstration and visual exhibition of the ancient Magyar traditions emerged. Whereas the first two effects were a continuation, or more specifically an intensification, of Magyarization, the third involved a new aspect of science, namely, propaganda. National revivalism at the turn of the nineteenth century utilized all the propaganda it could get. The question was, what sort of message was to be carried to the public, and how could ethnography deliver it?

An ethnographic exhibit staged in Budapest in 1896 by János Jankó contained twenty-four houses in a village setting, twelve of which were Magyar, and twelve of other nationalities (Kresz 1968:13). The buildings themselves were stereotypes of the better-known regional styles. In no way did the handsome structures erected at the ethnographic exhibit reflect actual social conditions, or reveal what Leó Beöthy had observed a few years earlier: "While the construction of palace-like stables continues for horses, thirty or even one hundred people live together, often in a single cave-like dwelling or a dilapidated room" (Beöthy 1876:90). Nor was there any indication that Hungary was having grave problems with its nationalities. At the exhibit an earlier notion called the tranquil "little Europe" principle re-emerged, a notion that the Hungarian empire was an egalitarian and democratic society in which all nationalities retained their character and perpetuated their culture (see Jankó 1897; Kovács 1896). Zoltán Kodály voiced his feelings about the exhibit as follows, "Even though I could hardly comprehend its significance at the age of thirteen, one of the most impressive accomplishments of the Ethnographic Society was the Millennial Village" (1959:531). A similar opinion was voiced by an international jury consisting of prominent men of science (Viski, et al. 1928:vi).

The demonstration of surviving ancient elements in Hungarian society was equally important. In this regard, one of the "purest and oldest forms of ancient occupation, fishing" – as still practiced by Magyar peasants – was demonstrated by Ottó Herman on an artificial pond (Városligeti tó) in Budapest, in conjunction with Jankó's exhibit.

These exhibits together contained 10,000 articles, a staggering figure for an outdoor museum. The gathering of the material had been a nation-wide project, involving many amateur ethnographers and other enthu-siasts under the leadership of Herman and Jankó. Their efforts, however, could not have succeeeded without the technical support of the Ethno-graphic Society and the financial aid of the government which Herman had requested at the Parliamentary meeting of November 29, 1890 (Kresz 1967: 13; Viski, et al. 1928:vi). The ethnographic exhibit of the Millennial Celebrations was a concerted effort of science and government for the expression of certain political ideas, namely, that Hungarian leadership within the Carpathian Basin was not merely desirable, but necessary as well, for it facilitated the perpetuation of a harmonious socio-political process within a multi-ethnic society. As rendered in the exhibit, these ideas apparently were resoundingly accepted, at least by the Magyar population. The question was whether the nationalities believed them or not. Perhaps they did at the time, but twenty years later at the Paris Peace Conferences, their representatives painted a picture of "little Europe" which showed slight resemblance to the Magyar rendering in the Millen-nial Exhibition and in the columns of *Ethnographia*, the official journal of the Hungarian Ethnographic Society.

2. THE HUNGARIAN ETHNOGRAPHIC SOCIETY (HES)

The need for an organization to structure the rapidly expending activi-ties of folklore collectors had been apparent at least since 1865, when negotiations for an ethnographic section in the National Museum began. Nothing tangible resulted until 1887, "when under the leadership of Pál Hunfalvy, thirty-one of our scientists decided to found the society" (Ortutay 1959:532). Within two years, the HES held its first meeting.[1]

[1] Originally the HES had fourteen founding and 438 regular members. Membership fluctuated throughout the years. In the period 1910–1914, there were over 1,000 mem-bers, but by 1933, membership had fallen to about 300. In 1959, membership again fell below 300 (Ortutay 1959:533). Even without tracing the geographic distribution of all the members, the enormous drop from 1,000 to 300 following Hungary's territorial losses in 1921 indicates that Hungarian ethnographers were by no means from Budapest alone but were from all over the country. This distribution profile, however, was considerably altered between the two World Wars when the capital city underwent a disproportionately greater academic and institutional growth than did the other regions.

The HES was the brainchild of Antal Herrmann, the most energetic, albeit overly optimistic, organizer of the time. Herrmann concurred with Hunfalvy on the extent of special departments which were to facilitate the widest possible scope of research. In the subsequent twenty-one "ethnic" and eight subdisciplinary departments (see Table 1), all interests

Table 1. Structure of the Hungarian Ethnographic Society (Source — *Ethnographia* 1890:60–68)

Protector (trustee): His Royal Highness Archduke Joseph (Habsburg)
Executive Board: Chairman — Pál Hunfalvy
      Vice Chairmen — Sándor Gömöri Havas and Aurél Török
      Secretary — Lajos Katona
      Treasurer — Samu Borovszky
Electors: Thirty members
Editor of the HES periodical *Ethnographia*: László Réthy

Department	Chairman	Rapporteur
Magyar	M. Jókai	S. Baksay
		L. Réthy
Székely	B. Orbán	P. Király
		F. Kozma
Csángó	A. Odescalchy	L. Szadeczky
Palóc	J. Nyáry	K. Mikszáth
		S. Pintér
Southern-Hungarian-German	J. Schwicker	A. Herrmann
		J. Szentkláray
Transdanubian German	I. Schneller	S. Kurz
Transylvanian-Saxon	G. Teutsch	O. Meltzl
		J. Wolff
Croatian	I. Josipovics	I. Bojnisic
		M. Cop-Marlet
		F. Kraus
Serbian	F. Nikolics	O. Asbóth
		A. Hadzsics
		I. Popovics
Bulgarian	K. Szimbusz	L. Koszilkov
		A. Strausz
Slavonic		D. Bachát
		S. Czambel
Ruthenian	G. Firczák	L. Csopey
		G. Drohobeczky
		M. Zloczky
Polish	E. Zalusky	L. Fialowsky
Vendic	I. Szalay	F. Göczy
Romanian	A. Marienescu	G. Alexics
		O. Mailand
		G. Moldován
Greek	M. Lyka	G. Tialios
Armenian	A. Molnár	L. Patrubányi
		K. Szongott
Gypsy	Archduke Joseph Habsburg assistant chairman: E. Ponori Thewrewk	A. Herrmann

148   MICHAEL SOZAN

Department	Chairman	Rapporteur
Bosnian	J. Asbóth	A. Strauss
		L. Thallóczy
Finno-Ugric	J. Budenz	B. Munkácsi
		J. Szinnyei, Jr.
		B. Vikár
Turko-Tatar	A. Vámbéry	I. Kunos
		J. Thúry
Folklore-Folk Psychology	A. Meltzl	L. Katona
Material Ethnography	J. Zichy	Mrs. Z. Gyarmathy
		O. Herman
		J. Xantus
Folk Music and Folk Dance	G. Zichy	I. Bartalus
		G. Káldy
		H. Kuhác
Physical Anthropology	A. Török	K. Pápay
Demography	K. Keleti	A. György
		J. Körösi
		G. Thirring
Palaeo-ethnology	F. Pulszky	R. Frölich
		Z. Torma
		M. Vosinszky
Graphics	B. Székely	A. Feszty
		J. Huszka
		I. Roskovics

Committee for the founding of the Hungarian Ethnographic Museum:
Chairman: J. Xantus
Members: O. Herman
A. Herrmann
K. Pápay
J. Szendrey
A. Török
Founding members: 14
Regular members: 498

seemed to be well represented. The "little Europe" principle had come through, at least in the structuring of the organization and in Hunfalvy's remarks at the first meeting, codified in Article 1, Section 3:

The study of the state of Hungary; the people who once inhabited and are now living in Hungary; the origin, development and present conditions of the nation's minorities, their national and physical character; the manifestations of national spirit and folk life, which are diverse and numerous (Hunfalvy 1890:3).

President Hunfalvy's further remarks asserted that although ethnography was a historical science, it relied on linguistics, physical anthropology, and archeology. Noteworthy in his phrasing is the equal emphasis on the study of both the past and the present, and on the spiritual and physical attributes of the people of Hungary.

Conspicuously absent from the society's program was even the slightest

reference to late nineteenth century ethnological theories. The only exception was L. Katona's innovative article in the first issue of *Ethnographia*
(1890) which, however, did not attract followers. There is no indication
that the intentions of the members of the HES went beyond historical
and synchronic description of the people of the Carpathian Basin, even
though most contemporary ethnological and anthropological theories
were known. *Ethnographia* carried book and trade journal reviews in
abundance, but personal views regarding theory and method rarely
showed in the interpretations of Katona, Hermann Munkácsi, and the
other reviewers. The scarcity of expressed views makes it difficult to gen-
eralize about the ideologies present in the HES, although a few obvious
signs allow certain conclusions.

First, in the early years of the HES, the notion prevailed that the oral
tradition of the folk was a survival of an ancient belief system, possibly
the fragments of a Magyar mythology which, if properly researched and
then synthesized, could be put into its original form. This was, of course,
the old Grimmean formula, subsequently restated by Andrew Lang (1887)
in a more modern package. Lang's reductionalism was followed by
folklorists for the very important reason that it promised to insure that
ancient Magyar religion would fall into the monotheistic class and therefore be equal to Aryan proto-culture. Hungarian folklorists drifted into
historicism (with an implicit mentalism) by way of comparative literature
and linguistics, and Hungarian ethnographers began to view information
about their Siberian tribal relatives from Lang's point of view. Meanwhile,
Wundt, who may have been the most important theoretician of the time,
was looked upon with great suspicion. Katona, for instance, questioned
Wundt's principle that the primitive mind was analogous to that of the
child: "We must take into consideration the fact that despite many
similarities, the children of civilization are brought up in an altogether
different social mileu, and despite the naivete of the mature native, he
is capable of exercising a great deal more critical and abstract reasoning
than our children."

Reductionalism attracted some students of peasant material culture,
such as J. Huszka, who attempted to reconstruct archaic peasant art
in Hungary from Persian and Indian motifs (1894, 1898). On the other
hand, conflicting with the reductionalist theory was the approach of
"the father of Hungarian material ethnography," Ottó Herman, and his
longtime adversary, János Jankó. Darwinian evolutionists by virtue
of their background in the natural sciences, both assumed that Hungarian
society had evolved from simple to complex. Their intensely minute analyses of peasant tool assemblages relied on a utilitarian-evolutionary

scheme: the simpler the object, the more primitive it was.

A number of ideas were shared by members of the HES at large. The most conspicuous was their reluctance to draw up general laws or principles about the nature of Hungarian peasant society or its culture. They felt that there were simply not enough data for generalization. More descriptive historical and contemporary data were needed. This, however, was not a unique characteristic of Hungarian ethnographers. Eastern, Central, and Western European ethnologists had similar interests. Let us not forget that at about the same period, the English Ethnological Society also "devoted itself...for the most part [to] purely classificatory and historical, or even merely descriptive [inquiries]. There was no attempt to detect laws of social or psychological differentiation. On the contrary, a demonstrably historical explanation was looked for, if an explanation was sought at all" (Burrow 1966:122).

The topics of national character and *ethnos* were approached through such questions as "To what race do we belong?" and "How came we to be?" These were considered to be historical questions. From the time of Hunfalvy, archival (and very little archeological) investigations and substantial comparative linguistic and folklore research exhausted the ethnographers' interest in the problem of *ethnos*. Even those who conducted fieldwork among the Hungarian cognate people living in Siberia acquired linguistic material first and ethnographic data second. The best field workers were either bona fide linguists such as B. Munkácsi or specialists in oral tradition such as L. Kálmáy, G. Sebestyén and B. Vikár. Etymological research was in vogue, as exemplified by the following titles: "The origin of the term Magyar" (*Ethnographia* 1890, 1895); "Ancient Hungarian terms for metal" (*Ethnograhia* 1894); "The origin of the term Székler" (*Ethnographia* 1890, 1896); "The origin of the term Croatian" (*Ethnographia* 1890); "The origin of proper names" (*Ethnographia* 1890).

Tracing of origins necessitated the use of the comparative method. In terms of today's standards, of course, nineteenth century comparative ethnography was rudimentary, and did not entail more than the juxtaposition of similar cultural elements from even the most disparate societies. Some improvements were in evidence after 1890, when diffusionist theories appeared, but even here we find little more than historiography. Both folklorists and material ethnographers adopted diffusionist theories. Jankó and Herman, for example, recognized the priority of borrowed elements from geographically close societies, over and above Eastern civilizations. They bowed to Ratzel, while Katona disputed the Grimmean thesis of racial retention and claimed that the exchange of stories and other traditions is a function of history, time, and geographic space, rather than of race.

Few, if any, ethnographers disagreed with the belief that only the most thorough description of the peasant society could lead to its understanding. B. Vikár's statement on this issue serves as a good example: "Without the exact and systematic recording of the variants we will never be able to unlock the secrets of Hungarian folklore. Until this vital task is completed all our predictions and conclusions will remain but hasty comments."

Non-interpretive descriptions may have been the strength of Hungarian ethnography in the early years. The detail and accuracy of the observed phenomena render most of the early publications useful to some extent for present-day research. The wealth of reporting on "folk customs" – a term applied to non-urban, non-Western traditional behavior forms and material culture – comprised the bulk of the articles in *Ethnographia* as well as other publications. With the exception of a few regional monographs, such as those by Jankó, Gönczy, Dudás, and the writers of the county monographs, folk customs were gathered from individual villages rather than in a cross-regional manner. The Palóc village communities in particular were the most popular subjects for study since the inhabitants were regarded as the purest Magyar peasants, and the best descriptive ethnographer of the period was G. Istvánffy, an expert on the Palócs. Between 1890 and 1911, he published seventeen articles on their customs, religion, and folklore, in addition to a monograph (1897). Increasingly, however, other regional groups, such as the people of Göcsej, the Széklers, the Sokács, and the Csángós, were "discovered." The description of their folk customs included rites of passage ceremonies, "superstitions," folklore, and a limited number of essays on family and kinship. The Millennial issue of *Ethnographia*, for instance, contained papers on the following subjects under the general heading of "Lectures and descriptive accounts":

a. Rites of passage ceremonies (7 articles)
b. Superstitious beliefs, holiday traditions (12 articles)
c. Oral traditions – legends, stories, folk songs (6 articles)
d. Material culture – costumes, house, furniture, etc. (3 articles)
e. Family and kinship (3 articles)

Although these articles were as "dry" as any descriptive literature can be, they sometimes revealed the particular biases and value judgements of the late nineteenth century ethnographer. The folk was usually depicted as rudimentary or primitive, at times as suspicious, lecherous, backward, and for the most part uneducated. At other times they were described as honest, naive, moral, brave, and industrious. Even Jankó, who was otherwise well known for his objectivity, occasionally made sweeping generalizations and meaningless value judgements. His observation on the Sokács, for example, contained the following: "As a truly pastoral people, they are brave. Reaching suddenly for the sword is in their blood. The love of freedom was implanted in them by pastoral life, while clan traditions upheld the institution of patriarchy. Simple, open-hearted, natural and hospitable, the Sokác is capable of being generous. He is honest, and respects others. All his actions and feelings are guided by upheavals of passion. These are all characteristics of the Serbs" (1896:156).

Since the principle of salvage ethnography superseded sociological and ethnological objectives, the role of interpretive approaches remained indecisive. Naturally, the foci of descriptive ethnography have undergone considerable change since the early HES years, and some of those early investigations have little meaning for modern ethnographers. At the same time, the principal objectives of ethnography were established at the turn of the century. Unlike the problems of method and research technique (the most grossly neglected issues in the HES), there was an important and hitherto unrecognized struggle between ideologies concerning the objectives of future study of Hungarian society and culture. The problem can be traced back to the 1820's, when two political ideologies clashed, the one maintaining that Hungary was a multi-ethnic nation-society, and the other that it was a single cultural unit under Magyar leadership. Whereas commonly shared, although vague, historical and comparative approaches tended to foster a certain amount of unity in the HES, the issue of the complex nation-society concept versus the Magyar society concept all but destroyed the effectiveness of the organization. More than that, the ideological split within the HES was so deep that only an energetic, last-minute effort to reorganize the society saved it from disintegration.

First we shall deal with the idea of the complex nation-society. Hunfalvy and Herrmann were very emphatic that Hungary was a nation with a multi-ethnic composition, although they did not deny the leading role of the Magyars in the Carpathian Basin. Magyar leadership, however, was purposely underplayed by both Hunfalvy and Herrmann in the founding principles of the HES, which strengthened but did not insure the "little" Europe formula in ethnographic research.

L. Réthy's one-year editorship of *Ethnographia*, along with his articles, testified to the kind of effort that was necessary to uphold the multi-ethnic, or complex nation principle. In his essay on the formation of the

Hungarian state, he emphasized that "Hundreds of thousands of people participated in a common effort to create a Hungarian state, which now has a common national tradition, ideology and blood" (1891). Offering a long list of outstanding individuals that ranged from Miklós Zrinyi, the defender of Szigetvár against the Ottoman Turks, to the Hunyadi family and many other "good Hungarians," all of non-Magyar ethnic origin, he maintained that the greatness of Hungary was a function of its multiethnic composition. Challenging contemporary policy making and growing chauvinism, he declared:

No matter how lay politicians explain the relationship of the Magyar race to other nationalities, and the latters' to one another... the natural factors of 1) ethnic independence, 2) common interest in work, material and cultural well-being, and before the law, and 3) striving toward common customs, life styles, language, and individual achievement, are at continuous work today as much as they have been for a thousand years. When we analyze the Hungarian society, the most striking phenomenon is its ability to assimilate nationalities (Réthy 1891:175).

For Réthy, the ethnogenetic study of the Magyar group (or any other nationality) held little value for ethnographic research: "We are no longer a Ural-Altaic people but a European complex society like our western neighbours" (1891:178). Therefore, the study of ethnic groups ought not to be restricted to the study of minority group-character, but rather it must be carried out on the national level: "This is an ethnological level standing above everything else" (1891:179).

Since the majority of the HES members were Magyar, many of whom were not entirely free of chauvinism, the maintenance of the "little Europe" principle became increasingly difficult. P. Hunfalvy, L. Réthy, A. Herrmann, G. Nagy, A. Strausz, and V. Semayer, the leaders of the multi-ethnic faction, found themselves confronted by the "Magyarites": O. Herman, Munkácsi, Katona, and others. Few details are available on how Réthy's melting-pot theory was received. Only the eventual results are clear. Within two years (1889–1891), the "little Europe" faction suffered a permanent defeat by the Magyarites. Réthy's resignation from the editorship of *Ethnographia* was announced "with regret" (1891:1), while Hunfalvy's death allowed O. Herman (no relation to A. Herrmann) to gain the presidency of the HES. Under its new leadership, the HES was reorganized. The ethnic departments disappeared, and the subdisciplinary departments became meaningless titles. The scientists from sister disciplines abandoned the organization, now concerned predominantly with the Magyar group. By 1896, the HES had changed its name from "Magyarországi Néprajzi Társaság" [Ethnographic Society of Hungary] to

"Magyar Néprajzi Társaság" [Hungarian Ethnographic Society], poignantly revealing the nature of the transformation. Publications reflected the change as evident in *Ethnographia*. In two years randomly selected, one from before 1895 and the other after, the multi-ethnic approach seemed to lose to Hungarology by a ratio of 1:1.5 to 1:3 (*Ethnographia* 1891, 1907).

Although a charge of racism could be (and has been) justifiably leveled against some of the new leaders of the HES, the merit of pursuing such investigation would be dubious at best. Let it suffice to say that from Herman's presidency until the time of the east-central European scope research of S. Solymossy, G. Róheim, Z. Kodály, and B. Bartók, it was simply assumed that the survival of the Magyar race in the "Slavic Sea" was a proof of superiority. The Magyar example illustrated the Darwinian (or the Malthusian-Spencerian) "struggle", and the "survival of the fittest." Magyar culture, or folk psyche, was considered to be like an organism – and Hunfalvy, Katona, and Réthy were quick to capitalize on organismic theories – which absorbed only those influences that were consistent with its make-up. Until the mid-1920's, the Eastern "great" civilizations were considered decisively more important sources of diffusion for the Hungarian culture than the Slavic and Western infiuences, although some ethnographers such as Katona, Strausz, and Munkácsi demonstrated the role of Slavic cultural impact on Magyar society.

Equally important for the future of Hungarian ethnography was the split between scientists preoccupied with the research of material culture, and those folklorists interested in "spiritual culture". In essence, the cleavage demonstrated a trend of specialization in ethnography, rather than an ideological or conceptual diversification. There was little disagreement on purpose and objectives which, to be sure, remained the study of those manifestations of peasant life that were either demonstrably or intuitively considered ancient. Both folklorists and materially oriented ethnographers were very much like archeologists, who uncovered assemblages – in material ethnography it was sets of tools, house furniture, musical instruments, and so on, while in folklore it was variants of stories, ballads, etc. – and attempted to derive them from certain historical or prehistorical forms. The archeological perspective was most apparent in A. Herrmann's call for the establishment of an ethnographic museum which, like the Magyar Népköltési Gyüjtemény [Hungarian Folklore Collection], was to "protect and demonstrate the peasant genius" (Herrmann 1890:20). According to Herrmann, because the folk was conservative, its products were indicators of a bygone age: "These objects are the carefully guarded sacred artifacts of domestic life; they are the fossil remains of folk culture which are to be considered as geological and archival evidence aiding our understanding of the hazy past" (1890:20).

Vigorous campaigns by J. Xantus to establish an ethnographic section within the National Museum bore fruit as early as 1872. Xantus was one of the most energetic collectors of artifacts, and he collected in Borneo, Siam, China, Japan, and the United States. His acquisitions, along with those of the natural scientist L. Biró, constitute a substantial part of the ethnological section of the Ethnographical Museum of Budapest. For a time, Xantus was also employed by the Smithsonian Institution for gathering material for its department of natural sciences. Only through the efforts of O. Herman, J. Jankó, V. Semayer, and Zs. Bátky, however, did Xantus' campaigns result in a viable institution for both storing material culture and training younger ethnographers. Semayer's curatorship (1902 –1919) was especially valuable for the advance of material ethnography. He organized regional museums and traveled widely, representing Hungary all over the world. He also followed Jankó's plan which called for the gathering of no more artifacts than were necessary to demonstrate the differences between Hungarian and other cultures.

In sum, the "tranquil" decades around the turn of the nineteenth century witnessed a transformation from an earlier ethnographic interest in Hungary as a multi-ethnic society to an interest in Hungary as a Magyar nation. This evolution did not take place in a vacuum but rather occurred within the larger socio-political process of Magyarization. Often at the expense of their own nationalities and of modern Western ethnological theories, ethnographers pursuing the path of Magyarization assumed a leadership within their scientific community that was to last until the time of this writing. The blind patriotism and chauvinism of the turn-of-the-century Magyar ethnographer is a thing of the past, but folk science in Hungary as in east-central Europe generally remains the study of the ethnographer's own society, allowing little cross-cultural research and generalization.

REFERENCES

ARANY, L., P. GYULAI
1872–1882   *Magyar népköltési gyüjtemény* [Hungarian folkpoetry collection]. Budapest.
BÁRÁNY, G.
1969   "Hungary: from aristocratic to proletarian nationalism," in *National-*

ism in eastern Europe. Edited by P. Sugar and I. J. Lederer, 259–309. Seattle: University of Washington Press.

BEÖTHY, L.

1876 *Nemzetlét: tanulmány a társadalmi tudományok köréböl Magyarország jelen helyzetének megvilágitására és orvoslására* [National existence: study on the illustration of present conditions of Hungary and for their remedy]. Budapest.

BURROW, J. W.

1966 *Evolution and society*. Cambridge: Cambridge University Press.

DUDÁS, G.

1896 *Bács-Bodrog vármegye egyetemes monografiája* [Universal monograph of Bács-Bodrog county]. Zombor.

GÖNCZY, F.

1914 *Göcsej s kapcsolatosan Hetés vidékének és népének összevontabb ismertetése* [The region and people of Göcsej and Hetés]. Kaposvár.

HERMAN, O.

1898 *Az ösfoglalkozások. Halászat és pásztorélet* [Ancient occupations. Fishing and pastoralism]. Budapest.

1899 A magyar ösfoglalkozások köréböl [From the Magyar ancient occupations]. *Természettudományi Közlöny*, 231–262.

1909 *A magyarok nagy ösfoglalkozása. Elötanulmányok* [The great Magyar occupation. A preliminary study]. Budapest.

HERRMANN, A.

1890 Hazai néprajzi muzeum alapitásáról [Concerning the establishment of an ethnographic museum]. *Ethnographia* 1:20–26.

HUNFALVY, P.

1890 Elnöki megnyitó [Presidential address]. *Ethnographia* 1:2–7.

HUSZKA, J.

1894 Népies ornamentikánk forrásai [The sources of our peasant ornaments]. *Ethnographia* 5:155–160.

1898 Tárgyi ethnographiánk östörténeti vonatkozásai [Prehistoric aspects of our material ethnography]. *Ethnographia* 9:41–62.

ISHIDA, E.

1965 European vs. American anthropology. *Current Anthropology* 6:303–318.

ISTVÁNFFY, G.

1897 *A matyó nép élete* [The life of the Matyó people]. Miskolc.

JANKÓ, J.

1892 *Kalotaszeg magyar népe* [The Magyars of Kalotaszeg]. Néprajzi Tanulmány 5.

1893 *Torda, Aranyosszék, Toroczkó magyar (székely) népe* [The Hungarian (Székler) people of Torda, Aranyosszék, and Toroczkó]. Budapest.

1896 Adatok a Bács-Bodrog megyei sokáczok néprajzához [Data on the Sokács of Bács-Bodrog county]. *Ethnographia* 7:34–64, 132–165.

1897 *Az ezredéves kiállitás néprajzi faluja* [The ethnographic village of the Millennial Exhibit]. Budapest.

1900 *A magyar halászat eredete* [The origin of Hungarian fishing]. Budapest.

1902 *A Balatonvidék népei* [The people of Lake Balaton]. Budapest.

KÁLMÁNY, L.
1881   Mythologiai nyomok a magyar nép nyelvében és szokásaiban. A hold nyevhagyományainkban [Mythological traces in the Hungarian language and customs. The moon in our oral tradition]. *Akadémiai Értekezések* 14:5.

KATONA, L.
1890   Ethnographia, ethnologia, folklore. *Ethnographia* 1:69–87.

KODÁLY, Z.
1959   Elöadás az MNT 70. évfordulóján [Lecture at the Seventieth Anniversary of the HES]. *Ethnographia* 70:531.

KOVÁCS, G.
1896   Néprajzi kiállitás [Ethnographic exhibit]. *Ethnographia* 7:253–259.

KRESZ, M.
1968   A magyar népmüvészet felfedezése [The discovery of Magyar folk art]. *Ethnographia* 79:1–36.

LANG, A.
1887   *The making of religion.* London.

MOLNÁR, E., editor
1967   *Magyarország története* [The history of Hungary]. Budapest.

MUNKÁCSI, B.
1892   A votyákok között [Among the Votyak]. *Ethnographia* 3:93–108.

ORTUTAY, G.
1959   Hetvenéves a Magyar Néprajzi Társaság [On the Seventieth Anniversary of the HES]. *Ethnographia* 70:529–562.

RÉTHY, L.
1891   A magyar nemzet alakulása [The development of the Hungarian nation]. *Ethnographia* 2:171–181.

SEBESTYÉN, G.
1902   *A regösök. Regös énekek* [The regös. Regös songs]. Budapest.

SUGAR, P., I. J. LEDERER, editors
1969   *Nationalism in eastern Europe.* Seattle: University of Washington Press.

SZABÓ, I.
1940   *A magyar parasztság története* [The history of the Hungarian peasantry]. Budapest.

VIKÁR, B.
1910   Ösköltészetünk élö emlékei [Living relics of our ancient poetry]. *Ethnographia* 21:65–82, 129–138, 201–210.

VISKI, K., et al.
1928   *Magyar népmüvészet* [Hungarian folk art]. Budapest.

The Rise of Social Anthropology in India (1774-1972): A Historical Appraisal

L. P. VIDYARTHI

This paper aims to highlight some of the basic factors in the genesis and stages of development of social researches in India. An attempt is made to record and review the researches that have been conducted by social anthropologists on Indian society and culture. In the light of earlier appraisals as well as new facts, three phases in the development of Indian social anthropology are identified. These phases are: (1) Formative [1774–1920], (2) Constructive [1920–1949], and (3) Analytical [1950-present]. While illustrative materials characterizing each of these phases are given, the more recent trends in Indian social anthropology are especially highlighted. The paper ends by linking the developments of Indian social anthropology to British and then American influences, and concludes with a statement of the need to develop a "synthetic approach" in Indian anthropology.

PREVIOUS REVIEWS OF INDIAN SOCIAL ANTHROPOLOGY

Various attempts to review the researches in social anthropology in India have been made from time to time by scholars such as Roy (1921), Majumdar (1950b, 1956), Ghurye (1956), Dube (1956, 1962), Bose (1963), Vidyarthi (1966a, 1966b), and Sinha (1968). Roy attempted a bibliographical account of the publications on tribal and caste studies as early as 1921. In his paper he referred to the materials published in the form of

Editor's note: This paper includes several minor changes of phrasing which Professor Vidyarthi has not had an opportunity to approve. The editor of the volume assumes responsibility for all such editorial considerations.

(1) articles in magazines, (2) compilations in handbooks of the different regions, and (3) monographs on tribes. Roy's effort, although the first attempt of its kind, recorded fairly systematic information about the early publications in this field, thus documenting the exclusive dominance of the British administrators, foreign missionaries, travellers, etc. in conducting anthropological researches in India.

After a lapse of two and a half decades, Majumdar (1947) in a memorial lecture at Nagpur University reviewed the development of anthropology and brought out the impoverished progress of Indian anthropology under the continued efforts of British anthropologists. In these two review papers, mention of American scholars in any context was conspicuous by its absence.

In another review article of a generalized type, Majumdar (1950b) tried to relate the developing science of anthropology in India (which to him at that time was essentially the study of primitive people) to the theories of culture developed in England as well as in America. He pointed out several areas of research in India in the light of existing theories and he suggested further scope for research.

The most significant review article by Majumdar (1956) was in the form of a supplementary paper to Ghurye's presentation in the UNESCO volume. In this paper he presented a very competent appraisal of teaching and research in anthropology in India in the context of the development of cultural theories elsewhere. One of his comments in this regard deserves to be reproduced here:

Social anthropology in India has not kept pace with the development in England, in the European continent or in America. Although social anthropologists in India are to some extent familliar with the work of important British anthropologists, or of some continental scholars, their knowledge of American social anthropology is not adequate (Majumdar 1956:164).

Ghurye in the same volume evaluated the emergence of Bombay as a center for sociological studies, and of Calcutta and Madras as centers for social anthropological studies, while he looked upon Lucknow as a composite center for economic, social anthropological, and sociological studies. Since both Ghurye and Chattopadhyay received their research degrees under W. H. R. Rivers in 1923 and became the heads of department in Bombay and Calcutta respectively, Ghurye traced the initial stimuli for the development of sociology and anthropology in India from Cambridge, and made the following observation:

It augurs well for India that if, in Bombay, sociology includes social anthropology, and in Calcutta, social anthropology is extended to include sociology to some extent as perhaps, source of inspiration came from the same teacher (Ghurye 1956:154).

Along with these two review articles which were written and discussed at an international level in 1952, Professor Dube also presented his proposal enumerating "the urgent tasks of anthropology in India," before the Fourth International Congress of Anthropological and Ethnological Sciences held in Vienna in 1952. In his paper (1956: 273–275), Dube made a reference to the unfortunate prejudice and distrust of the social workers and popular political leaders toward the anthropologists, and he made a case study of the vanishing tribe, its folklore and art, village studies, caste dynamics, etc. He also suggested an active cooperation among the government, the universities, and individual scholars both Indian and foreign, and he presented a proposal for the formation of a central organization at an international level for attacking the basic problems of social anthropological research in India.

Perhaps expanding and revising the same paper in the light of later developments, Dube contributed another paper on social anthropology in India in 1962. In the course of his critical evaluation in the light of the characteristics of the two earlier phases in social anthropology, he highlighted the weaknesses of the contemporary Indian social anthropology as they were reflected in techniques of research and methodology. Here his main concern was with "what ought to be rather than what is," and in view of this he put forward a number of suggestions of theoretical, methodological, and substantive nature (Dube 1962). In the same volume, Bailey (1962: 254–256) wrote an exploratory paper. His main concern was to highlight the inadequate researches that had been done in India "in proportion to the richness of social anthropological laboratory situations that demand adequate research in the field of structural explanation of the complex society."

The latest and the most comprehensive publication on this topic was by Bose (1963) in the form of a booklet prepared under the auspices of the Indian Science Congress Association. In this publication, along with a brief reference to earlier researches, Bose reviewed the progress of anthropology in India during the previous half century and presented the materials in three sections: (1) prehistoric archeology, (2) physical anthropology, and (3) cultural anthropology. Devoting considerable attention to the review of researches in cultural anthropology, he enumerated the major researches done in the fields of (a) village studies and (b) marriage and family, but he leaned heavily toward a discussion of (c) caste. While his attempt to relate the various Indian social anthropologists in terms of prevailing schools was not taken far, his mention of theoretical anthropology remained confined to his own theory of culture. For want of space, unfortunately, other theories of culture and civilization were not mentioned. On the whole, although Bose's appraisal of social anthropology in India was undoubtedly the latest and the most substantive, it tended to remain incomplete insofar as it created an appetite that it could not afford to satisfy.

In his two papers, Vidyarthi reviewed the rise of social anthropological researches in India and highlighted the recent trends in social anthropology. Improving upon earlier classifications, he categorized the history of social anthropology into Formative (1774–1919), Constructive (1920–1949), and Analytical (1950-present) periods, and went on to emphasize in detail the recent trends in village studies, caste studies, studies of leadership and power structure, of religion, of kinship and social organization, of tribal village and applied anthropology. This paper, originally presented during the Seventh International Congress of Anthropological and Ethnological Sciences in Moscow, for the first time made a systematic attempt to review the various phases in the development of Indian anthropology (Vidyarthi 1966a).

In his second paper, published in the same year in the light of similar materials (1966b), Vidyarthi referred to recent trends in Indian social anthropology and pointed out the approaches of anthropologists toward integrating the knowledge of various disciplines for a proper understanding of man and society. He made a special mention of the various efforts of the social scientists to study the problems of tribal and rural communities in India. He also made a plea that Indian social science should not overlook what may be termed its "Indianness." This Indianness in the field of social science referred to our distinct cultural milieu and value attitude system as well as a body of ideas of Indian thinkers reflected in ancient scriptures which are full of social facts and which should be used in the understanding of cultural process and civilizational history of India.

In a paper presented during a conference in New York, Sinha (1968) lent his support to Vidyarthi's three-fold division of phases. He also confirmed the imitative nature of social anthropological researches in India and referred to the fact that in general, Indian anthropologists have been prompt in responding to the latest developments in the West without caring to pursue the earlier phases of constructive endeavors that have their logical aims in an Indian context. Acknowledging this craze of imitating the West, Sinha made a search to establish certain Indian traditions in social and cultural anthropology. In the study of the total pattern of Indian civilization he mentioned a few scholars such as Bose (for his contributions to the classification of India into two basic zones of material culture cutting across the linguistic divisions, a pyramidal form of Indian unity in diversity, non-competitive economic ideology and the Hindu mode of tribal absorption, interrelationship between the villages and supra-local centers), Srinivas (Sanskritization, spread, dominant caste), Karve (agglomerative character of the Hindu society), Sinha (Indian society as evolutionary emergent from a tribal base), and Vidyarthi (study of sacred complex). Continuing his search for India's contribution to research methodology, Sinha observed that Indian anthropologists in general have not paid much systematic attention to devising a special methodology for studying the unique layout of the cultural patterns and processes of the sub-continent. However, he pointed out a few exceptions in this regard: Das (rigorous utilization of genealogical method in the study of Purum social organization), Bose (application of spatial distribution techniques in the dating of Indian temples, utilization of the tools of human geography in studying cultural historical problems, use of family histories in the study of social change in urban centers), Chattopadhyay and Mukherjee (use of statistical techniques in studying social change), Karve (combination of textual analysis with field data in the study of kinship), Vidyarthi (study of sacred complex utilizing such concepts as sacred center, cluster and segment, etc.). In the light of an appraisal of the various phases and trends in Indian anthropology, Sinha made a strong case for pursuing the natural history tradition for completing the basic descriptive outline of the forms of behavior of the Indian people, and for building a super-structure of analytical and incisive studies of specific problems on that base. He further observed that "It is only on the basis of such ground work that the Indian scholars will be able to effectively participate in the international adventure of expanding the frontiers of knowledge in anthropology" (Sinha 1968).

In addition to these papers written from time to time on the development of social anthropology in India, we come across a few full length review articles and a number of introductory observations in many books on the different topics of social anthropology in India. Among the authors of review articles, special mention may be made of Dumont and Pocock who, in a series of publications, attempted to highlight significant research areas in Indian social anthropology. Their first publications (1953, 1957) reviewed critically the village studies as well as the kinship studies in India. While they reviewed these two sets of studies in a wider context of world literature, the selections from India were from *Village India*, edited by Marriott (1955), and from *Kinship organization in India* by Karve (1953). Similarly, their second volume (Dumont and Pocock

1958) was devoted to a review of literature on caste with special reference to the work of Bougle (1908) and Hocart (1950). The third volume (Dumont and Pocock 1959) dealt with theoretical discussions of the various concepts of religion in India. Drawing material from the work of Srinivas (1952), Stevenson (1954), Marriott (1955), and Elwin (1955), the two scholars entered into discussion of the concept of purity and pollution, levels of Hinduism in relation to "its ultimate value," and then the institutional function of priests, and so on. In their own ways, each of these three volumes definitely reviewed the contributions to "Indian sociology," but as has been rightly commented by Bailey (1959), their perspective was too narrow and suffered from the "very worst kind of inverted ethnocentrism" on the parts of the editors. However, one finds in these volumes an appraisal of the sociological and social anthropological studies in India in the context of world literature, especially African studies, as they are of significance from the angle of critical comparison.

Finally, the trends of social anthropological studies have been sporadically reviewed here and there in a few prefaces and introductions to specific books on tribal, caste or village studies, and although scattered, they also provide some information and opinions on the trends of social anthropological researches in India. Mention, for example, may be made of Vidyarthi (1964) for tribal studies; Prasad (1957), Srinivas (1962), Mathur (1964) for caste studies; Srinivas (1955), Majumdar (1956) for village studies; and Dube (1965) for leadership studies. Thus, although sporadic and casual efforts have been made from time to time to review the development of anthropology in India, and although scattered materials by several authors on this topic are available, the efforts in this paper to present a comprehensive and up-to-date appraisal of the course of development of social researches in India are the first of their kind.

THE PHASES OF DEVELOPMENT

Any historical study covering a reasonable span of time needs to be categorized in terms of meaningful chronological phases. While it was too early for Roy (1921) to classify the ethnographic studies in terms of time perspective, he categorized studies in terms of the sources of publication, that is, magazines, handbooks, monographs, and so on, and then in terms of the nationality of the authors. Nor in the more recent writings of Dube and Bose do we find any explicit attempts on their parts to categorize material in terms of meaningful historical sequences. Dube (1962) referred to three phases of development in social anthropology: an earliest phase of compilation and publication of volumes on tribes and castes containing brief and often sketchy accounts of the divergent customs and practices of the various groups, a second phase characterized by detailed monographic studies of individual tribes mostly through personal observations, and the beginning of a third phase after the national independence, marked by considerable quantitative advancement and some qualitative achievement. Bose (1963) also referred to three such phases of writings: (1) encyclopaedias of tribes and castes; (2) descriptive monographs; and (3) analytical studies of villages, marriage and family, caste, civilization, and so on. These classifications by far need not be considered to be of much significance since they were not attempted seriously and did not review the anthropological literature in light of trends prevalent in the respective periods. The determination of phases of anthropological trends in terms of theory, methods and substantive data needs to be attempted in terms of multiplicity of traits so that they may bring out the cumulative as well as the distinctive features of each phase.

An attempt to classify the course of development in terms of the dominant trends of the historical periods was made by Majumdar who cared to suggest landmarks in the course of development of anthropology. Borrowing terms from Penniman (1935), Majumdar (1950a) divided anthropological researches in India into three phases: Formulatory (1774–1911), Constructive (1912–1937), and Critical (1938-present). In determining the beginning of the Formulatory period, the establishment of the Asiatic Society of Bengal was the only obvious choice since it marked the beginning of scientific traditions for the study of "nature and man" in India.

The beginning of Majumdar's second phase was marked by the publication of the first full-length monograph on the Mundas by S. C. Roy, an Indian national who also happened to be a great force in molding the anthropological career of Majumdar himself. In recognition of this in a later writing, Majumdar (1959) wrote of Ranchi as a place of pilgrimage for himself. To me the Constructive period seems to begin around 1920, for the department of sociology was opened at Bombay in 1919 with F. Geddes as its head, the department of anthropology at Calcutta began in 1920 with R. Chandra as its head, and the first full-fledged Indian journal of anthropology was begun by the late S. C. Roy in 1921. All these developments in and around 1920 brought a new temper to the development of anthropology in India, and it seems to me that the Constructive period should be dated from that year.

Majumdar conceived of a third phase, a Critical period, beginning in 1938 when the Indian and British anthropologists met together on the occasion of the Silver Jubilee of Indian Science Congress in Lahore and carried out a stock-taking of anthropological developments in India, exchanged notes,and planned jointly for future anthropological researches in India. According to Majumdar, this event marked the beginning of a critical approach. In the same year Majumdar published his own problem-oriented monograph on the Ho tribe (Majumdar 1937). Originally submitted as a doctoral thesis in Cambridge University, in its analysis of cultural dynamics the monograph reflected a departure from traditional descriptive studies. When Majumdar later wrote his essay proposing stages in Indian anthropology, he could not have anticipated the accelerated developments that took place during the two decades following India's independence and owing especially to the new collaboration with and the interests of American anthropologists, particularly in the American initiation of collaboration with Lucknow University and with the Central Ministry of Community Development. American scholars such as Oscar Lewis (as consultant to the Ministry of Community Development) and Morris Opler came to India on a large scale anthropological mission. Moreover, several Indian anthropologists such as Dube and a few others visited anthropological institutions in the United States. The period also saw the publication of M. N. Srinivas' book, *Religion and society among the Coorgs of South India* (1952), which proved to be of great importance from an analytical perspective. In view of all these considerations it seems relevant to rename this period an Analytical period instead of Critical period as envisaged by Majumdar.

To be precise, then, the course of the development of social anthropology needs to be studied in terms of three phases: Formative period (1774–1919), Constructive period (1920–1947), and Analytical period (1948–present). I do not imply that each phase has completely replaced its predecessor. As a matter of fact, there have been strikingly different rates of development in the different parts of India, and an acquaintance with this fact needs to be emphasized. To clarify this point it may be mentioned that although the formulatory period began in Assam and other north-eastern border areas long ago, those areas have just emerged from the constructive phase of descriptive ethnography. Similarly, in contemporary social researches being conducted in different parts of India by various agencies and individuals with different purposes, the co-existence of all three phases is quite evident in the compilation of glossary about tribes and castes, monographic and descriptive studies characteristic of constructive periods, as well as in theoretically sophisticated analytical researches.

THE BEGINNING: THE FORMATIVE PERIOD

We owe the beginning of anthropological investigation in India to the Asiatic Society of Bengal. Credit goes to Sir William Jones who organized the society in 1774, became its founder president, defined the scope of the society as the study of "nature and man" in India, and piloted a number of researches and publications on this broad subject.

Since then, British administrators, missionaries, travelers, and a few other anthropologically oriented individuals collected data on tribal and rural groups, and wrote about their life and culture in the *Journal of the Asiatic Society of Bengal* (1784), *Indian Antiquary* (1872), and later in the *Journal of the Bihar and Orissa Research Society* (1915) and *Man in India* (1921). Along with other historical and geographical information, they also collected ethnographic data and published a series of district gazetteers, handbooks on tribes and castes, and then a number of monographs, especially on the tribes of Assam. During the census of 1931 and of 1941, some British and Indian anthropologists were associated in the collection of anthropological data on the tribes and castes of different parts of India.

British scholar-administrators posted in different parts of India, such as Risley, Dalton, and O'Malley in East India, Russell in middle India, Thurston in South India, and Crooks in northern India, wrote encyclopaedic inventories about the tribes and castes of India which even today provide the basic information about the life and culture of the peoples of the respective regions. The importance of these accounts can be judged from the fact that the Anthropological Survey of India has outlined a plan to reprint some of them with suitable additional notes. In addition to these handbooks, administrators such as Campbell (1856), Lathum (1859) and Risley (1891) published general books on Indian ethnology. The purpose of these volumes was to acquaint government officials and private persons with classified description of tribes and castes with a view to ensuring effective colonial administration.

These generalized works about the land and people were followed by efforts to prepare detailed accounts of specific tribes and in some cases castes in the different regions, as in the study of Chamar by Briggs (1920). Among those who made such studies were Shakespeare (1912), Gurdon (1912), Mills (1937), Parry (1932), Grigson (1938) and a few others who wrote competent monographs on specific tribes. A few missionaries, among them Bodding (1925) and Hoffman (1950), were attracted to ethnographic and linguistic researches. All of these scholars were especially influenced by such early British anthropologists as Rivers (1906), Seligmann (1911), Radcliffe-Brown (1922), and Hutton (1931) who had published monographs based on their work among the tribes of India.

Early Indian Anthropologists

Under these influences, the first Indian national to write exhaustive monographs on the tribes of India was S. C. Roy, who published his first epoch-making work on the Munda tribe (1912). This was followed by a series of five monographs on the Oraon (1915), the Birhor (1925), Oraon religion and customs (1928), Hill Bhuinya (1935), and the Kharia (1937). These works by Roy were acknowledged by the British anthropologists of the day as competent studies, and Hutton in his presidential address to the Indian Anthropological Institute in Calcutta on January 5, 1938, described Roy as "the father of Indian ethnology." Under the intellectual inspiration of the British anthropologists and the financial encouragement of the then British governor of Bihar, Sir Edward Gait, Roy did outstanding work in Bihar. After Roy, R. P. Chanda published a book on the Indo-Aryan race in 1916, which evoked great interest in the study of the cultural history of India.

THE CONSTRUCTIVE PERIOD

Social anthropology in India definitely underwent a phenomenal change when it was included in the curricula of the important universities in Bombay (sociology in 1919) and Calcutta (anthropology in 1921). These two centers for sociological and anthropological researches attracted trained scholars, stimulating them to undertake significant researches. Soon obscure subjects like kinship and social organization were studied by Ghurye (1943, 1952, 1954), K. P. Chattopadhyay (1921, 1926), Srinivas (1942, 1946), Majumdar (1937), Karve (1940), and a few other anthropologists such as P. N. Mishra and L. K. A. Iyer, K. P. Chattopadhyay, T. C. Das, and D. N. Majumdar in the East and North India, and G. S. Ghurye, Irawati Karve, L. K. Ananthakrishna Iyer, and A. Aiyappan in the West and South India provided the initial stimulus for the organization of scientific anthropological research by conducting field expeditions, writing books and articles, and by training researchers for anthropological study of tribal and rural cultures.

A big jump came in 1938 when a joint session of the Indian Science Congress Association and the British Association, on the occasion of the

Silver Jubilee of the former body, reviewed the progress of anthropology in India. Eminent anthropologists from abroad deliberated with Indian anthropologists and discussed plans for future research in India. During this period a few anthropologists completed their doctoral work and soon provided new theoretical leadership. Critically analyzing their data, for example, Majumdar in his work on the changing Ho of Singhbhum (1950a), Srinivas in his study of marriage and family in Mysore (1942) and N. K. Bose in his publication on "Hindu methods of tribal absorption" (1961 [1929]) brought about a certain amount of theoretical sophistication in Indian anthropological research. The appearance of Verrier Elwin's series of problem-oriented publications on the tribes of Madhya Pradesh, Orissa and then on the religion of the Savara of Orissa (1939, 1942, 1943, 1947, 1952) gave further recognition to Indian anthropology, while von Furer-Haimendorf's publication on the tribes of Hyderabad and other successive publications (1943, 1945a, 1945b, 1946a, 1946b) provided additional refined models for Indian workers.

Indian anthropology, which had been born and brought up under the dominant influence of British anthropology, matured during its Constructive phase also under a British influence. During this period, except for a few studies of Indian institutions such as caste (Briggs 1926; Iyer 1929; Hutton 1946), the tradition of tribal studies which had begun in the work of enlightened British scholars, administrators, and missionaries continued under British and Indian anthropologists until the end of the 1940's. Similar to the anthropology being taught at Cambridge, Oxford, and London, Indian anthropology was characterized by ethnological and monographic studies with a special emphasis on research in kinship and social organization.

THE ANALYTICAL PERIOD

After the second global war and especially following India's independence, contact between American and Indian anthropologists significantly increased. For example, Morris Opler of Cornell University, Oscar Lewis of the University of Illinois, David Mandelbaum of the University of California, and many of their students came and stayed in India with their research teams. The effect of this contact was the creation of an atmosphere: (1) for the systematic study of Indian villages with a view to testing certain hypotheses, (2) for refining some of the methodological framework developed elsewhere, and then (3) for assisting community development programs in the Indian villages.

Village and Caste Studies

The American scholars not only produced valuable theoretically-oriented works on Indian rural cultures, but also inspired both young and old Indian anthropologists to take up similar researches on Indian villages and caste systems. The beginning of this phase may be dated from the publication of Srinivas' book, *Religion and society among the Coorgs of South India* (1952), which was exemplary in making a departure from the descriptive phase to the analytical phase as well as from tribal studies to non-tribal community studies. Another marker of the new period was Iravati Karve's book on the Hindu kinship system (1953). During the next decade, others such as Dube and Majumdar took up theoretically sophisticated studies of rural communities, and in a real sense, the literature of Indian anthropology began to be integrated with the world anthropological literature.

Action Research

The tribal and rural community development program of the Government of India gave further fillip to the Indian social scientists to study and evaluate the process of change in tribal and rural India. In such development programs, the concepts of action anthropology formulated by Sol Tax for the first time partially replaced the principles of applied anthropology which had developed during the British colonial administration. In some of the later writings on tribal policy and programs by Majumdar (1949), Dube (1960), Elwin (1952), Vidyarthi (1957, 1969, 1960, 1968), the influence of action anthropology in India has come to be established as an important discipline from theoretical, substantive, and action points of view.

Socio-Psychological Research

Under the American influence and under the guidance of B. S. Guha, a graduate of Harvard University, the study of culture and personality found a place in the Anthropological Survey of India. As part of the survey, two psychologists, Uma Choudhary (1955) and P. C. Ray (1951, 1953, 1955, 1957, 1959, 1966), made field studies with a view to establishing racial differences, personality types, and other socio-psychological characteristics among the tribals. Such research received further stimulus when the American anthropologist, Geetal P. Steed (1955), conducted a study in a Hindi village in Gujrat and G. M. Carstairs (1957), a British psychiatrist, conducted field research among the different communities of Rajasthan. The work of some of the social psychologists in universities such as Ranchi and Allahabad gave additional impetus to this kind of work.

Folklore Researches

Until the systematic treatments of Verrier Elwin, folklore research in the form of sporadic collections of tribal folk songs and tales had been merely appended to monographs on other topics. With the passage of time the social elements hidden in the folklore were also unearthed by a few anthropologists and several scholars of different literatures especially in Bhojpuri, Assamese, and Marhathi. A number of publications began bringing out the social, historical, and behavioral usages of folklore.

Studies of Power Structure and Leadership

The attempt to analyze power structure and decision-making in Indian rural society is also of recent origin. Here again the credit goes to the American Oscar Lewis and his Indian collaborator who initiated the study of faction and leadership with their two volumes on North Indian (Lewis 1954) and South Indian (Dhillon 1955) villages respectively. Published under the auspices of the Planning Commission, these two widely-discussed volumes brought to light the varied roles of kin and caste-oriented factions in decision making. Moreover, these studies inspired a number of American, British, and Indian scholars to take up additional studies of rural leadership in different parts of India.

Anthropology of Religion in India

Another field of social anthropology which reflects the British and American influences, and which needs to be mentioned separately, is religion. An objectively-based study of primitive religion in India was initiated by Majumdar, and his explanation of Bongaism in *Affairs of a tribe* (1950a) paralleled other modern anthropological trends in the study of religion (Sarana 1961). The study of religion in the context of Indian villages was first made by Srinivas who in his book *Religion and society among the Coorgs of South India* (1952) developed the concept of Sanskritization to explain the process of change in the Hindu village. A full-length study of a tribal religion was published by Elwin (1955) on the Savara tribe of Orissa, in which he supported the concept of "spiritism" suggested earlier by S. C. Roy (1928).

Anthropological interest in the study of religion was focused in the preparation of two volumes, *Aspects of religion in Indian society* (Vidyarthi, editor 1961) and *Religion in South Asia* (Harper 1964). Both volumes included papers based upon original investigations of different aspects of tribal and rural religion. The Majumdar memorial volume appropriately opened with an essay on "Professor Majumdar and the anthropology of Indian religion" by Gopala Sarana, and is dedicated to his memory. Marriott, Aiyappan, Sharma, and Srivastava contributed papers which threw light on some of the dominant and distinguishing characteristics of Indian religion and philosophy. The papers that followed were of more specific nature and the units of study were mostly limited to respective villages. Carstairs and Mathur described the complexes of religious beliefs and practices in three typical villages of Rajasthan and a Malwa village respectively. Singh wrote about religion in a Sikh village, while Vidyarthi described the sacred complex of a tribal village. Other papers covered still smaller units, although their theoretical implications were of wider consequence. Madan, Atal, Singh, Chattopadhyay, Sahay, and Sinha analyzed religious features such as festivals, cults, and deities in such a manner that they demonstrated great methodological significance. Thus, as Bose has observed, Vidyarthi's volume covered a wide range — from the way religion is practiced by folk in different parts of India to analyses of certain complex beliefs present among tribal peoples and which have been modified through contact with "Hinduism."

Harper's volume originated in a conference on Religion in South Asia, held August, 1961. The subsequent book consisted of nine papers by Mandelbaum, Ames, Berreman, Kolenda, Opler, Gumperz, Beals, Yalman, and Harper. Publication of the volume brought to light the various approaches of the respective authors, and in general it is bound to stimulate further research in Indian religion.

A work somewhat different in kind from these first two volumes was edited by Milton Singer. *Traditional India: structure and change* included papers which dealt with both textual and contextual analyses of oral and recorded traditions. Although the theme of the book was to understand the image of "new India" in the light of her rich and deeply rooted heritage, almost all of the papers had some bearing on religious traditions, which obviously have been a common idiom in Indian history. These papers dealt with the various dimensions of Indian civilization and analyzed aspects of cultural media and cultural performances, including religious ones. A few of the papers, however, dealt exclusively with aspects of religion in specific communities, as in McCormack's paper on the media of communication found among the Lingayatsect and in Raghavan's more general paper on the methods of religious instruction in South India. Other papers examined the Anavils of Gujrat, the Chamar of Senapur, and the Nayar.

A full-length study of the sacred city of Gaya as a dimension of Indian civilization has been attempted by Vidyarthi (1961b) within a framework of the theories of Redfield and Singer. The study is an aid to the understanding of religion in India in terms of the great traditional life of the communities.

Many of the village monographs cited above include materials on religion, and its importance in village life is evident in all these studies. In one such village study, Senapur Planalp did extensive research exclusively on religious life and values as part of his doctoral work at Cornell University, and he subsequently presented a full-length description of religious life in a Hindu village (1956).

Urban Studies

The researches of Robert Redfield, Milton Singer, and McKim Marriott of the University of Chicago provided theoretical and methodological direction toward understanding the folk and peasant communities in India as dimensions of Indian civilization. Their work contributed to a reinterpretation of the "great" and "little" traditions of India and led to an anthropological study of "great" and "little" communities of various dimensions. Under the influence of the Chicago school of anthropology, Indian anthropologists began to study both traditional and modern cities with a view to first understanding them as part of Indian civilization and to then analyzing them in terms of the folk-urban continuum.

Studies of the process of urbanization, industrialization, and city planning have been undertaken as such research schemes have been financed by the National Planning Commission. With Milton Singer's methodological study of Madras, Marriott's study of Wai Town near Poona, and Martin Oran's study of Jamshedpur, the importance of the study of cultural roles of cities came into prominence. With financial assistance from the Planning Commission, some anthropologists took up urban studies, and the scope of anthropology was broadened from the study of isolated primitive tribal communities to rural and then to urban and industrial centers. The studies of Calcutta by Bose (1958), Kanpur by Majumdar (1961), Lucknow by Mukherjee and Singh (1961), and Gaya and Ranchi by Vidyarthi (ed. 1961, 1969) reflect the dual impetus that Indian anthropologists have received from the Chicago anthropologists and from the Planning Commission.

Professional Training and Cooperation

Finally, and also under the American influence (Tax, et al. 1953), the universities have realized the need to integrate the various branches of anthropology for the purpose of training and research. In all the Indian universities there is an integration in the teaching of anthropology with of course a bias for specialization in specific branches of anthropology. Additionally, many social scientists have felt the need for collaboration in order to gain a comprehensive understanding of the social and cultural phenomena of Indian communities, and in some recent researches and publications in the areas of village and city studies, religion and leadership, and social change and planning, a trend toward interdisciplinary studies has been conspicuously evident. With the recent constitution of the Indian Council of Social Science Research and with the current efforts of the Ministry of Education to reorganize the Anthropological Survey of India, this trend has been strengthened and is likely to become more so in the future.

CONCLUSION

On the basis of the survey undertaken in this paper, it is apparent that social research in India, which had originated and developed under British influence, is now mainly flourishing under the stimulation received from the United States and other countries. While British social anthropology continues to provide useful models in the study of kinship and marriage, the British functional approach to tribal and rural studies has been supplemented by the American cultural-historical approach. Such an approach has been necessary as interest in India's emergence from its traditional structure has increased. As these newer approaches have developed, the descriptive phase of tribal studies has been replaced by the analytical study of different communities and by the attempt to formulate terms and concepts and to advance theories and methods for the general understanding of Indian society and culture. The administrative anthropology of the colonial pattern has been reorienting toward academic interests, and with this, a new quest for interdisciplinary approaches to understand the complexity of Indian society has become evident. Again following the lead of certain American scholars, there is now more "network studies" and "part-whole" analysis and less of "isolate studies," a trend which has led to an emphasis on the similarities rather than the differences among the various Indian communities. As a whole, social anthropology in India has made satisfactory progress during the past two decades and has been recognized by the universities and the government as an important discipline which studies peoples at all levels of cultural development in their wholeness but with precision and empirical orientation.

The journey of Indian anthropology still continues. It has gone ahead under the influence of and in collaboration with British and then American anthropologists. Of course these non-Indians will continue to wield powerful influence in expanding the scope of anthropology in India in the future. Science knows no barriers and the science of man in India has still much to learn in the fields of theory and method from the other scientifically advanced countries of the world. But this does not mean that social anthropology in India should overlook what may be termed its "Indianness." Perhaps to some extent social anthropology has not done so, because it has not progressed under the spell of unthinking imitation. Because of this salient feature, Professor Kroeber has said that India has listened to England, America, and to herself. The result, we may say, has been a synthetic approach (Majumdar 1959: 173). Such a synthetic approach may be conceptualized in terms of our unique cultural milieu, value-attitude system, and heritage and historical experiences. We have had our own sets of social thinkers who have given thought from time to time to the social problems and who have also given direction in solving them. Among such social thinkers was Mahatma Gandhi whose teachings and ideals seem to Jaiprakash Narayan (1964) as the submerged part of an "ice-berg" which the social sciences ought to explore. Along with the thinkers, social scientists ought also to consider the ancient scriptures such as the Vedas, the Upanishad, the Smritis, the Puranas and the epics — all full of social facts and all in need of careful study to help understand the development of the "Indianness" of social anthropology in India as it is especially used in the study of the cultural processes and civilizational history of India.

REFERENCES

AIYAPPAN, A.
1961   "Thinking about Hindu way of life," in *Aspects of religion in Indian society*. Edited by L. P. Vidyarthi, 38–44. Meerut: Kedarnath Ramnath.
ATAL, YOGESH
1961   "The cult of Bheru in a Mewar village and its vicinage," in *Aspects of religion in Indian society*. Edited by L. P. Vidyarthi, 140–150. Meerut: Kedarnath Ramnath.
BAILEY, F. G.
1959   "For a sociology of India," in *Contribution to Indian sociology*, volume three. Edited by Louis Dumont and D. Pocock, 101. The Hague: Mouton.
1962   "The scope of social anthropology in the study of Indian society," in *Indian anthropology: essays in memory of D. N. Majumdar*. Edited by T. N. Madan and Gopala Sarana, 254–256. Bombay: Asia Publishing House.
BODDING, P. O.
1925   *The Santal medicine*. Memoirs of the Asiatic Society of Bengal 10(2).
BOSE, N. K.
1958   Social and cultural life of Calcutta. *Geographical Review* 20.
1961   "Hindu methods of tribal absorption," in *Cultural anthropology*. Bombay: Asia Publishing House. (Originally published in 1929.)
1963   *Fifty years of science in India: progress of anthropology and archaeology*. Calcutta: Indian Science Congress Association.
1968   *Calcutta: 1964. A social survey*. Bombay: Asia Publishing House.
BOUGLE, C.
1908   *The essence and reality of caste system*. Paris: Alen.
BRIGGS, W. G.
1920   *The Chamars*. Calcutta: Association Press.
CAMPBELL, J.
1856   Ethnography of India. *Journal of the Asiatic Society of Bengal* 35:1–152.
CARSTAIRS, G. M.
1957   *The twice-born*. London: The Hogarth Press.
1961   "Pattern of religious observances in three villages of Rajasthan," in *Aspects of religion in Indian society*. Edited by L. P. Vidyarthi, 59–113. Meerut: Kedernath Ramnath.
CHANDA, R. P.
1916   *Indo-Aryan races: a study of the origin of Indo-Aryan people and institution*. Calcutta, Rajsahi: Virendra Research Society. (Reprinted in 1969 under Indian Studies.)
CHATTOPADHYAY, G.
1961   "Carak festival in a village in West Bengal," in *Aspects of religion in Indian society*. Edited by L. P. Vidyarthi, 151–165. Meerut: Kedarnath Ramnath.
CHATTOPADHYAY, K. P.
1921   Some Malayalam kinship terms. *Man in India* 1:53–55.

1926   An essay on the history of Newar culture. *Journal and Proceedings of the Asiatic Society of Bengal* n.s. 23(3).

CHOUDHURY, UMA

1955   A comparison of Santal mental test reactions in rural and urban areas. *Bulletin of the Department of Anthropology* 4(1):67–68.

COHN, B. S.

1958   "The Chamar of Senapur," in *Traditional India: structure and change.* Edited by Milton Singer, 413–421. Special issue of the *Journal of American Folklore* 78.

DHILLON, H. S.

1955   *Leadership and groups in a South Indian village.* New Delhi: Planning Commission.

DUBE, S. C.

1956   "The urgent task of anthropology in India," in *Proceedings of the Fourth International Congress of Anthropological and Ethnological Sciences* (held at Vienna in 1952), 273–275.

1960   "Approaches to the tribal problems," in *Indian anthropology in action.* Edited by L. P. Vidyarthi. Ranchi: Council of Social and Cultural Research, Bihar.

1962   "Social anthropology in India," in *Indian anthropology: essays in memory of D. N. Majumdar.* Edited by T. N. Madan and Gopala Sarana. Bombay: Asia Publishing House.

DUBE, S. C., *editor*

1965   *Emerging patterns of rural leadership in southern Asia.* Hyderabad: National Institute of Community Development.

DUMONT, LOUIS, D. POCOCK

1953   "Critical Essays," in *Contribution to Indian sociology,* volume one. Edited by Louis Dumont and D. Pocock. The Hague: Mouton.

1957   *Kinship contribution to Indian sociology.* The Hague: Mouton.

1958   "Hocart: on caste relation and power," in *Contribution to Indian sociology,* volume two. Edited by Louis Dumont and D. Pocock. The Hague: Mouton.

1959   "Religion: critical essays," in *Contribution to Indian Sociology,* volume three. Edited by Louis Dumont and D. Pocock. The Hague: Mouton.

ELWIN, VERRIER

1939   *The Baiga.* London: John Murray.

1942   *The Agaria.* London: Oxford University Press.

1943   *Maria murder and suicide.* London: Oxford University Press.

1947   *The Muria and their Ghotul.* London: Oxford University Press.

1955   *A philosophy of NEFA,* second edition. Shillong: NEFA Administration.

GHURYE, G.

1943   A note on cross cousin marriage and rural organization in Kathiawar. *Journal of the University of Bombay* 5(1): 88–90.

1952   *Social change in Maharashtra, part one.* Sociological Bulletin.

1954   *Social change in Maharashtra, part two.* Sociological Bulletin.

1956   "The teaching of sociology, social psychology and social anthropology," in *The teaching of social science in India,* 148–153. UNESCO.

GOUGH, E. KATHLEEN
1958 "Cults of the dead among the Nayar," in *Traditional India: structure and change*. Edited by Milton Singer, 446–478. Special issue of the *Journal of American Folklore* 78.

GRIGSON, W. V.
1938 *The Maria Gond of Bastar*. London: Oxford University Press.

GUMPERZ, J. J.
1964 "Religion and social communication in village North India," in *Religion in South Asia*. Edited by E. B. Harper. Seattle: University of Washington Press.

GURDON, P. R. T.
1912 *The Khasi*. London: Macmillan.

HARPER, EDWARD B., *editor*
1964 *Religion in South Asia*. Seattle: University of Washington Press.

HOCART, A. M.
1950 *Caste: a comparative study*. London: Methuen.

HOFFMAN, J.
1950 *Encyclopaedia Mudarica, volume thirteen*. Patna: Government Printing Press.

HUTTON, J. H.
1931 *Census of India*, volume F, India part three B: *Ethnographic notes*. Simla: Government of India.
1946 *Caste in India: its nature and origins*. Cambridge: Cambridge University Press.

IYER, L. K. ANANTAKRISHNA
1929 The Kahars of Mysore. *Man in India* 9:171–172.

JAY, EDWARD
1959 The anthropologist and tribal welfare: Hill-Maria — a case study. *Journal of Social Research* 2: 82–89.

KARVE, IRAVATI
1940 Kinship terminology and kinship uses of the Maratha country. *Bulletin of the Deccan College Research Institute* 2–4:327–389.
1953 *Kinship organization in India*. Poona: Deccan College.

KOLENDA, P. M.
1964 "Religious anxiety and Hindu," in *Religion in South Asia*. Edited by E. B. Harper. Seattle: University of Washington Press.

LATHUM, R. G.
1859 *Ethnology of India*. London: Van Voorst.

LEWIS, OSCAR
1954 *Group dynamics in a North Indian village*. Delhi: Planning Commission.

MADAN, T. N.
1961 "Herath: a religious ritual and its secular aspects," in *Aspects of religion in Indian society*. Edited by L. P. Vidyarthi, 129–139. Meerut: Kedarnath Ramnath.

MAJUMDAR, D. N.
1937 *A tribe in transition: a study in culture pattern*. London: Longmans Green.
1947 *The matrix of Indian culture*. Lucknow: Universal. (Sri Mahadeo Hari Bathodkar Foundation lecture delivered in 1946).

1949 The changing canvas of tribal life. *The Eastern Anthropologist* 3:40-47.
1950a *Affairs of a tribe: a study in tribal dynamics.* Lucknow: Universal.
1950b Anthropology under glass. *The Journal of the Anthropological Society of Bombay,* special issue (1-16).
1956 "Special report on the teaching of social anthropology," in *Teaching social science in India,* 161-173. UNESCO Publication.
1958 *Caste and communication in an Indian village.* Bombay: Asia Publishing House.
1959 "The light that failed," in *Anthropology and tribal welfare.* Edited by L. P. Vidyarthi. Ranchi: Council of Social Science Research, Bihar.
1961 *Social contours of an industrial city.* Bombay: Asia Publishing House.

MANDELBAUM, DAVID G.
1964 "Process and structure in South Asian religion," in *Religion in South Asia.* Edited by E. B. Harper. Seattle: University of Washington Press.

MARRIOTT, MCKIM
1955 "Little communities in an indigenous civilization," in *Village India.* Edited by McKim Marriott. Chicago: University of Chicago Press.
1961 "Changing channels of cultural transmission in Indian civilization," in *Aspects of religion in Indian society.* Edited by L. P. Vidyarthi, 15-25. Meerut: Kedarnath Ramnath.

MARRIOTT, MCKIM, editor
1955 *Village India.* Chicago: University of Chicago Press.

MATHUR, K. S.
1961 "Meaning of religion in a Malwa village," in *Aspects of religion in Indian society.* Edited by L. P. Vidyarthi, 114-128. Meerut: Kedarnath Ramnath.
1964 *Caste and ritual in a Malwa village.* Bombay: Asia Publishing House.

MC CORMACK, W.
1958 "The forms of communication in Virasaiva religion," in *Traditional India: structure and change.* Edited by Milton Singer, 325-335. Special issue of the *Journal of America Folklore* 78.

MILLS, J. P.
1922 *The Lhota Naga.* London: Macmillan.
1937 *The Rengma Naga.* London: Macmillan.

MUKHERJEE, R. K., BALIJIT SINGH
1961 *Social profiles of a metropolis.* Bombay: Asia Publishing House.

NAIK, T. B.
1958 "Religion of the anvil of Surat," in *Traditional India: structure and change.* Edited by Milton Singer, 389-396. Special issue of the *Journal of American Folklore* 78.

NARAYAN, JAIPRAKASH
1964 Gandhism and social science. *AVARD, News Letters* 6(5).

OPLER, MORRIS E.
1964 "Particularization and generalization on process in ritual and culture," in *Religion in South Asia.* Edited by E. B. Harper. Seattle: University of Washington Press.

PARRY, N. E.
1932 *The Lakhers.* London: Macmillan.

PENNIMAN, T. K.
1935   *A hundred years of anthropology.* London: Gerald Duckworth.
PLANALP, SENAPUR
1956   "Religious life and values in a Hindu village." Unpublished doctoral dissertation, Cornell University.
PRASAD, N.
1957   *Myth of the caste system.* Patna: Patna University Press.
RADCLIFFE-BROWN, A. R
1922   *The Andaman Islanders.* Cambridge University Press.
RAGHAVAN, V.
1958   "Methods of popular religious instruction in South Asia," in *Traditional India: structure and change.* Edited by Milton Singer. Special issue of the *Journal of American Folklore* 78.
RAY, P. C.
1951   Differences in concrete intelligence among the Jaunsaris. *Journal of the Asiatic Society* 16:45–52.
1953   Maze test performance of the Bhils of Central India. *Bulletin of the Department of Anthropology* 2(1):83–90.
1955   The tensional feeling among the Abors and Gallong indicated by the Rorschach. *Indian Journal of Psychology* 30: Part 1–2, 95–103.
1957   Effect of culture-contact on the personality. *Structure of Anthropology* 6 (2).
1959   *The children of the Abor and Gallong.* Delhi: Education and Psychology Monograph.
1966   "The Lodha and their spirit-possessed men: psycho-socio-cultural factors in tribal transformation." Paper read before Summer School in Anthropology held at Darjeeling.
RISLEY, H. H.
1891   *Tribes and castes of Bengal.* Calcutta: Bengal Secretariat Press.
RIVERS, W. H. R.
1906   *The Todas.* London: Macmillan.
ROY, S. C.
1912   *Mundas and their country.* Calcutta: City Book Society.
1915   *The Oraons of Chotnagpur.* Ranchi: Bar Library.
1921   Anthropological researches in India. *Man in India* 1:11–56.
1925   *The Birhor: a little known jungle tribe of Chotanagpur.* Ranchi: Man in India Office.
1928   *Oraon religion and customs.* Ranchi: Man in India Office.
1935   *The Hill Bhuiyas of Orissa.* Ranchi: Man in India Office.
1937   *The Kharia.* Ranchi: Man in India Office.
SAHAY, K. N.
1961   "Christianity and cultural processes among the Oraon of Ranchi," in *Aspects of religion in Indian society.* Edited by L. P. Vidyarthi, 323–340. Meerut: Kedarnath Ramnath.
SARANA, GOPALA
1961   "Professor Majumdar and the anthropology of Indian religion," in *Aspects of religion in Indian society.* Edited by L. P. Vidyarthi, 1–13. Meerut: Kedarnath Ramnath.

SELIGMANN, C. G., B. SELIGMANN
1911 *The Veddas of Ceylone.* Cambridge: Cambridge University Press.
SHAKESPEARE, J.
1912 *The Lushai Kuki clan.* London: Macmillan.
SHARMA, K. N.
1961 "Hindu sects and food pattern in north India," in *Aspects of religion in Indian society.* Edited by L. P. Vidyarthi, 45–58. Meerut: Kedarnath Ramnath.
SINGER, MILTON, *editor*
1958 *Traditional India: structure and change.* Special issue of the *Journal of American Folklore* 78(281).
SINGH, I. P.
1961 "Religion in Daleke: a Sikh village," in *Aspects of religion in Indian society.* Edited by L. P. Vidyarthi, 191–219. Meerut: Kedarnath Ramnath.
SINGH, T. R.
1961 "Hierarchy of deities in an Andhra village," in *Aspects of religion in Indian society.* Edited by L. P. Vidyarthi, 166–171. Meerut: Kedarnath Ramnath.
SINHA, SURAJIT
1961 "Changes in the cycle of festival in the Bhumij village," in *Aspects of religion in Indian society.* Edited by L. P. Vidyarthi, 341–368. Meerut: Kedarnath Ramnath.
1968 "Is there any Indian tradition in social/cultural anthropology: retrospect and prospect." Paper presented during Wenner-Gren conference on The Nature and Function of Anthropological Traditions.
SRINIVAS, M. N.
1942 *Marriage and family in Mysore.* Bombay: Asia Publishing House.
1946 The social organization of South India *Man, Journal of the Royal Anthropological Institute* 46.
1952 *Religion and society among the Coorgs of South India.* London: Oxford University Press.
1962 *Caste in modern India and other essays.* Bombay: Asia Publishing House.
SRINIVAS, M. N., *editor*
1955 *India's villages.* Bombay: Asia Publishing House.
SRIVASTAVA, R. S.
1961 "The chief currents of contemporary Indian philosophy," in *Aspects of religion in Indian society.* Edited by L. P. Vidyarthi, 20–37. Meerut: Kedarnath Ramnath.
STEED, GEETAL P.
1955 "Notes on an approach to a study of personality formation in a Hindu village," in *Village India.* Edited by McKim Marriott, 102–144. Chicago: University of Chicago Press.
STEVENSON, H. N. C.
1954 Status evaluation in Hindu caste system. *Journal of the Royal Anthropological Institute* 84:45–65.

TAX, SOL, *et al.*
1953   "Anthropology as a field study," in *An appraisal of anthropology today.* Edited by Sol Tax, 342–356. Chicago: University of Chicago Press.

VIDYARTHI, L. P.
1957   Anthropology, authority and tribal welfare in India. *Eastern Anthropology* 11(1): 14–34.

1961a   "Sacred complex in a hill tribe village," in *Aspects of religion in Indian society.* Edited by L. P. Vidyarthi, 241–267. Meerut: Kedarnath Ramnath.

1961b   *Sacred complex in Hindu Gaya.* Bombay: Asia Publishing House.

1964   *Cultural contours of tribal Bihar.* Calcutta: Punthi Pustak.

1966a   Researches in social science in India: some preliminary observations. *Social Science* INFORMATION 5(1). Paris.

1966b   Social anthropological researches in India: some preliminary observations. *Journal of Social Research* 9(1): 1–74.

1969   *Cultural configuration of Ranchi: study of pre-industrial city of Tribal Bihar.* Calcutta: Bookland.

VIDYARTHI, L. P., *editor*
1960   *Indian anthropology in action.* Ranchi: Council of Social and Cultural Research, Bihar.

1961   *Aspects of religion in Indian society.* Meerut: Kedarnath Ramnath.

1968   *Applied anthropology in India.* Allahabad: Kitab Mahal.

VON FURER-HAIMENDORF, C.
1943   *The Chenchus: jungle folk of Deccan.* London: Macmillan.

1945a   "Tribal populations of Hyderabad yesterday and today," in *Census of India 1941,* volume thirty-one. Hyderabad: Government Central Press.

1945b   *The Reddis of the Bison Hills: a study in acculturation.* London: Macmillan.

1946a   The agriculture and land tenure among the Apatanis. *Man in India* 26: 181–195.

1946b   Notes on tribal justice. *Man in India* 26: 181–214.

Ruth Benedict, Anthropologist: The Reconciliation of Science and Humanism

JUDITH MODELL

Anthropology offered Ruth Benedict a special reconciliation of the ambiguities she discovered in her own temperament. In 1947, when as retiring president she gave a farewell speech to the American Anthropological Association, she characterized anthropology as halfway between humanities and science, demanding the approaches of both for a complete understanding of culture. The tolerance she perceived for two ways of thought illuminates both the nature of the discipline and its rewards for a woman like Ruth Benedict. The distinction between science and humanities had roots in Benedict's childhood, as a representation of conventional sex roles: the masculine, the mind which abstracts and classifies, and the feminine, the mind which considers "human emotions, [and] symbolic structures," attitudes and feelings (Benedict in Mead 1966:463).

The distinction Benedict made grew out of her observations of the males and females in her immediate environment, her own temperamental response to their different behavior and attitudes, and growing awareness of what her culture expected of her as a woman. Her evaluation of the character of her mother, and what she knew about her father, fell automatically into the context of turn of the century American definitions of appropriate sex roles. As she grew up, Ruth Fulton realized the extent to which her private assessments were formed and reinforced by society's distinctions. At once sensitive to her variation from expected patterns of behavior, she yet could not compromise with them. The failure of a marriage and the end of World War I sent her back to school and she discovered anthropology, by chance, a discipline whose flexible methodology suited her personal uncertainty. The receptiveness of anthropology to idiosyncratic encounters with data gave Benedict the opportunity to unify private dichotomies while introducing a significant theoretical concept. In addition, the discipline then, as now, welcomed women and generally provided a refuge for those who felt marginal to the mainstream of American culture. My argument is not that anthropology was unique in this offering, nor that Ruth Benedict held a unique relationship to her career, but that the coming together of a personality and a discipline at a particular time in the development of each sheds light on both the history of anthropology and the possible routes to fulfillment for a woman of Ruth Benedict's type and time.

I do not define Ruth Benedict as a feminist, since her arguments pertain to any individual in some way marginal to his culture, but I think she knew that much of her dissatisfaction grew from an inability to accept feminine roles as defined by her society. Without that sense of dissatisfaction, Benedict would not have gone back to school, nor would she have so perfectly accepted the subject she chose to study. My argument goes beyond Margaret Mead's, in *An anthropologist at work* (1966), in emphasizing the relationship of Ruth Benedict's changing self-conception to her anthropological work.[1]

In her 1947 speech Ruth Benedict remarked appreciatively on the use of life history for integrating a scientific and a humanistic approach. I in turn will use her life history to illustrate her own points about the reciprocal interaction between an individual and a society: "The unique value of life histories lies in that fraction of the material which shows what repercussions the experiences of a man's life — either shared or idiosyncratic — have upon him as a human being molded in that environment" (Benedict in Mead 1966:469). Benedict's life history (the fraction I present) shows how her life was molded by her culture, and how she turned back to that molding to illuminate the process for others. The lesson of her life history is for a general as well as a professional audience, for it teaches women about achieving their potential within society's limitations, it teaches any individual about the ways of accommodating to cultural expectations, and it teaches anthropologists about the unexplored offerings of their discipline.

Ruth Fulton was born in 1887, a child of the late Victorian era. A year

---

[1]   Much of my evidence is based on the material that Margaret Mead put together in *An anthropologist at work* (1959). My references are to the 1966 Atheling Edition, New York. (Cited as Mead 1966). Mead notes both the importance of Benedict to her discipline and the importance of the discipline in shaping Benedict's sense of herself as a woman in American society. My argument goes beyond hers in emphasizing the relation of the latter to Benedict's anthropology.

and a half later, another daughter was born to Bertrice and Frederick Fulton, in December 1888. Three months later Frederick Fulton died. He had just begun a promising career in medical research, and in investigating a malaria epidemic contracted a fever which was never adequately diagnosed. He was 32 when he died, and his wife three years younger. During his illness the small family had moved to Bertrice Fulton's parents' farm in the Chenango Valley in New York State (Frederick Fulton's family lived in the same neighborhood). After Dr. Fulton's death, his widow and two small girls stayed in her parents' house.

The trauma of a father's early death was exacerbated for Ruth by the reactions of the adults around her. Their responses set up patterns in her own development which persisted through her life, affecting her marriage, her writing, and finally her anthropology. Bertrice Fulton marked bereavement with dramatic gestures. She brought the small child in to look at her father in his coffin, and implored her to remember his face (Mead 1966: 98). The impact of this scene lasted, a fact which Ruth realized and incorporated into her developing self-consciousness. In 1934, when at 47 she wrote an autobiographical piece for Margaret Mead, the first sentence mentions Dr. Fulton's death (Mead 1966:97). She remembered from early childhood, contrasting the calm beauty of Frederick Fulton's face with the frantic emotional response of her mother, and once she upset her religiously Baptist grandparents by insisting that a picture of Christ was a portrait of her father (Mead 1966:107).

Meanwhile, every March, Bertrice Fulton passionately mourned the death of her husband. Frightened by these outbursts in her mother, her one parent, Ruth Fulton condemned them. She also consequently (if unconsciously) set up a dichotomy between masculine and feminine, in which the latter stood for an excessive emotionalism she rejected, and the former a contentment she desired.

Nothing disturbed the ideal picture Ruth Fulton created of her father. He had died early in a career devoted to others, a life whose worth his daughter never questioned. For her, the calm of death became associated with the kind of achievement he had promised. The masculine, in her tentative definition, linked scientific objectivity and selflessness to the unshakeable contentment she had read in her father's face. Contrasting with this was her mother's selfish grief, and intense involvement with the emotional turmoils of a small family. As a child Ruth Fulton attempted to associate as closely as possible with her father's world, and to deny her mother's. Unlike her outgoing and cheerful sister Margery, who became adept in the household tasks prescribed for girls and necessary, to some extent, on a farm, Ruth refused to practice domestic skills. While Margery sewed clothes for Ruth's naked dolls, Ruth ran off to the fields to be with her grandfather. With the cooperation of Grandpa Shattuck, the small girl kept most of these trips a secret from her mother and grandmother.

As a baby Ruth Fulton had had measles, which left her partially deaf. The inability to hear what was said, combined with an unwillingness to get involved, distanced Ruth Fulton further, especially from her mother. (Perhaps her grandfather's booming ministerial voice overcame Ruth's defect.) Her mother impatiently, and with some accuracy, attributed withdrawal to unfriendliness. Ruth's deafness was not discovered until she was five years old and enrolled in public school; by that time patterns of contact in the family had been well-established. Then Ruth Fulton learned to read and discovered another way of escaping from prescribed tasks and the pressures to conform.

From time to time Bertrice Fulton insisted that Ruth participate in family life. In her autobiographical essay, Benedict recalled vividly the painful aspects of these encounters, but at the same time she was attracted by the companionship of family life. If the young girl suspected she failed to meet certain expectations, there was no one around to support a disregard of them. Ruth Fulton asked questions, challenging her environment, and looking for her proper place within it. More and more, too, as she grew older, she was drawn into her mother's female world. There were tasks to be done, and everyday life demanded her participation on that side of the dichotomy — even if she read poetry while washing dishes (Mead 1966:112). Ruth shared, in fact, the emotionalism she condemned. This showed itself first in recurring temper tantrums. Each time she was called back to family life (she noted in 1934), she reacted with violent outbursts of temper. These imitated with unconscious cruelty her mother's annual mourning ceremonies. When Ruth was eleven, stomach aches and vomiting replaced the tantrums, and also occurred regularly. Then, at twelve, her menstrual periods began and took on the same six-week rhythm as her vomiting. The ambiguity that characterized Ruth Fulton's attitude toward femininity had psychic and physiological manifestations well before the grown woman verbalized these conflicts.

By the time she was an adolescent Ruth Fulton found other ways of accommodating to a world in which she felt out of place. Conventions existed, alternative to the ones at home yet accepted as appropriate for women of her time and her background. She realized, still without thinking specifically about reasons, that certain ways of adjusting were more acceptable than others partly because they indicated choice and control. To rebel against what her family expected of her as an older daughter in a fatherless family by escaping into fields or fantasy simply inspired anger.

But the private fantasies of a lonely six-year old took on a different value when the fifteen-year old converted them into short stories and poetry. The people Ruth Fulton knew judged writing an appropriate alternative for girls, and she herself equated literary talents to her sister's domestic and, later, artistic skills. To the idea that a man's achievement lay in a world outside himself she began to add the idea that a woman can substitute satisfaction in a world of imagination and symbol for the conventional rewards of family and domesticity. A second dichotomy, between imaginative and practical endeavor, refined the earlier differentiation between male and female qualities.

While Ruth Fulton's definition of male and female patterns was thus becoming more precise, she still had to understand her own personality within these definitions. The comfort she found in writing and reading conflicted with her gnawing suspicion that accomplishment in an external world — the male way — had a measurable value that insured its worth. She wanted a way of evaluating her activities in order to avoid what she feared: the narrow pursuit of self-fulfillment.

Ruth Benedict's definition of masculine and feminine had a biographical base before she added the intellectual framework. The traits she specified as masculine and feminine came in response to her upbringing, and to her immediate family situation. But the family also transmitted cultural values, and an individual biography acquires resonance within a general social context. Ruth Benedict's idiosyncratic assumptions reflected cultural patterns before she had any inkling of the process involved. An early manifestation of the interaction was the child's angry inability to assume the feminine role personified in her mother. With this went an unconscious compensation, as the little girl idealized the absent, male role. In rejecting her mother's life, the daughter partly reacted to personality differences. Underneath this, however, and largely unconscious, lay a puzzled resistance to the conventional patterns her mother tried to inculcate. These patterns were not rigid or restrictive in the sense of announcing woman's place in the home and woman's role as wife and mother. What was conveyed was a more subtle, therefore harder to detect and evaluate, pattern of expectations about individual goals.

By the early twentieth century in America, when Ruth Fulton was growing up, women had a fair degree of educational equality with men. Women's colleges had been established throughout the previous half century, and Bertrice Fulton herself belonged to one of Vassar College's earliest graduating classes. The real dilemma, as Ruth came to realize in her mother's life and after she herself went to Vassar, in her own, was the use a woman could make of her education. Even if — which was not always true — the actual subjects taught to women matched those taught to men, the context into which they brought this training differed. With the exception of a minority of students, most women left Vassar expecting to get married and raise children, at least as the main focus of their life, with careers subsidiary. What could be more important to the future of American society than that women be fitting companions for men and proper mothers to future generations? This ideology dominated Ruth Fulton's college years, when President James Monroe Taylor outlined his ideal of the "well-rounded" woman. Vassar graduates were to be "cultured but human, not leaders but good wives and mothers, truly liberal in things intellectual but conservative in matters social," as his successor paraphrased it, adding: "And this most of them dutifully became" (Mac-Cracken 1950:24). Vassar students, coming largely from the upper classes, intended to adopt the manners of their parents. The women who did rebel against the established order were forced to become radical by being denied moderate modes of action, and Vassar graduates founded and perpetuated extreme left women's groups, such as the National Woman's Party. If Ruth Fulton admired her classmate Inez Milholland Boussevain for publicizing the feminist cause by riding horseback down Fifth Avenue in New York City, she could not follow this example. Her response to stereotyped sex roles was still couched in uncertainty. Ruth Fulton Benedict needed a standard by which to measure the choices available to men and women in her culture before she explored pragmatic social change.

Her education at Vassar did not teach her a way of countering the approval society granted to the choice made by the majority of her classmates. Margery Fulton made that choice. The summer after the sisters graduated (1909), Margery married Robert Freeman, a minister from California. She had two children and went back to a successful career in teaching. Ruth made a different choice, but only later knew its complicated motivations. Mainly she persistently resisted the model set by her mother. If Ruth Fulton was unable to break out of social conventions, she was equally unable to accept the compromises they demanded from a woman. If she used her mother as a model Ruth concluded that women found first fulfillment in husband and children, and only a secondary satisfaction in realms outside the family. She saw, too, the risks of goals that depended upon others, and began to wonder whether women chose or were forced into their roles by nature as well as society. Were women somehow less well-equipped for confronting the world? Did biological differences underlie the separate male and female routes to self-fulfillment? Ruth jotted down these questions, plus miscellaneous ideas and shaky

hypotheses, in notebooks, journals, and on odd pieces of paper. She wondered, further, whether the dilemma was peculiar to her, and to her times
and culture. Would she as a woman have been happier in another century,
another place? Did other societies allow for a greater scope of individual
difference? These questions went back to childhood, when Ruth Fulton
dreamed of living in ancient Egypt or on a lovely farm just over the hill.
They were the questions she would ask as a young teacher and then a
young wife. Finally, they were the questions that informed her anthropology.

Ruth Fulton did, after finishing Vassar, make her plans within alter-
natives acceptable for women in her situation. She spent the year 1909–
1910 in Europe (suitably chaperoned), then went back to Buffalo to live
with her mother. That year (1910–1911) she took still another step into
women's proper sphere, and did volunteer social work. It was as if,
finding she had to accept a female role, Ruth Fulton punished herself by
accepting its severest limitations. She also was following her mother's
pattern of doing social work as a prelude to serious commitment. Journal
entries and notes reveal how much Ruth disliked this work, and suggest
that had she been paid she might have felt differently. A salary gave work
a defined value. At the end of the year she accepted a teaching job in
Pasadena and though she continued to live with her family (her mother
also moved to her sister's), her sense of independence grew. She did not
question the worth of teaching as a career, but doubted the potential of
any career for exacting a peimanent commitment from a woman. Ruth
compared teaching to the choice of marriage, still suspecting that the
majority of women in her culture had been ideally prepared for one role
and not for the other. In a 1912 journal entry she decided:

So much of the trouble is because I am a woman. To me it seems a very terrible
thing to be a woman. There is one crown which perhaps is worth it all — a great
love, a quiet home, and children…. We have not the motive to prepare ourselves
for a 'life-work' of teaching, of social work — we know that we would lay it
down with hallelujah in the height of our success, to make a home for the right
man (Benedict in Mead 1966:120).

Throughout these four years (1910–1914) Ruth Fulton tried to judge her
own capacities and establish her own values against the background of
family and social pressures. She blamed part of her problem on the conditions set for women in her society, part on temperamental peculiarities,
and believed an answer would come in an adjustment between the two,
not a radical break with either. In California, too, Ruth Fulton had little
communication with other women who might be sharing the confusions
she discovered in herself. Her sister's life seemed settled (Mead 1966:119),

and in contrast to the Freemans' contented domesticity, the teachers she met complained constantly about their fate. The old maid teachers, as she referred to them, bitter and resentful, told and retold "all their twenty-year old conversations with men" (Benedict in Mead 1966:120). Ruth Fulton Benedict never found it easy to confide in others and consequently (if involuntarily) denied herself the comfort of common struggle. The women's suffrage movement had not engaged her energies and she did not become truly politically active until the late 1930's, when World War II loomed on the horizon and she followed Boas in applying anthropological knowledge to the world crisis. Increasingly, during the years in California, Benedict turned to writing as a route to self-knowledge. She had written stories since adolescence and gradually replaced those with poetry. In her first year of teaching, she also began a journal, but a journal's unrelieved privacy could not resolve the ambiguities poetry could. Though Ruth Benedict did not explicitly formulate the argument, she shared intuitively what she discovered in reading: the idea that keeping a diary became an outlet for women unable to find, within social restrictions, other means of expressing themselves.

For Ruth Fulton Benedict, fully to understand the significance of writing poetry meant dealing again with her culture's standard of appropriate roles for women. To know where poetry stood in her own life, she had to relate literary expression to the ordinary routes of achieving self-satisfaction allocated to men and women by her society. For three years she taught adolescent girls to read standard literary classics. She assigned them her favorite books, by male writers whose encounters with the world she admired for their expansive embracing of variety (e.g. journal entries on Shakespeare in Mead 1966). But she also wanted to know that what students read affected their lives, or teaching became a work of futility.

In writing poetry, too, Benedict looked at her relationship to a literary tradition dominated by males. Where did she, as a woman writer, stand in respect to, for instance, Walt Whitman, whose exuberant poetry she particularly liked? The differences she perceived between herself and Whitman fit back into her old masculine-feminine pattern. Her sex might absolve her of responsibility. "Does this sense of personal worth, this enthusiasm for one's own personality, belong only to great self-expressive souls?" she asked in 1922. "Or may I perhaps be shut from it by eternal law because I am a woman and lonely?" (Benedict in Mead 1966:123).

But Ruth Benedict had been struggling against the very point that women intrinsically lack a strong sense of personal worth. She tried as a poet to separate the conviction of achieved selfhood from sexual stereotypes. Her early poems, in sonnet form, analyze emotions under strict technical control. Form, she was learning, can utilize emotion and make it productive. Suppression was not the only way of dealing with the painful private responses she felt her society and her literary tradition relegated to the female realm. Benedict took another important step when she submitted her poems to various editors. This, too, fit into a recurring pattern. As Ruth Fulton had needed the external approbation a salary symbolized, so she needed the justification of writing that publication symbolized (e.g. letters to Sapir, in Mead 1966). Throughout the 1920's her poems were published in respectable journals such as *Poetry*, the *Dial*, and the *New Republic*.

To appreciate the benefits of an external evaluation of her work Ruth Benedict did not have to achieve personal fame. She submitted poetry under a pseudonym. She wrote as a female, Anne Singleton, which suggests she knew that taking a masculine name would be an easy mask and an avoidance of the dilemma she had set out to solve. Benedict knew the solution lay in realizing the potential of the feminine side of her nature, not in denying it. To characterize opposing elements the poet still used her society's sexual differentiation; the imagery in Anne Singleton's poems extended the debate of Benedict's prose. A tree was often the central image, and poems investigated the tension between tall, searching, outward reaching branches and budding, fertile, fruit-bearing qualities. The tension fed back into private writings where the woman wondered whether poetry would ever provide perfectly satisfactory expression to both sides of her nature. In her journal, in 1913, she contrasted William and Mary Wordsworth (the poet's sister) as a way of questioning from another perspective whether a woman can be as great a poet as a man, or whether her talents lie elsewhere, "in the supreme power — to love." Once more, Benedict was asking whether a woman's ultimate satisfaction comes from being rather than acting: "In the quiet self-fulfilling love of Wordsworth's home, do we ask that Mary Worthsworth should have achieved individual self-expression?" (Benedict in Mead 1966:130).

She would ask this question again, after she had been married for several years. For in June 1914 Ruth Fulton made the choice about which she had formerly felt ambivalent, and married Stanley Benedict. A diary entry records her immense joy at the decision, suggesting relief at having come to an end of debate. Less than a year later she knew that love had not silenced questions about herself, and she turned back to journal and poetry to search for an answer. A new subject dominates these writings, as Ruth Benedict tried to gauge the extent to which she associated happiness as a wife with being a mother. Did a marriage need children, she asked, in order fully to satisfy a woman? Was the failure to have children at the root of her growing dissatisfaction? The Benedicts' inability to have children had a biological basis, if a distinction between that and psychic resistance holds. Ruth Benedict had learned to anticipate self-satisfaction from loving another, and looked at her unhappiness within that cultural framework.

She observed, too, her husband's contentment with his life, and thought in terms of finding an equivalent for herself. For a woman, the assumed equivalent of a man's commitment to a career lay in being a wife and eventually a mother. But even before Ruth Benedict gave up hoping for children she suspected that factors in her temperament militated against that obvious answer. She was attracted by Stanley Benedict's world of work and colleagues, and her husband's commitment reminded Ruth of what she envied in her father's life. Both men were research scientists, with the opportunity to make an achievement recognized by the world. Unable easily to relinquish her desire for children, Ruth Benedict tried to merge two ambitions and to convince herself that to be satisfied as a mother she needed another task as well. "I must have my world, too, my outlet, my chance to put forth my effort" (Benedict in Mead 1966:136). She had followed her mother's pattern in the outer form of her life, but resisted the emotional commitment her mother made. Vassar had fostered the idea that childrearing was a proper end for educated women, and Ruth Benedict had long questioned that social offering. When she undertook a new project, in the early years of her marriage, she discovered just how pervasive this exalting of wife and motherhood was.

Turning back to books and writing as a way of understanding herself, Ruth Benedict decided in 1914 to study the ways women in other times had accommodated to society's demands and restrictions. She picked three women she knew had confronted their restlessness in its relation to social conventions — Mary Wollstonecraft, Margaret Fuller, and Olive Schreiner — but completed only the first essay. What she knew about writing poetry she now learned about writing biography, that without a response her debates about identity turned fruitlessly in upon themselves. Whether or not she called her focus a masculine one, the writer increasingly needed an external, unbiased reaction to her work. Because she decided that communication was an essential part of judging this endeavor, Benedict wanted promise of publication for the essays before she finished them (see letters in Mead 1966).

In addition, the specific content of her material on Wollstonecraft stirred up rather than settled questions about women's roles and rewards. Benedict had responded initially to Wollstonecraft's feminism because it did not reject domesticity to demand battle on a barricade. In her interpretation of the eighteenth century woman she reached the conclusion that

Mary Wollstonecraft's passion for Gilbert Imlay and her preoccupation with their baby girl finally distracted the woman from the principle that guided her life. Out of disillusion with her subject the biographer learned for herself the value of building one's life upon a firm integrating idea. Ruth Benedict put the many drafts of her manuscript away, absorbed once again in her own dilemma.

The difficulties of these years, and the collapse of the Benedicts' marriage, took place against a background of turmoil. World War I severely disrupted ordinary patterns of life and for Ruth Benedict challenged the worth of her activities. During these years Stanley Benedict did research in connection with the war effort, and his wife contrasted this to her own charity work in a Westchester suburb, finding the latter ludicrous. Nor did writing poetry satisfy her urge to contribute to the course of external events. Ruth Benedict had not, however, lost her sense that education ultimately promised possibilities of change, though she doubted the use of traditional education. Years in all-girls' schools raised questions about the relevance of classroom learning to the actualities of a woman's life. A book on three feminists raised similar questions, since its audience probably already sympathized with that mode of adjustment. Benedict increasingly saw the issue in terms of the patterns of reward by which society encouraged individual adaptation. To gain insight into this process, Benedict realized that she had to know about the variety of ways, in different times and places, individuals learn to behave in assigned roles and to display culturally appropriate attitudes.

In 1919, unable to justify her previous projects and wanting just to do something, Ruth Benedict enrolled in two courses at the New School for Social Research. In 1946, with the wisdom of hindsight, she wrote that World War I determined her choice of anthropology.[2] The war, she said, convinced her of the need to pay attention to national character differences. The superficial analysis of nearly 30 years later belies the complexity of Ruth Benedict's motivation. Even at the time she made the choice Benedict

[2] The statement was part of a biographical sketch written for the American Association of University Women (Letter in Ruth Fulton Benedict Papers, Vassar College).

After Ruth Benedict's death in 1948, her papers were deposited in the Vassar College Special Collections Library. Eleven boxes are open to scholarly use; in addition there are two boxes of notes on mythologies, and two more boxes which are closed until 1984. The eleven available boxes contain extensive correspondence to and from Ruth Benedict, drafts and manuscripts, notes for books, articles, and lectures, unpublished poetry, journal pages, and a variety of other miscellaneous material (e.g. scrapbooks, book reviews, datebooks). I have consulted the papers to make use of documents Margaret Mead either did not publish or did not emphasize in her interpretation in *An anthropologist at work*. My use of these materials in interpretation and comment throughout this piece should be apparent.

did not realize its complicated connections to past preoccupations, nor could she predict the impact the subject would have on her future. She needed something to do, the admission policy of the New School was liberal, and anthropology presented an attractive program. Ruth Benedict discovered almost by chance an initiation into adulthood that brought together both unconscious and conscious long-standing concerns.

As a child Ruth Fulton had sensed her failure to fit into roles thought appropriate to her sex and time. As she matured, the woman made her intuitive insight part of a conscious intellectual stance on individualism within a society. Ruth Benedict knew, by the time she went to Vassar in 1905, that hers was not a radical temperament and that she could not easily embrace the violent overthrow of conventions. She left political activism to those temperamentally equipped for the struggles of power, and sharpened her analytical approach to the question of stereotyped roles. Her answer would be the liberal one of adjustment, not violation of expected behavior patterns. She brought into anthropology a personal dissatisfaction with women's roles in American society and from this perspective studied the relationship of any individual to surrounding institutions. Does the pattern set by society affect all individuals the way she saw it affecting herself and the women she knew? The sexual distinctions began to fade as Ruth Benedict realized the enormity of the question she had formulated.

Benedict's teachers at the New School were Elsie Clews Parsons and Alexander Goldenweiser, and with them she learned two very different anthropologies. Dr. Parsons' dry and distant attitude toward her subject overlay what had essentially been a personal conversion (Kroeber 1943: 252–255). Discovery of anthropology was unexpected, in some ways tangential to the main thrust of this woman's career. A sociologist by profession, Mrs. Parsons became intrigued, on a vacation with her husband, by the Pueblo Indians of the American southwest (she was near 40, and had received her doctorate from Columbia University over a decade earlier). The reasons for this fascination would appeal to her student Ruth Benedict, since it depended upon insight into the delicate and diverse ways children learn defined behavior roles. Behind this lay a deeper, and not explicitly announced, awareness that knowledge of varying patterns of socialization offered a woman a way of controlling responses to her own culture.

Alexander Goldenweiser was a Russian-Jewish immigrant who felt himself to be on the fringes of American society. Judging from what she wrote about him later, and about Sapir and Boas, Benedict detected an analogy between their marginality and that of American women in general. She explicitly suggested the effect of marginality on the anthropological work of Sapir and Boas, and suspected that the relationship held for her earlier teachers. Benedict had wisely, if fortuitously, entered a profession which gave scope to the interaction between personal and academic choices. Goldenweiser differed from Parsons in intellect and personality, as with impulsive and imaginative leaps he swept from tribe to tribe, making bold assumptions about interconnections (Mead 1966:8). As a student of both, Benedict looked again at the sexual stereotypes established in her own society, which she had accepted and used to characterize temperament. The implications of an earlier dichotomy broadened.

To add to her appreciation of what she learned came acknowledgement of her achievement as a student. Both Goldenweiser and Parsons suggested she do advanced work in anthropology, and they persuaded Boas to accept her into Columbia's Ph.D. program. Parsons gave her student encouragement in another way as well. In the older woman Benedict met someone who had molded her life around a conscious commitment and who, in her strength, encouraged others not necessarily to follow in her footsteps but to find a commitment of their own. Bertrice Fulton had seemed to her daughter to have been pulled along by external forces, in the early death of her husband and in the measures she took to rebuild her life after that. Ruth struggled to gauge the inevitability of choices for women and at 25, in Pasadena, found an alternative in the way her headmistress had assessed the limitations of her life and accepted, open-eyed, the compromises it demanded. "You have much to expect of life," Miss Orton told Ruth Fulton in 1912, as she advised the young woman to leave teaching for a life that held promise of purpose and contentment (Mead 1966:128).

In 1921 Ruth Benedict became a student of Franz Boas. She was not his first female student, and until World War II nearly half of Columbia University's anthropology degrees went to women (22 of 51, 1901–1939; see Thomas 1955:703–705). Boas virtually controlled entrance to the anthropology program and he welcomed women students; in the field they could get information denied to men and often, importantly, they did not need the financial support and economic certainty that men did. Between Boas and Benedict there developed a mutual dependency and intellectual exchange that lasted until his death in 1942. The emotional tie was as important to Benedict as the academic, and kept her from chafing as other students did under the patronizing dominance of "Papa Franz."

What Boas asked her to do academically suited her temperamentally. For their dissertations most of his students in that decade traced the spread of a trait from culture to culture. Ruth Benedict studied the diffu-

sion of the spirit quest among North American Indian tribes. Her dissertation, *The concept of the guardian spirit in North America* (*AAA Memoir
29*, 1923), is workmanlike, thorough, and an acknowledged contribution
to the discipline. Underneath the writer's presentation of new material
lay a private concern with the meaning of adulthood in society. The
merging of social with religious rites in the Indian quest particularly
appealed to Benedict, to the woman who as a child tested the comforts of
religious mysticism and as a poet tried the significances of personal vision.
In Plains culture the men sought visions, and finding a vision equipped
them for an adult role. A symbolic, emotional experience brought with it
the achievement of mature status as defined by their society. The relationship between an individual's private revelation and social recognition
belonged to Ruth Benedict's oldest debates about her own life.

After reading her dissertation Edward Sapir wrote to Benedict, "Let
me congratulate you on having produced a very fine piece of research"
(Sapir in Mead 1966:49). The compliment was important to a woman who
needed external appreciation for her endeavors, and the letter initiated a
friendship that had long-lasting effects. Sapir, Benedict discovered, was
an anthropologist whose heart in some ways, for some years, belonged to
poetry. The correspondence and conversation begun for professional
reasons in the spring of 1922 revealed other personal affinities. The two
realized that they shared a sense of being out of tune with existing American conventions, Sapir because he felt his German-Jewish background and
Benedict because she knew the disadvantages to a woman of wanting
more than marriage and family. Both sought in poetry, and in anthropology, not an escape from individual discomfort, but a route towards
expanding the individual statement into one of universal significance.

As poets they knew the importance of symbolic structures for bridging
gaps between the known and the unknown, in oneself and in one's world.
Long before, as a student at Vassar (in 1909), Benedict had written: "Man
is always reaching out beyond the world he sees and hears.... Yet the
tools man works with are only crude, and this world of aspirations and
ideals demands perfection, and so there must necessarily remain much
that transcends the thought and language of man. It is with the sense of
this limitation that he has fashioned symbols" (Benedict in Mead 1966:
113). Sapir, like Benedict herself, refined and developed this idea through
his anthropology and his poetry. He moved more quickly than Benedict
into analyzing the impact of unconscious motive upon social forms.
Benedict's investigation into the psychic underpinnings of symbolic structures, in an individual and a society, came later, and meshed then with her
own full appreciation of the function of formal ritual for dealing with

potentially disruptive ambiguities. Benedict looked closely at the psychic roots of social conventions only after she made peace with her role as a woman in twentieth-century American society.

In 1922 Margaret Mead decided to study anthropology at Columbia (Mead 1972:115). Her subsequent importance to Ruth Benedict goes well beyond the credit that redounds to a teacher from an outstanding student, though Benedict certainly appreciated the justification of her work provided by a responsive student. The slight stammer and awkwardness that marred Benedict's classroom performance disappeared after a while from private conversation, and there she defended her ideas candidly and carefully. She had consistently doubted the value of isolated soul-searching, associating it with the fear of facing the world she believed women had been trained in. Margaret Mead brought the private searching of poetry into the open (she, too, wrote poetry during the 1920's). She convinced Ruth Benedict that poetry was work, and work to be done well involved discussions with others. In a group of poets and anthropologists Benedict learned that her way of encountering confusion was shared by others. She found colleagues, like those she had envied Stanley Benedict, and talked with them of dilemmas she had once debated privately, thus discovering affirmation of her own quest.

Benedict's attitude toward writing poetry changed. The change shows in the poetry itself, in a surer use of private metaphor to communicate meaning. Letters to Sapir, written at the same time as the poetry, reinforce the impression that during the 1920's Benedict gradually learned the place of poetry in her life as a woman. She found a way of accepting her culture's cliché that women are naturally intuitive and introspective. When introspection led to effective participation in a world outside of self, qualities which Ruth Benedict had divided because the division seemed obvious biologically and culturally, now came together. She had made a separation into feminine and masculine to reject the first, and she had defined worth in terms of the second. But the more she confronted the world, the less could she preserve these early dualisms. Benedict did not totally replace one perspective with another; rather, she learned to accept the ambiguities of identity as essential to individual growth and membership within a society. Increased anthropological knowledge intertwined with confidence in her own insights, providing a personal integration that had public impact.

As confidence in herself as a professional woman grew, Benedict moved physically and psychically away from her husband. The movement began in their first years of marriage, and throughout the 1920's Ruth Benedict felt real despair at her inability to communicate with Stanley Benedict.

She had, at that time, few close friends with whom to discuss the significance of love, marriage, and children (datebooks in the Vassar collection show increased contacts were another benefit of anthropology courses). The pessimistic conclusions she reached in her journal about motherhood were based on her own unhappiness and on observations of the women in her family. Being a daughter and not a mother shaped her analysis of the role, and she talked of how intense maternal concentration threatened equally the child and the mother. Such women ended up living a daughter's life vicariously, pressuring the child to succeed where the mother failed. "No, it is wisdom in motherhood as in wifehood to have one's own individual world of effort and creation" (Benedict in Mead 1966:136). To assume that a marriage with love and children would have completely satisfied Ruth Benedict is to disregard the insights she gained into the complex definitions of that role in American society.

With her students Ruth Benedict found an ideal motherhood. Although many of those she taught at Columbia and Barnard were women, she did not have the sense of futility she had in California when what was taught in the classroom had little effect outside it. Again, the evidence is implicit, in the number of years Benedict taught anthropology and in the students she influenced. To teach anthropology, Benedict added her experiences to a theoretical statement of the flexibilities inherent in social processes. Through the unspoken example of integration in her own life she came closer to the goal she had set for education: to teach individuals how to test their own capacities for self-realization. Not simply a matter of persuading students to read and learn from reading (she enjoyed that in Pasadena) Benedict discovered in anthropology that teaching effects rearrangements in the interaction between an individual and a culture.

Throughout the 1920's and 1930's, as Benedict came to know and be known by students, her appearance changed. Sensitive to the donning of masks in life and in art, she would not have denied the significance of the way a woman presents herself to the world. When Mead first saw her in the classroom, Benedict wore a grey dress, and all changes in clothes were rung on the same theme. With professional confidence she feared less that caring about looks proved her female vanity. She relaxed, and her beauty flourished. Mead comments on this, dating one change at 1926. After a summer of particular difficulty with Stanley Benedict, Ruth Benedict cut her hair, recreating an old beauty as she symbolically announced self-assertion (Mead 1972:163). When one today asks former students and colleagues about Ruth Benedict, practically all mention her appearance. Most comment on her beauty, all on her delicacy and femininity. She never, as these people remember, lost the gracious manners and tone of a well-bred woman. The deafness fit in, too, with Benedict's changing presence in the world. The defect that had driven the small girl into awkward escapes from conversation and contact became, in the woman, a mode of intense listening. She learned to lip-read, and the intensity with which she studied people's faces gave them a gratification which she realized in their reciprocal friendship. The courtesy, the sensitive attention to another's spoken and implied attitudes, were qualities Ruth Benedict placed under the rubric of feminine. Strengthened in a world of masculine achievement, she relaxed the strictures on qualities she had, in self-doubt, allocated to one sex and rejected.

In 1934, after fifteen years of studying and teaching anthropology, Ruth Benedict published *Patterns of culture*. The book, I think, marked a turning point in her career and in her life analogous to the first field trip for other anthropologists. It tied together various threads of past thoughts and goals in what it said and in what it achieved in an external context. Only after she published the book and announced her commitment to a guiding principle could Benedict go on to achieve what she did in anthropology.

For one thing, Benedict cared about publication. She did not write poetry, or the three biographical essays, for herself as sole audience, and the need to communicate remained a vital part of her self-conception. Writing was essentially an educative process for Ruth Benedict, and she dismissed the idea that one could learn about oneself without learning about and influencing others. The embracing of this idea, she felt, had long given women a false sense of accomplishment. She knew that learning meant interacting with one's world, or education became futile for both the teacher and the student. If she could not utilize this faith in bringing up her own children, she could apply it in the classroom and in the books she wrote.

Ruth Benedict wanted *Patterns of culture* to reach a wide audience. Her letters to the publishers include suggestions about format, type, and color to make the book as attractive as possible. She also planned its content to appeal to a lay as well as a professional audience, and presented anthropological data in vividly balanced prose. The poet guided the scientist, a joining of forces symbolized in the title itself. Benedict chose the word "patterns" purposefully, rejecting other possibilities such as "configurations." "Patterns" was a good anthropological word (Sapir used it in his 1922 letter to her, describing the logical sequel to her dissertation: Mead 1966:49), and Ruth Benedict cared for a poem by Amy Lowell called "Patterns." In Lowell's piece, a woman in stiff brocade walks through a formal garden, hating the patterns that restrict but dreading the chaos if safe structures collapse. Lowell's ambivalent vision of boundaries resembled Anne Singleton's, and Lowell's poem ends with natural impulse beaten down by society.

Benedict, in her book, extended the poet's perception of inevitable tension between individual impulse and social control to reveal its constructive side. The anthropologist moved beyond the hostility expressed by Lowell's female persona in this poem to show that the very patterns which are on one face restrictive, on another provide the material for self-development. Each culture chooses, Benedict went on to explain, a dominant pattern of behavior and attitude. Each individual takes his cues from this pattern and molds his life accordingly: "His culture provides the raw material of which the individual makes his life" (Benedict 1959 [1934]: 252). In responding to and building on the traditions of his culture, an individual discovers the only viable path to maturity.

Benedict introduced a secondary concept in *Patterns of culture*. Again turning to literature, she adopted from Nietzsche's *Birth of tragedy* the contrast between Apollonian and Dionysian. The Dionysian breaks through ordinary bounds to attain most valued moments; the Apollonian "knows but one law, measure in the Hellenic sense" (Nietzsche in Benedict 1959 [1934]: 79). Benedict had admired Nietzsche before she welcomed his description of contrasting types as bearing directly upon her own concern with social control and individual impulse. As a dramatic metaphor the antithesis between Apollonian and Dionysian has value, but in applying the terminology to three different cultures in her book Benedict discovered its inadequacy. She ended up, in fact, depending more upon psychoanalytic than on literary terms, and characterized the Dobu as paranoiac, the Kwakiutl as megalomaniac. Only the Zuni remained quietly Apollonian. The concept used by Nietzsche did convey a general tone, plausibly of Zuñi culture, and though Ruth Benedict praised where he condemned, Nietzsche's "fine phrase" gave the anthropologist a way of integrating the formless data of field notes.

The phrases Benedict used, however, confused some of her readers. She saw both the value and the limitation of a symbolic framework for conveying complex ideas. A metaphor served in communication only if its limits were recognized, and Benedict assumed her readers shared her sensitivity to accepted fictions. In *Patterns of culture* she briefly defended the use of an image or analogy which "brings to the fore the major qualities" that differentiate one thing from another, without the confusion of detail (Benedict 1959 [1934]: 79). The risk in her aim to merge art with social science was that the scientist would not tolerate art's demand for selection and distortion, and that the lay reader would not look behind art's description to the underlying reality.

Anthropologists, since 1934 when the book came out, have challenged Benedict's concept of "patterns," and the accuracy of her characterizations of Dobu, Zuñi, and Kwatiutl cultures. The anthropological debate, constantly altered by the accumulation of data and the adoption of new techniques, has led to more precise definition of "pattern" and related terms. Benedict introduced a metaphor to clarify her insight into the way individual behavior takes its cues from cultural institutions, and ramifications of both word and theory have echoed through anthropology. Students and non-students, admirers and critics, use Benedict's descriptive concept as the basis for investigating, from manifold points of view, the interaction between individual behavior and cultural norms.

Benedict appreciated the book's general popularity as much as its contribution to her discipline. *Patterns of culture* sold well, was translated, and was reissued in numerous paperback editions (including a 25-cent one right after World War II). She had written it with great care, editing her prose with fine literary skill (as she edited the dissertations of her students, enlivening for them page after page of ethnographic material). She wanted people to enjoy reading the book, and to take its lessons willingly. These lessons had particular relevance to an America suffering through a severe economic depression and on the brink of a Second World War. In doubt and uncertainty about the running of their own society, readers looked to other ways of managing life. But the lesson Benedict taught had a focus beyond the situation in a specific country at a specific time. She spoke to all individuals who questioned their relationship to society and the degree to which society molded their behavior and attitudes. As a woman, she had known the limitations placed, explicitly and implicitly, on what she could do in life. From that perspective, she looked at any individual who felt his private needs sharply out of tune with external demands. The book was in no sense a plea for women's rights — none of Benedict's work fits that description. It was a plea for the tolerance of differences, from a woman who felt keenly her own differences from the major trends in her society.

Patterns of culture was also a plea for utilizing the insights into how different personalities are formed. By outlining several ways in which a culture determines the nature of individual growth, Benedict implicitly suggested ways of adjusting the patterns to incorporate greater diversity. She had learned, with despair in studying literature and with optimism as an anthropologist, that education could bring about a new approach to the world. This meant knowing oneself and one's world, and discovering an ideally productive relationship between the two.

Anthropology, combining for Benedict the insights of literature with the findings of a science, taught her about the existence of disparate strains in her own temperament. What she had first observed in Parsons and Goldenweiser — that personality configurations determined the work they did in anthropology — became true of her own relationship to the career she had chosen. Her solution came about on several levels, for as she learned about the relationship of masculine to feminine in her character, she found both sides gratified in her career. If publication and publicity represented the masculine, Benedict had achieved that with a contribution to science; she had proved at the same time that a woman's self-expression did not crumble on confronting the world.

In 1947 Ruth Fulton Benedict gave her farewell speech to the American Anthropological Association. For what would be one of her last public statements, she summarized the ways in which anthropology integrated personal ambivalences, and suggested a road the discipline could take in the future. Santayana, she said, first introduced her to anthropological ways of thinking, and his work can still guide young anthropologists. But Santayana had been important to Benedict beyond his studies of cultural diversity. As a student at Vassar she read his *Life of reason* (published in 1905 when she was a freshman). Then, through the early painful years of her marriage, she referred back to passages in the book to clarify her thoughts about the meaning of love and parenthood in an individual's life. Finally, in 1947, as a successful anthropologist and a contented woman she took a new lesson from *The life of reason*. She had learned through private struggle and professional striving to appreciate the philosopher's thesis that an individual acts not in opposition to society but in interdependence with its institutions (Benedict in Mead 1966:466). She came to share his position that the creative and original personality must build on the traditions provided by his culture, and that harmony in any individual results from an acceptance of temperament and situation. "This natural harmony," she quoted from Santayana, "between the spirit and its conditions is the only actual one; it is the source of every ideal and the sole justification of any hope" (Mead 1966:466).

Ruth Benedict's life shows a temperament achieving harmony with itself and with its world. This woman came to self-realization within a setting that seemed to deny her spirit its proper expression. Through first looking closely at herself in poetry and journals, next through the study of women in other periods, and finally in a fortuitously ideal career, Ruth Benedict found that her spirit could flourish in the bounds established by her culture. When she encountered anthropology in 1919, at 32, she immediately realized part of its significance to her. The subject bore upon her enduring intellectual preoccupation with the differences among individuals and how they responded to social patterns. Anthropology also brought Benedict's temperamental dilemma into the open, balancing personal against academic insights, and the desire for achievement against the search for contentment. In unifying the feminine, the intuitive and private quest, with the masculine, the desire to make an achievement the world would acknowledge, anthropology provided the foundation for personal satisfaction and gained an invaluable disciple.

For the conflict that had remained unresolved in poetry, in marriage, and in her studies of other women, Benedict found a resolution in 1934 with the publication of *Patterns of culture*. From then until her death in 1948, Benedict taught vast numbers of people about the different ways of living within a pattern: the lesson of her own successful accommodation.

REFERENCES

BENEDICT, RUTH FULTON
  1923   *The concept of the guardian spirit in North America.* Memoirs of the American Anthropological Association 29:1–97.
  1959   [1934] *Patterns of culture.* Boston: Houghton Mifflin.
BENEDICT PAPERS
  n.d.   *Ruth Fulton Benedict papers.* Vassar College Special Collections Library.
KROEBER, ALFRED L.
  1943   Elsie Clews Parsons. *American Anthropologist* n.s. 45:252–255.
MacCRACKEN, HENRY NOBLE
  1950   *The hickory limb.* New York: Scribner and Sons.
MEAD, MARGARET
  1966   *An anthropologist at work: writings of Ruth Benedict* (Atheling edition). New York: Atherton Press. (Originally published 1959.)
  1972   *Blackberry winter: my earlier years.* New York: William Morrow.
SPIER, LESLIE
  1943   Elsie Clews Parsons. *American Anthropologist* n.s. 45:244–251.
THOMAS, WILLIAM L. *editor*
  1955   *Yearbook of anthropology.* New York: Wenner-Gren Foundation for Anthropological Research.

Typological Realism in A. L. Kroeber's Theory of Culture

TIMOTHY H. H. THORESEN

My contention in this paper is that A. L. Kroeber's theory of culture derived logically from his assumptions about perception and from his understanding of the practical implications of those assumptions, his methodology. By methodology I mean something closer to the philosophy of science than to the exercise of technical skills, and Kroeber's best single statement of methodology is to be found in his 1935 paper, "History and science in anthropology." What follows here is a synthesis based on that 1935 paper. It is intended to be only suggestive, a preliminary mapping out of some thoughts which will be more fully explored and documented in a larger work.

The key element in Kroeber's discussion of "history "and "science" in anthropology was his conviction that ultimately social-cultural-historical phenomena cannot be completely explained within a behavioristic psychology that treats the human mind as a passive receptor and transmitter of sense impressions. Kroeber admitted the difficulty of even discussing something called the human mind, but, he insisted, "it remains a factor in our basic task none the less" (Kroeber 1935:566). The implications of this factor were never developed. Presumably it would enter into the exercise

A number of the ideas suggested in this essay require much fuller exposition and supporting documentation than was possible to present here. The interested reader should refer to the very useful obituaries by Steward (1961), Hymes (1961), and Rowe (1962), to the biographical studies by Theodora Kroeber (1970) and Steward (1973), and to my analysis in my dissertation (Thoresen 1971). Relevant bibliographies are included in each of these, with the most complete in Steward (1961). The larger work in preparation will be a book-length interpretation of A. L. Kroeber's anthropology.

For their criticisms of earlier versions of this essay, I wish to thank Ilse Bulhof, Loris Essary, Dickson Pratt, Alice Thoresen, and Alexander Vucinich.

of both history and science, and scattered through Kroeber's early papers is the word "apperception" with various referents indicating its application to the perceptual process in general.

Apperception as a refracting link between percepts and concepts, however, had special application to Kroeber's understanding of historical method. Contrasting history and science as synthetic and analytic respectively, he found historical activity as "essentially a procedure of integrating phenomena as such." The issue was the old problem of reductionism, that of "dissolving phenomena in order to convert them into process formulations" (Kroeber 1935:546). For both history and science, however, Kroeber recognized a distinction between method and material. History was not characterized by anything intrinsic to the historical data — such as temporal sequence — but by a stance or strategy taken by the historian. History and science were therefore two kinds of mental activities, or more properly, similar mental activities which sought different end products. "Nature," the thing itself, remained unchanged under either treatment; while the result of history was a statement of pattern, the result of science was a statement of process. Importantly, statements of pattern and statements of process seem for Kroeber not to have been logically or hierarchically related; one did not lead to the other since they were fundamentally different kinds of statements. Process statements were fragmenting. They entailed a selective re-ordering of perceived phenomena in accord with some set of criteria nct intrinsic to the perceived situation. For purposes of comparison and measurement some kind of classificatory grid, paradigm, or taxonomy was imposed on the phenomena. In contrast, pattern statements were descriptive reintegrations of a body of phenomena presumably or hopefully in terms of the discovered order found within the phenomena. Furthermore, there was no single prescribed principle of order to be used. Several were always to be found, and with reference to cultural material the historian or anthropologist could just as validly present descriptively synthetic statements of spatial order as of temporal order. Such statements would necessarily be "in their essence subjective findings;" at best would "only approximate truth or certainty" (Kroeber 1935:547). Nevertheless, neither historical nor scientific statements were more true or false than the other. Rather, both were subject to the accuracy with which they dealt with their respective phenomena, and neither ever dealt with all the phenomena of a given situation. There was always the matter of selection and the selective criteria.

Kroeber's distinction between history and science could therefore be loosely phrased in terms of the Aristotelian contrast between specific and general. Certainly Kroeber's stated emphasis on the historiographical

principles of continuity and uniqueness implied more than mere direction
of interest. History's concern with differences contrasted with science's
concern with similarities. But the distinction again requires the word
stance or strategy. The historian in effect created his subject. Not arbitrarily, of course, but the conceptual bounds of the subject were not fixed by
the subject itself. Any given set of phenomena could be integrated into
various patterns, and into several simultaneously. Thus, in several papers
published in the early 1920's, Kroeber could write without self-contra-
diction, of Yurok culture, Northwest culture, American culture, and
ultimately of civilization as a whole. Yet, there was no logical subordination in this expansion of temporal and spatial parameters. BOTH principles
— uniqueness and continuity — were implied, while any latent contradiction between these principles was resolved in terms of point of view. Between the individual psyche and that complex whole called culture or
civilization there were no "natural" units. Laws of culture, as Kroeber
repeatedly insisted, would be laws of psychology. Obviously the same laws
would hold in the study of culture itself.

Nevertheless, Kroeber also insisted that the apperceived patterning in
cultural phenomena was neither arbitrary nor accidental. Hence the title
phrase for this essay: typological realism. The apperception of cultural or
historical patterns was highly analogous to "those biological activities
covered by the old term 'natural history'" (Kroeber 1935:546). Processes
such as "convergence, degeneration, areal grouping" were to be found in
both natural and cultural history, and Kroeber seems to have understood
the conceptual bases of both as essentially similar. That raised the species
problem. Kroeber's resolution was offered in the context of his work on
the history of American Indian languages in the 1910's. He had stated that
while there was probably no such entity as a biological species from a
philosophical, that is, ontic, consideration, "species" was nevertheless a
useful conceptual tool which allowed inferences of both order and change.
The application to language stocks and groupings was direct (see Kroeber
1913). The wider application to civilization was implicitly genetic and
uniformitarian, and always with reference to civilization as a whole.
Culture units were therefore necessarily arbitrary and yet not so arbitrary.
They were constructs — types — which more or less fit the situation and
the phenomena. Most significantly, the truth of any given descriptive integration of that phenomenon—such as a culture—was not to be measured
by the criterion of certainty but by that of consensus, as in a rather neat
equivocation Kroeber exposed the heart of his method: historical deter-
minations "differ from one another in seeming more or less probably true,
the criterion being the degree of completeness with which a historical

interpretation fits into the totality of phenomena; or if one likes, into the totality of historical INTERPRETATIONS of phenomena." (Kroeber 1935:547. Emphasis added.)

The working out of these several ideas was spread through several decades. Given the overall orientation, Kroeber's statement in 1952 that theory was for him always a by-product is quite understandable (see Kroeber 1952:3). His was not an analytic imagination. That is no reflection on his acute sense of theoretical problem but rather an observation that when given a theoretical problem, Kroeber was prone to use a particular set of conceptual tools in attempting its resolution. Those tools were indicated as early as his doctoral dissertation, about which he once suggested that it "foreshadowed" his basic theory of culture (Kroeber 1952: 12). The larger context into which that dissertation fit was a widespread concern for determining the origins of cultural phenomena, and in the 1890's one of the cultural domains in which origins were most actively sought was primitive art. On the basis of his work among the Arapaho (see Kroeber 1901), Kroeber registered a protest against that search in two forms. One was that on the basis of his own field work he had not found any consistent, meaningful system of symbolism among the Plains Indians that would substantiate the assumptions regarding the evolution of mind as held by his predecessors working for the Bureau of American Ethnology (compare Mooney 1903). His second protest was logical although it too grew out of his field methods and his implicit documentation of style areas. He argued that the search for origins was a search for specific or efficient causes, and that not only did his data not allow an isolation of efficient causes, but more generally such an isolation was not the proper business of an anthropologist. Instead, he affirmed the need for the study of culture as a whole, the only "organic" unit. Parts could be known only in terms of the contextual and historical whole. Determination of efficient causes for cultural phenomena without reference to the cultural whole was, he believed, logically absurd.

Alternatively to the search for cultural origins, Kroeber's research strategy — the documentation of style areas and the determination of cultural tendencies, an imprecise word that in context seems to have meant something similar to both trends and functions — became the basis of his work in California even before he had completed his doctorate. With the establishment of the Department of Anthropology in the University of California in 1901, and soon thereafter the Archaeological and Ethnological Survey of California in 1903, the professional, although at times financially precarious, nature of Kroeber's researches was apparent. Initially the work was quite literally a mapping of the territory, a task which was first evident in language studies and the bounding of language areas (see Dixon and Kroeber 1903). With reference to both language and culture traits the effort was simply taxonomic, while the chief analytic problem was assessing the influence of the natural environment. Significantly, environment proved to be a variable of the same order as those considered in the art question, and was rejected as a determining efficient cause. Alternatively, the distribution of both language and culture traits patterned non-randomly with the result that Kroeber found himself documenting "types" of culture which had only a rough correlation with natural (usually drainage) areas of land surface (see Kroeber 1904). Analytically, California ethnology lent itself to a methodological orientation derived from a combination of Kroeber's studies in biology and literature, that is, a natural history approach to classification and a phenomenological emphasis on description and apperceptive response. The central conceptual tool in the actual ordering of culture traits was what Kroeber called "type."

The significance of Kroeber's typological approach was compounded about 1908 or 1909 when he overtly introduced a time perspective into his studies. He had of course always recognized the temporal dimension of his material but had in effect suppressed its importance for lack of an adequate conceptual frame. But, toward the end of Kroeber's first decade in California, Nels Nelson, then an undergraduate under Kroeber, reopened the temporal questions in California archeology when he essentially confirmed Max Uhle's chronologic inferences from seriation studies. Uhle's work had demonstrated that cultural phenomena patterned by type through both space and time; proper attention to the patterning allowed temporal inferences. A few years later in the study of American Indian languages, Edward Sapir began pushing forward the dynamic element latent when both grammar and lexicon were used in contructing a taxonomy of languages. Degrees of linguistic similarity were a strong indication of degrees of descent. Archeology and linguistics thus provided the missing rationale for a genuinely historical approach to ethnology. The methods of both were based on typological or natural history ordering and the conversion of synchronic taxonomies into diachronic inferences of genetic relations among the taxons. The extension of the inferential logic to ethnological data was only methodologically appropriate in the effort to recover the unrecorded history of aboriginal America.

The results of Kroeber's areal-typological methods began to appear by the end of the 1910's in a number of superficially different but essentially similar studies, all of which Kroeber would have called culture history: California kinship (Kroeber 1917a) and languages (Dixon and Kroeber 1919), Zuñi pottery seriation (Kroeber 1916a, 1916b) and social organization (Kroeber 1917c), pattern in dress fashion change (Kroeber 1919), *Anthropology* (Kroeber 1923), and the *Handbook of the Indians of California* (Kroeber 1925 [completed in 1917]). By 1920 the method had crystallized, and the rest of Kroeber's distinguished career was spent in at times almost a playful trying out of variations and extensions of his basic conceptual tools. The California Culture Element Distribution Survey of the 1930's and Kroeber's several papers on statistical method from the same period reveal his implicit understanding of his analytic units as constructs, while he also indicated his assumption that the data themselves — the brute facts — were irrefutable and that their patterning was therefore meaningful (for example, see Kroeber 1934, 1940, and Kroeber and Chretien 1937). The meaning of such meaning remained something of a problem, however. Earlier he had presented his *Handbook* as a "history," intended to reconstruct and present the "scheme" within which the aboriginal Californians had lived their lives. His method was to overlay trait distributions and to correlate trait complexes into centers or "hearths." Throughout, he assumed that somehow the discovered patterns among the cultural phenomena were meaningful both cognitively and affectively to the culture bearers under study. How, or why, was a matter for the psychologists. Pending such study, Kroeber operated with an elusive *als ob*: although he had discovered, constructed, or integrated the observed phenomena from a necessarily "etic" point of view, the resultant patterns could be treated AS IF they were truly meaningful to the observed ethnic groups.

That *als ob* is the key to Kroeber's "Superorganic"(see Kroeber 1917b) as well as to his *Configurations of culture growth* of over two decades later (Kroeber 1944). Significantly, the patterns surveyed in that 1944 book were derived almost wholly from secondary sources, from consensus. Nevertheless, given such consensus the discovered patterns were real enough, and the pattern idea became the basis for much of Kroeber's discussion of the nature of culture in his well-known textbook (see Kroeber 1948, especially Chapter 7). There he emphasized several of the points brought out above: the continuity of culture as a whole, the validity of using the term culture for units less than the whole, the distinctness of culture from psychology, the importance of recognizing culture as a product of mental activity. His various metaphors tended strongly toward motion and change: the stream of mental activity, or the growth of culture. Conceived in such terms, the pattern was perceived as such only by the historian or anthropologist (compare Bidney 1942, 1944). Yet the final significance of the pattern was the constraint it imposed on thought and activity, on behavior. Consequently, as Kroeber insisted in various papers, it was not merely an abstraction. It was a matter of genuine ideas held by real people with actual consequences. Even though only the anthropologist saw the pattern as a whole, the typological construct behaved as if it were a genuinely autonomous level of reality. At the same time, Kroeber protested, such a "superorganic" had a conceptual but not an ontic reality. This "retraction" of his alleged "reification" of culture late in Kroeber's career (see Kroeber 1952:23), however, is better explained by a changed professional climate of opinion with its new and different questions than by any inconsistency on the part of Kroeber. Kroeber's interest was always in phenomena "as such," as he called the epiphenomenal patterning among the phenomena "culture" and the study of the phenomena "history." The enterprise as a whole was premised on the principle of apperception and the cluster of corollaries that I imply in the phrase, "typological realism."

REFERENCES

BIDNEY, DAVID
    1942   On the philosophy of culture in the social sciences. *The Journal of Philosophy* 39:449–457.
    1944   On the concept of culture and some cultural fallacies. *American Anthropologist* 46:30–44.
DIXON, ROLAND B., ALFRED L. KROEBER
    1903   The native languages of California. *American Anthropologist* 5:1–26.
    1919   Linguistic families of California. *University of California Publications in American Archaeology and Ethnology* 16:47–118.
HYMES, DELL
    1961   Alfred Louis Kroeber. *Language* 37:1–28.
KROEBER, A. L.
    1901   Decorative symbolism of the Arapaho. *American Anthropologist* 3:308–336.
    1904   Types of Indian culture in California. *University of California Publications in American Archaeology and Ethnology* 2:81–103.
    1913   The determination of linguistic relationship. *Anthropos* 8:389–401.
    1916a Zuñi culture sequences. *Proceedings of the National Academy of Sciences*, volume two, 42–45.
    1916b Zuñi potsherds. Anthropological Papers of the American Museum of Natural History 18:1–37.
    1917a California kinship systems. *University of California Publications in American Archaeology and Ethnology* 12:339–396.
    1917b The superorganic. *American Anthropologist* 19:163–213.
    1917c Zuñi kin and clan. *Anthropological Papers of the American Museum of Natural History* 18:39–205.
    1919   On the principle of order in civilization as exemplified by changes of fashion. *American Anthropologist* 21:235–263.

1923   *Anthropology.* New York: Harcourt, Brace.
1925   *Handbook of the Indians of California.* Bureau of American Ethnology Bulletin 78.
1934   Blood-group classification. *American Journal of Physical Anthropology* 18:377–393.
1935   History and science in anthropology. *American Anthropologist* 37:539–569.
1940   Statistical classification. *American Antiquity* 6:29–44.
1944   *Configurations of culture growth.* Berkeley: University of California Press.
1948   *Anthropology* (revised edition). New York: Harcourt, Brace.
1952   *The nature of culture.* Chicago: University of Chicago Press.

KROEBER, A. L., C. D. CHRETIEN
1937   Quantitative classification of Indo-European languages. *Language* 13:83–103.

KROEBER, THEODORA
1970   *Alfred Kroeber: a personal configuration.* Berkeley: University of California Press.

MOONEY, JAMES
1903   Review of *The Arapaho* Part I, by Alfred L. Kroeber. *American Anthropologist* 5:126–130.

ROWE, JOHN HOWLAND
1962   Alfred Louis Kroeber 1876–1960. *American Antiquity* 27:395–415.

STEWARD, JULIAN H.
1961   Alfred Louis Kroeber 1876–1960. *American Anthropologist* 63:1038–1060.
1973   *Alfred Kroeber,* New York: Columbia University Press.

THORESEN, TIMOTHY H. H.
1971   "A. L. Kroeber's theory of culture: the early years." Unpublished doctoral dissertation, University of Iowa.

Biographical Notes

VITOMIR BELAJ (Yugoslavia).   No biographical data available.

ROBERT E. BIEDER (1938–   ) is Associate Director of the Center for the
History of the American Indian at the Newberry Library. He received his
Ph. D. in 1972 from the University of Minnesota in American History and
Anthroplogy with a dissertation on "The American Indian and the
development of anthropological thought in the United States, 1780–
1851." He is currently revising the dissertation for publication. He is a
co-founder and member of the editorial board of *The History of Anthropology Newsletter*. His publications are in history and in the history of
anthropology.

EMILIE DE BRIGARD (1943–   ) was educated at Radcliffe College and the
University of California, Los Angeles. She works as a film consultant and
curator and is currently preparing an illustrated book, *Anthropological
cinema*, for publication by the Museum of Modern Art, New York.

DON D. FOWLER (1936–   ) is Research Professor of Anthropology in
the Desert Research Institute, University of Nevada System, Reno,
Nevada. He received his B. A. from the University of Utah in 1959 and
his Ph. D. in anthropology from the University of Pittsburgh in 1965.
He is also a Research Associate of the Smithsonian Institution. His
publications include works on the history of anthropology, the anthropology of the American West, and the cultural ecology of arid lands.

JACOB W. GRUBER (1921–   ) has taught anthropology at Temple

University, where he is now Professor, since 1948. His academic degrees are from Oberlin College (B.A., M.A.) and the University of Pennsylvania (Ph. D.). Although regarding himself as a general anthropologist, his particular interests are in archeology and in the history of anthropology and the natural sciences of the nineteenth century. As his publications suggest, his primary interest is in the relationship between the products of science and the social matrix from which they emerge.

STEPHEN FORD HOLTZMAN (1937–   ) received his B.S. from the California Institute of Technology in physics, his Ph. D. from the University of California, Berkeley, in anthropology. He has been Assistant Professor at Brandeis University and at Northern Illinois University. His interests are the history of anthropology, fossil man, primate social behavior, and urban anthropology.

JUDITH MODELL (1941–   ) received her B.A. from Vassar College, 1963, with a concentration in English Literature, in which field she received her M.A. from Columbia University in 1965. Having written on Virginia Woolf and Katherine Mansfield as writers of personal documents, she moved to more general interest in women's studies, particularly the role of women professionals. As a graduate student in anthropology at the University of Minnesota, she has concentrated in social anthropology and the history of anthropology, undertaking a dissertation on Ruth Fulton Benedict. She is an editor of *The History of Anthropology Newsletter*.

JANOS NEMESKÉRI (Hungary). No biographical data available.

MICHAEL SOZAN (1938–   ) was born in Budapest. He received his B.A. in sociology from Union College, Schenectady, New York in 1965, an M.A. from Syracuse University in 1968, and his Ph. D. in Anthropology from Syracuse University in 1972. He has been Professor of Anthropology at Slippery Rock State College, Pennsylvania, since 1971. His main field of interest is peasant societies and his publications include works on culture change in peasant societies, the history of East European ethnographic tradition, and other problems of the sociology of knowledge.

GEORGE W. STOCKING, JR. (1928–   ) received his B.A. from Harvard College in 1949, and his Ph. D. in American Civilization from the University of Pennsylvania in 1960. Until 1967, he taught history at the University of California, Berkeley; and since 1968 he has taught history and anthropology at the University of Chicago, where he is now Professor of Anthropology. He is the author of *Race, culture, and evolution: essays in the history of anthropology* (1968); editor of J. C. Prichard's *Researches into the physical history of man* (1973), and also of *The shaping of American anthropology: a Franz Boas reader* (1974) He is currently working on the history of British social anthropology from Tylor to Radcliffe-Brown.

THOMAS G. TAX (1946–   ) studied history at the University of Chicago where he received his B.A. in 1968 and his Ph.D. in 1973. His interests include U.S. social and cultural history and the history of anthropology. He is currently living in Chicago, Illinois.

TIMOTHY H. H. THORESEN (1944–   ) received his B.A. from St. Olaf College in 1966, his M.A. from Purdue University in 1968, and a Ph.D. in American Civilization from the University of Iowa in 1971. He taught Anthropology and American Studies at the University of Texas, Austin, from 1971 to 1974. Currently he is a Research Associate in Anthropology at the University of California, Berkeley, where he is preparing a book-length interpretation of A. L. Kroeber's anthropology and where he is also involved in field research in the anthropology of religion. His special interests include the history of anthropology and the social anthropology of the United States.

LALIT P. VIDYARTHI (1931–   ) received his doctorate from the University of Chicago and is now Professor and Chairman of the Department of Anthropology at the University of Ranchi, India. Currently (1974–1978) he is the President of the International Union of Anthropological and Ethnological Sciences and of the Xth International Congress of Anthropological and Ethnological Sciences to be held in India in 1978. Dr. Vidyarthi is the President of the Indian Anthropological Association, a Founder Member of the Indian Council of Social Sciences Research, Chairman of the Task Force on Development of Tribal Areas of the Planning Commission, and a member of the Central Council on Tribal Research, Institute of the Ministry of Home Affairs, Gov't of India. He is Founder Editor of *The Journal of Social Research, The Indian Anthropologist*, and *The Research Journal of Ranchi University*. His numerous publications include books and articles as well as many volumes which he has edited. His major field of research is the tribal culture of India: the Andman and Nicobar Islands; urban-industrial, political, and action anthropology; Indian civilization, the history of Indian culture, folklore, and village studies.

Index of Names

Index of Subjects

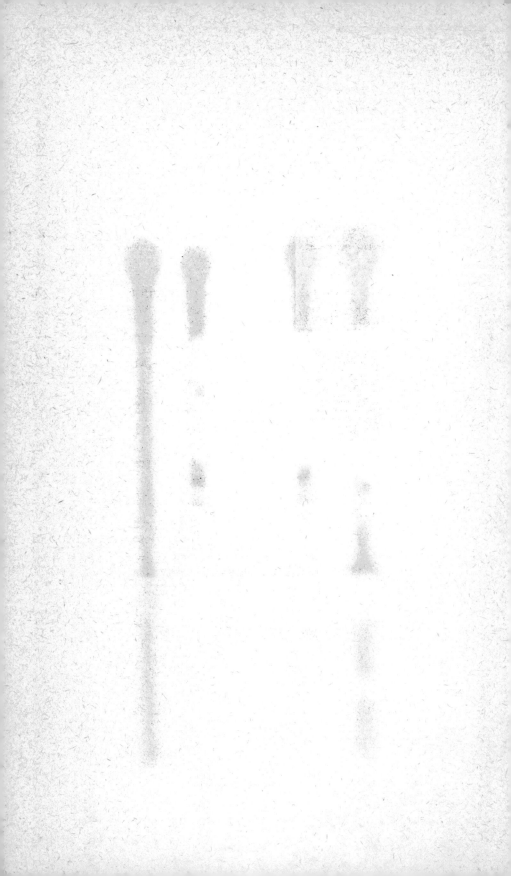